Franchising Globally

Also edited by Ilan Alon

Authored Books

GLOBAL MARKETING (*With Eugene Jaffe*) (Forthcoming)

SERVICE FRANCHISING: A Global Perspective

THE INTERNATIONALIZATION OF U.S. FRANCHISING SYSTEMS

Reference Books

A GUIDE TO TOP 100 COMPANIES IN CHINA, SINGAPORE: World Scientific (*With Zhang and Wenxian*) (Forthcoming)

BIOGRAPHICAL DICTIONARY OF NEW CHINESE ENTREPRENEURS AND BUSINESS LEADERS (*With Zhang and Wenxian*)

Edited Books

CHINA RULES: GLOBALIZATION AND POLITICAL TRANSFORMATION (*With Julian Chang, Marc Fetscherin, Christoph Lattemann, and John McIntyre*)

THE GLOBALIZATION OF CHINESE ENTERPRISES (*With John McIntyre*).

THE NEW GLOBAL SOCIETY, *series editor*,

1. GLOBALIZATION AND DEVELOPMENT (*Eugene D. Jaffe*)
2. GLOBALIZATION AND HUMAN RIGHTS (*Alma Kadragic*)
3. GLOBALIZATION AND LABOR (*Peter Enderwick*)
4. GLOBALIZATION AND POVERTY (*Nadejda Ballard*)
5. GLOBALIZATION AND THE ENVIRONMENT (*Howon Jeong*)
6. GLOBALIZATION, LANGUAGE, AND CULTURE (*Richard Lee*)

BUSINESS AND MANAGEMENT EDUCATION IN CHINA: Transition, Pedagogy and Training (*With John R. McIntyre*)

BUSINESS AND MANAGEMENT EDUCATION IN TRANSITIONING AND DEVELOPING COUNTRIES: A Handbook (*With McIntyre, John R.*)

BUSINESS EDUCATION AND EMERGING MARKET ECONOMIES: Perspectives and Best Practices (*With John R. McIntyre*)

CHINESE ECONOMIC TRANSITION AND INTERNATIONAL MARKETING STRATEGY

CHINESE CULTURE, ORGANIZATIONAL BEHAVIOR, AND INTERNATIONAL BUSINESS MANAGEMENT

INTERNATIONAL FRANCHISING IN INDUSTRIALIZED MARKETS: Western and Northern Europe (*With Dianne Welsh*)

INTERNATIONAL FRANCHISING IN INDUSTRIALIZED MARKETS: North America, Pacific Rim, and Other Developed Countries (*With Welsh, Dianne*)

INTERNATIONAL FRANCHISING IN EMERGING MARKETS: China, India and Other Asian Countries (*With Dianne Welsh*)

INTERNATIONAL FRANCHISING IN EMERGING MARKETS: Central and Eastern Europe and Latin America (*With Welsh, Dianne*)

Franchising Globally

Innovation, Learning and Imitation

Ilan Alon

George D. and Harriet W. Cornell Chair of International Business, Director, The China Center at Rollins College, Rollins College, Florida, USA

First published 2010 by
PALGRAVE MACMILLAN

Palgrave Macmillan in the UK is an imprint of Macmillan Publishers Limited,
registered in England, company number 785998, of Houndmills, Basingstoke,
Hampshire RG21 6XS.

Palgrave Macmillan in the US is a division of St Martin's Press LLC,
175 Fifth Avenue, New York, NY 10010.

Palgrave Macmillan is the global academic imprint of the above companies
and has companies and representatives throughout the world.

Palgrave® and Macmillan® are registered trademarks in the United States,
the United Kingdom, Europe and other countries.

ISBN: 978–0–230–23828–2 hardback

This book is printed on paper suitable for recycling and made from fully
managed and sustained forest sources. Logging, pulping and manufacturing
processes are expected to conform to the environmental regulations of the
country of origin.

A catalogue record for this book is available from the British Library.

Library of Congress Cataloging-in-Publication Data

Alon, Ilan.
    Franchising globally : innovation, learning and imitation / Ilan Alon.
        p. cm.
    Summary: "Franchising Globally is first of its kind to examine franchising
both from an entrepreneurial and from an international perspective. The
book includes theoretical discussions and practical examples of international
franchising as well as both micro and macro studies of franchising
environments in different parts of the world" – Provided by publisher.
    Includes bibliographical references and index.
    ISBN 978–0–230–23828–2 (hardback)
    1. Franchises (Retail trade) 2. International trade. I. Title.
HF5429.23.A375 2010
658.8'708—dc22   2009048423

10 9 8 7 6 5 4 3 2 1
19 18 17 16 15 14 13 12 11 10

Printed and bound in Great Britain by
CPI Antony Rowe, Chippenham and Eastbourne

Contents

List of Illustrations

Tables

Figures

Acknowledgments

This book is the outcome of work spanning several years and involving numerous supportive individuals. I will first like to acknowledge all my chapter co-authors, without whom this book would not be possible. This book features a compilation of my work on the topic and summarizes the extent of my contribution to the field of global franchising.

Individual chapters also benefited from the comments and reviews of various people and organizations. I would especially like to thank the anonymous reviewers and editors of Journal of Small Business Management, International Entrepreneurship and Management Journal, International Journal of Entrepreneurship and Small Business, Mercati e Competitivita, Management Online Review, and Ivey Business School.

Finally, if it was not for my dedicated family, wife and two beautiful children, I would not be able to muster the energy, time and intellectual capital that are required to put together a book of this sort. I thank God for blessing me with supportive family, friends, and colleagues, and for providing me with an auspicious environment for research. Rollins College is the premier liberal arts school in Florida, with an emphasis on global citizenship and responsible leadership.

Foreword

Forms of franchising have been around for a long time, dating back to the I.M. Singer (Sewing) Co. and the McCormick Harvesting Machine Co. (eventually, International Harvester), but it has only been in the last 40 years that we have been systematically studying franchisors in an attempt to help entrepreneurs and managers successfully build their franchised chains. In those years, we have come a long way toward understanding when franchising makes sense, what kind of contract terms will aid growth and survival, and how to recruit and work with franchisees successfully. As with much academic research, though, our knowledge is largely built on evidence from well-developed markets, especially the United States. Unfortunately, what works in the U.S., as so many have learned the hard way, often does not translate into international success – especially in emerging markets.

Professor Alon has devoted much of his career to reconciling what we know in a domestic U.S. context with on-the-ground realities in a diverse set of international markets. *Franchising Globally* builds upon and ties together much of what we learned in his prior books on international franchising with a specific focus on emerging markets. The book is a rare combination of well-executed academic analysis and case studies supported by detailed interviews, all deepened by Ilan Alon's breadth of experience and enriched by featured coauthors. The result is the construction of useful insights that are both academically rigorous and grounded in practice. The book should aid academics wishing to learn more about franchising in a variety of international contexts, and practicing franchisors pondering the possibilities of emerging markets. Let me highlight three particularly exciting features.

First, *Franchising Globally* combines in one place broad generalizable models that guide thinking about franchising in emerging markets with detailed information about specific firms and markets. From the broad models, we learn about the general context of emerging markets, factors that distinguish franchisees from independent entrepreneurs, antecedents to international franchising decisions, and commonalities and differences among important international markets. These offer academics a foundation for building better theories to explain franchise activities in emerging markets, and furnish managers with broad guidelines to consider in relation to their own firm's attributes. Each firm and potential market is unique, however, and what works in general often fails in the particular. This is where the cases step in. Managers can relate unique problems and challenges confronted by a specific firm in a specific market to their own unique situation, and academics might see the seeds of patterns that will form the baseline for future theory development. Together, these broad generalizable models and detailed cases provide a rich resource for considering expansion via franchising into emerging markets.

By blending the broad and generalizable with detailed cases, a second noteworthy feature of this book is that you can fruitfully pick and choose among chapters based on what interests you. If your interest is in whether and how it might make sense for a successful firm to expand from a developed market into an emerging market, the analysis in Chapter 3 can be read along with the cases that involve a potential entry in Chapter 9 and a failed entry attempt in Chapter 12. If your interest is hotels, the analyses in Chapters 3 and 5 can be fruitfully used in conjunction with the Best Western case in Chapter 10. Overall, there are many ways to mix and match the chapters in this book to satisfy your curiosity about a number of specific research questions, industries, and markets.

The third characteristic of this book that I find particularly worthy of mention is that there are chapters here on topics that are quite unique and not well understood. The term "franchising" is used in reference to a wide variety of contractual arrangements that this book accommodates. The case study on Best Western offers a detailed example of a franchise chain that has been highly successful, but lacks the command and control structure and profit motive behind most franchisors, and the examination of microfranchising describes how franchise arrangements are being used creatively to achieve important social objectives in less-developed regions.

Overall, I think you will find that the compilation of research studies and case analyses is among the best resources for those contemplating expansion into emerging markets. For academic researchers interested in franchising generally, Alon draws attention to the ways in which existing franchise theory does and does not pertain to these unique contexts, and for those interested in the evolution of entrepreneurship in emerging markets *Franchising Globally* sits at the ground floor where franchising coevolves with the basic legal and institutional structures needed to support it. Once again, Professor Alon has drawn our gaze beyond standard franchise contracts in developed countries into the places where franchising is going and the new ways franchising occurs. I am confident that you will enjoy the journey into the world of entrepreneurship and franchising in emerging markets.

James G. Combs
Jim Moran Professor of Management
Executive Director of the Jim Moran Institute for Global Entrepreneurship
Florida State University

Notes on Contributors

Ilan Alon is Cornell Professor of International Business at Rollins College and a visiting scholar at Harvard Kennedy School. His books on franchising include: *Service Franchising: A Global Perspective* (Springer, 2005); *International Franchising in Industrialized Markets: Western and Northern Europe* (CCH Inc., 2003); *International Franchising in Industrialized Markets: North America, Pacific Rim and Other Developed Countries* (CCH Inc., 2002); *International Franchising in Emerging Markets: China, India, and Other Asian Countries* (CCH Inc., 2001); *International Franchising in Emerging Markets: Central and Eastern Europe and Latin America* (CCH Inc., 2001); and *The Internationalization of US Franchising Systems* (Garland Publishing, 1999). Alon has taught franchising courses in China (Fudan and CEIBS), Italy (MIB), and India (IILM), and lectured extensively on the topic to various professional associations, including the International Franchise Association, International Society for Franchising, and the Academy of International Business. In the realm of consulting, Alon has been consulted by both for-profit franchising companies as well as government bodies such as the government of Croatia and USAID. In Croatia, he was responsible for introducing franchising education, as well as for training bankers, business consultants, franchisors, franchisees, and lawyers.

Mirela Alpeza, M.Sc., Ph.D candidate, is a Junior Researcher at the J.J.Strossmayer University of Osijek, Croatia; with her main field of research is entrepreneurship. Since 2003. Mirela has been a head of The Franchise Center, part of Center for Entrepreneuship in Osijek, where she teaches and offers consultations to potential franchisees and franchisors about the advantages and challenges of franchising. The Franchise Centre in Osijek runs Croatia's leading education program about franchising and publishes information about franchising offers on its franchising portal www.fransiza.hr, with wider regional coverage and impact. Mirela's publications include conference papers and articles about franchising and corporate entrepreneurship.

Gérard Cliquet is professor at the IGR-IAE (School of Business Administration) of the University of Rennes 1 (France). He obtained his Master's at the University of Paris Panthéon-Sorbonne and his Ph.D. at the University of Caen (France). He has published more than 30 articles in journals. He has been the editor of 11 books and contributed more than 30 chapters. He has contributed about 80 papers mostly to international conferences. Dr. Cliquet is president of a network of French-speaking business schools, the CIDEGEF.

Jim Combs (Ph.D., Louisiana State University) is Jim Moran Professor of Management and Executive Director of the Jim Moran Institute for Global Entrepreneurship at Florida State University. His research interests are primarily in the areas of franchising, research synthesis, and corporate governance in family firms. He has published more than 30 refereed journal articles in journals such as the *Academy of Management Journal, Strategic Management Journal, Journal of Management, Journal of Business Venturing,* and *Entrepreneurship: Theory & Practice.* He is currently an Associate Editor at the *Academy of Management Journal* and has served as a guest editor for *Organizational Research Methods.* He also serves on the editorial review boards of the *Academy of Management Journal, Journal of Management, Entrepreneurship: Theory & Practice,* and *Cornell Hospitality Quarterly.* He has served on the Executive Committee of the Business Policy and Strategy division as its Secretary and Newsletter Editor and as a member of the Southern Management Association's Board of Governors.

Aleksandar Erceg teaches the course on Franchising at the J.J. Strossmayer University of Osijek, Graduate Program in Entrepreneurship, Croatia. He was born in Osijek, Croatia, where he earned his M.Sc. in Entrepreneurship at the J.J. Strossmayer University of Osijek. Aleksandar's publications include conference papers and articles about franchising and operations management. Besides his academic studies he is also consultant/trainer at The Franchise Center – part of the Center for Entrepreneurship Osijek – where he teaches about franchising in Croatia and how to become franchisee/franchisor.

Cecilia M. Falbe received her Ph.D. from Columbia University. Her research and teaching interests are in the fields of organization strategy and implementation, strategic change and entrepreneurship. Dr. Falbe has published in *Administrative Science Quarterly,* the *Academy of Management Journal, Journal of Applied Psychology, ,* and the *Journal of Small Business Management* among others. She is the coeditor of two books on social issues and is conducting research on the effect of regulation on corporate strategy and governance. Recently she coauthored a book chapter on HR technology delivery systems and trends. She is a principle faculty member in the University at Albany's e-HR MBA program where she supervises student consulting engagements and teaches a change management course focused on systems implementation.

Allen H. Kupetz is the Executive-in-Residence at the Crummer Graduate School of Business at Rollins College, the number-one ranked MBA program in Florida and top 40 nationally, according to *Forbes* and *BusinessWeek*. His 2008 book, *The Future of Less*, earned him a reputation as a recognized leading thinker on the present and future impact of technology on individuals and corporations. Allen is also the president of Kpartnerz, Inc., an international management consulting firm.

Matthew C. Mitchell is Assistant Professor of International Business at Drake University in Des Moines, Iowa, USA. He holds an AB in Physics from Rollins College, an MBA in Management from Crummer Graduate School of Business and a PhD in International Business from the University of South Carolina. His research is situated at the intersection of international business, culture and political economy and he has written extensively on the topic. Matthew has travelled, lived, and worked in more than 55 countries and has been invited as a consultant and guest lecturer for multinational companies, NGOs, and universities around the world.

J. Mark Munoz is an Associate Professor of International Business at Millikin University in Illinois, and a Visiting Fellow at the Kennedy School of Government at Harvard University. He is also Chairman of the international management consulting firm, Munoz and Associates International, and focuses on business development in emerging nations. He has received several awards including three Best Research Paper Awards, a literary award, and a Teaching Excellence Award among others. As well as top-tier journal publications and book chapters, he has authored four books, *Land of My Birth*, *Winning Across Borders*, *In Transition*, and *A Salesman in Asia*.

Liqiang Ni received a B.Sc. in math from Fudan University in 1996, and a Ph.D. in statistics from the University of Minnesota in 2003. From 1996 to 1998, he worked as an auditor at the Shanghai office of Price Waterhouse Da Hua. Since 2003, Professor Ni has been on faculty in the Department of Statistics and Actuarial Science, University of Central Florida, Orlando, Florida. His research interests include statistical pattern recognition, dimensionality reduction, regression diagnostics, model selection, and econometrics. He is a member of International Chinese Statistical Association, Institute of Mathematical Statistics, and the American Statistical Association, as well as an Elected Member of the International Statistical Institute.

Rozenn Perrigot is an Associate Professor in the Marketing Department of the Graduate School of Business Administration at the University of Rennes 1. She is also an Affiliate Professor at the ESC Rennes School of Business. She is a member of the Center for Research in Economics and Management (CREM UMR CNRS 6211). Her research papers, published in academic journals, conference proceedings and as books chapters, deal with franchising and retailing.

Rachid Alami, Ph.D. and DBA, is an international consultant in business management and corporate strategy. He has more than 15 years' experience in consultancy and teaching. He teaches project management, operations management, and business strategy for universities and business schools. His research focuses on emerging markets and doing business with developing countries. He has worked in and managed industrial and financial project development on three continents for several multinational companies, and is currently the CEO of International Management Consultancy – IMC – providing business consultancy in Africa, the Middle East, and Canada.

Dr. Marc Sardy is Associate Professor of International Business and an Associate of The China Center at Rollins College. He holds AB in Economics from the University of Chicago, A MS in Statistics from CUNY, Zicklin School of Business and a PhD in International Finance from The University of Cambridge. Dr. Sardy's research areas include International Business and International finance and the entertainment industry. He has published many articles in these areas. He currently serves on several editorial boards.

Amir Shoham (Ph.D., Ben Gurion University) holds degrees in Economics and Business Administration from Ben Gurion University. He is currently on the faculty of the Department of Business Administration, College of Management and Department of Economics, Sapir Academic College, in Israel. Shoham also teaches in academic institutions in other countries including China, Singapore, and France. The courses he teaches include Managerial Economics, Introduction to Finance, International Finance, and International Financial Strategies. He sits on the Boards of Directors of two public firms. Recently, he has published articles in *JIBS*, *The Global Economy Journal*, and *Journal of Socio-Economics*. Born in Israel, he is an Israeli citizen.

Donata Vianelli is Associate Professor of Marketing at the University of Trieste, Italy. In the Faculty of Economics she is coordinator of the University Degree in Business and Management and she teaches various courses related to International Marketing and International Business. In the mentioned fields she has published more than 40 articles, book chapters and books both at a national and international level.

Youcheng Wang, Ph.D., is Associate Professor with the Rosen College of Hospitality Management, University of Central Florida. His research interest focuses on marketing, destination marketing systems, customer relationship management, destination image and branding, collaborative strategies, and technology management.

Dianne Welsh is the Charles A. Hayes Distinguished Professor of Entrepreneurship and Director of the North Carolina Entrepreneurship Center at The University of North Carolina Greensboro. She is coeditor of the first comprehensive volumes on global franchising in emerging and industrialized markets. Dianne is the author of more than 100 published manuscripts. She has been quoted in *Fortune*, *The Wall Street Journal*, and *Franchising World*. She has presented at a number of International Franchising Association Conferences. She is Past Chair of the International Society of Franchising and has served as guest editor for special journal issues on international franchising.

Introduction

Ilan Alon

Franchising around the world is quickly increasing. There is a dual process of international franchising and diffusion of local franchising systems through innovation, learning, and imitation. Alon (2005) discusses the development of service franchising as a global phenomenon with a focus on the use of franchising, franchisor clusters, master international franchising, and cases relating to Russia, Philippines, and China.

There has been an urgent call from both the franchise industry and the academic community for research on world franchising markets. The advent of franchising is a worldwide phenomenon that cannot be overlooked. In countries around the globe, franchising substantially affects the economy and is taking up a larger percentage of the retail trade daily. In some countries, franchising is becoming responsible for half of their total retail sales. A series of edited volumes about international franchising in developing and developed countries was published by Alon and Welsh (2001, 2003).

This book extends these works by adding to the repertoire of available analytical frameworks and enriching the country- and company-level studies of franchising in different regions. Each chapter is self contained, with a particular analytical model, country, and industry examined. The full spectrum of articles summarizes current theoretical streams applied to franchising, analyzes the particularities of franchising employed in different regions of the world, and highlights specific industry environments of franchising, most notably in the hospitality, food, and retail sectors. This book is unique in its investigation of salient themes relevant to franchising globally: internationalization, emerging markets, and entrepreneurship. The chapters divide into three parts:

   I. Franchising Approaches and Frameworks
  II. Area Studies of Franchising
 III. International Franchising Cases

In Part I, Chapter 1, coauthored with Dianne Welsh and Cecilia Falbe, discusses franchising in emerging markets. The first chapter will set the stage by reviewing the development of franchising over time and across countries. A sample of countries from around the world will be used as examples of the various regions: Eastern and Central Europe, South America, and Asia. We will examine the multiplicity of franchising permutations that evolved in various countries and the research covering these areas.

The chapter is an attempt to summarize the main research that has been conducted thus far on international retail franchising. It begins with an overview of the development of the literature and discusses the nature and scope of emerging markets, with particular reference to their impact on the stakeholders in international retail franchising. Next, it develops a conceptual model relating international retail franchising to its stakeholders. Then, a review of the research is divided into areas of the emerging world market: Central and Eastern Europe, Mexico and South America, Asia, and other areas that include India, Kuwait, and South Africa. The chapter concludes by discussing the next step toward developing a research base and improving understanding of emerging markets, as well as the opportunities and challenges for retail franchising and future research. Analytical frameworks for understanding franchising interactions in emerging markets will continue to be useful as long as these markets continue to show potential. Franchisors need to understand the full spectrum of stakeholders impacted by franchising.

Franchising may also contribute to entrepreneurship models. Chapter 2, coauthored with Marc Sardy, examines empirically the unique characteristics of franchisee entrepreneurs. Franchising has been long claimed by entrepreneurship researchers to be a form of entrepreneurship, one that provides a balance between autonomy and independence on the one hand and control and obedience on the other. This chapter provides a comparison between franchisees and nascent entrepreneurs and focuses on the personal characteristics of the entrepreneur, his/her experiences, and local resources. The well known PSED dataset is used in this chapter to show the empirical differences that exist between the two sets of entrepreneurs.

The chapter is unique in using the PSED dataset for deriving a better understanding of the nature of nascent entrepreneurs as compared to franchisee entrepreneurs. We used previous studies on the differences between the two groups and developed variables divided into three dimensions: (1) prior experience, (2) growth objectives, and (3) motivation and risk. Jonckheere-Terpstra tests, Chi-Square tests, F-tests, and logistic regression models detected differences in all three dimensions. The conclusion is that franchisee entrepreneurs in the United States of America are distinctive in their characteristics. As compared to nascent entrepreneurs, franchisee entrepreneurs have less experience, less confidence in their skills, less capital, more aspirations toward creating larger organizations, less confidence in their abilities to make the business a success, and more belief that their first year income will be stable.

Chapter 3, written with Liqiang Ni and Raymond Wang, provides another empirical validation of international franchising, with particular emphasis on the hotel sector. As mentioned earlier, in recent years, a number of articles and books have been written on the internationalization of franchising systems from around the world. Prominent among the studies is the central role that the U.S. took in the development of international franchising and, more specifically, in the hotel and restaurant industries which led the way. This chapter investigates the organizational determinants of internationalization in the hotel sector using logistical regression and a dataset of hotel chains over a period of time. The chapter proposes and tests an agency-based organizational model of international franchising in the hotel sector. Using data obtained from a Franchisor Questionnaire 2001–2008, we analyzed a panel of 121 observations of 19 U.S.-based hotel groups. Our analysis reveals that the hotel franchisor's decision to internationalize is positively related to the franchise ratio, franchise experience, and the use of multiunit franchising, and negatively related to the minimum investment needed and the scale of U.S. operations. Our model provides information on the factors affecting international franchising in the hotel sector, simultaneously advancing our knowledge on hotel groups' use of franchising as an international expansion strategy. Agency incentives and franchising resources are contributors to the desire to seek international franchisees. The use of multiunit franchising systems hastened the pace of globalization.

Studies linking environmental factors to companies' decision to internationalize showed that various political, social, and economic factors either attract or repel international franchising investment (Alon, 2005). The factors promoting international franchising have been established through past research on global franchising. These include economic, social, political/legal, and institutional frameworks associated with this development. For example, richer countries on a per capita basis, with stable legal and political systems and an entrepreneurial culture will absorb franchising more readily. Chapter 4, coauthored with Amir Shoham, looks at the mostly environmental factors responsible for internationalization, and uses these factors to cluster markets. Our results show that countries divide into eight clusters with similar international franchising market characteristics. A discussion of each cluster follows along with implications for franchising research.

Part II consists of four area case studies: Italy, Morocco, Croatia, and Less Developed Markets. The variety of franchising applications across multiple locations allows for an examination of franchising development in different institutional contexts: levels of economic development, culture, legal system, and industry.

Chapter 5, coauthored with Donata Vianneli, focuses on the environmental determinants that make up the Italian market, providing a milieu for franchising development. The chapter reviews the franchising literature with respect to the Italian hotel market and surveys hotel executives and experts to develop a map of the opportunities and threats that exist in this important tourism market. This chapter, along with Chapter 3, is especially relevant to multinational franchisors in the hospitality industry. While Chapter 3 focuses on the organizational determinants of internationalization, Chapter 5 examines the location-specific factors that seed franchising development.

Franchising in Africa is a little studied area. In this region of the world, where religion and cultural peculiarities still dominate, few franchisors, even world famous ones, have ventured, and a high proportion of those that have, have failed. Chapter 6, coauthored with Rashid Alami, discusses the franchising environment in Morocco, showing the opportunities and threats there, and analyzes why some franchising companies, like Subway, have failed, while others, such as McDonald's, have flourished. Skill in adapting to the cultural environment is especially important to the success of international franchising in the important African market. By studying some of the best-known U.S. fast-food chains that have entered Morocco through franchising, this chapter tries to shed light on the visible and invisible factors that influence international marketing success. In the African market, the key factors for success appear to stem from a number of variables such as adapting menus to local traditions and having a local business partner who can be trusted. We propose a business framework based on market research and previous models that scholars have developed for fast-food companies that want to mitigate risks and enhance their chance for success.

Chapter 7, coauthored with Mirela Alpeza and Aleksandar Erceg, explores franchising in the emerging market of Croatia, where franchising is still a young and transitioning sector. Companies involved in retailing, distribution, and wholesaling operations in Croatia are now becoming aware of the benefits (and costs) of franchising as an organizational method and are considering its adaptation to the Croatian context. Yet, franchising is underdeveloped in the country, with only a handful of active firms, lack of regulatory structure, lack of support from institutions, disinterested banks, and little experience in the marketplace. Our contribution is an assessment of the franchising model in the Croatian context.

In Chapter 8, coauthored with Matthew C. Mitchel, a new organizational form of franchising is introduced: microfranchising. Microfranchising is franchising on a small franchisee scale, often with a social agenda, that is appropriate for bottom-of-the-pyramid markets. In low-income countries, microfranchising is becoming a new distribution format for delivering everything from health services to telecommunications. The concept of microfranchising, while in its infancy, has drawn considerable interest worldwide. Furthermore, it has been successfully implemented in many formal and informal market environments by both nonprofit organizations and market-oriented actors. As is typical of emerging business models, the format needs to be further assessed in order to determine the best practices and viable models. This chapter draws lessons and insights from existing franchise literature as well as microfranchising research and case studies to determine effective business strategies. Microfranchising in less developed markets maybe another method for pulling potential entrepreneurs out of poverty and into the modern economic system.

Collectively, Chapters 5–8 contribute to the bank of recent area-specific studies of franchising. Through these studies we can see that franchising permutations have evolved to fit the unique institutional context and environmental conditions.

Starting Part III, Chapter 9, coauthored with Allen Kupetz, describes Ruth Chris' international ambitions and their need to conduct market analysis for development. Ruth Chris is a reputable, high-end, steak franchise which offers a differentiated, quality product and atmosphere. The chapter discusses the establishment of Ruth Chris in the U.S. and abroad, and gives the reader a framework by which to judge its future internationalization. The outcome of internationalization is assessed and a framework for analyzing market selection and mode of entry are evaluated.

Chapter 10, coauthored with Gérard Cliquet, Matthew C. Mitchel, and Rozenn Perrigot, discusses another form of franchising permutation in the hotel sector, exercised by Best Western. In the franchising literature, the hotel industry is often studied. Brands such as Mercure, Ibis, Comfort Inn, Courtyard, etc. use franchising extensively as a method of national and international growth . The hotel industry is global, with a high level of internationalization. The topic of internationalization remains important for the network operators in the hotel chains as a result of environmental differences and organizational constraints. They must try to adapt their chain to the country they want to enter in order to succeed, yet at the same time stick to the formula that made them famous. This is not always easy. One system, not organized as a franchise per se, is globally omnipresent, and exhibits some uniformity in its concept internationally. This system is the one employed by Best Western (BW). The system uses a quasi-franchising system to expand internationally, is registered as a nonprofit organization, and is expanding rapidly through affiliation networks. This system is unique and, thus, worthy of study. Chapter 10 can be profitably paired with both Chapters 3 and 5 for those particularly interested in hotels. While the earlier chapters focus on the theoretical aspects, the case study grounds them in the reality of a particular hotel franchisor.

Chapter 11, coauthored with Mirela Alpeza and Aleksandar Erceg, examines the decisionmaking process in franchising in a country where the practice is quite rare, Croatia. This chapter builds on the information in Chapter 7 by examining a specific case study, that of an American coffee franchising concept. Since franchising is little known in the country, the legal environment is not geared to it and the business environment only partially exposed to the idea, so it is remains a minor player in the economy. Despite the developmental challenges involved, two entrepreneurs, who were educated in the U.S., brought coffee franchising to Croatia, Starbucks style, and offered a unique coffee-bar experience that can only be found the upscale centers of American suburbia. What is even stranger is that they opened the concept store in Osijek, a relatively undeveloped region of Croatia. Their success in uncharted territory serves as a model for future entrepreneurs in developing countries.

In contrast to the success story of Chapter 11, Chapter 12 shows how a franchise system ran into trouble in another emerging economy, China.

Athlete's Foot entered the bustling Shanghai market in the 1990s when the market had just opened to foreign franchising concepts and retailing was flourishing. At the time, department stores in China started providing space for athletics shoes and franchisees willing to participate in the concept proliferated. Things did not stay rosy for long: competition stiffened, rents increased, suppliers integrated downstream, and shopping malls and department stores started offering more space for athletics shoes. As a result, the master franchisee faced bankruptcy.

Chapter 13 offers some final reflections on the evolution of franchising globally and offers some insightful comments and areas for future research.

References

Alon, Ilan (2005). *Service Franchising: A Global Perspective.* New York: Springer.

Alon, Ilan, and Dianne Welsh, Eds. (2001). *International Franchising in Emerging Markets: China, India and Other Asian Countries.* Chicago IL: CCH Inc. Publishing.

Alon, Ilan, and Dianne Welsh, Eds. (2003). *International Franchising in Industrialized Markets: Western and Northern Europe.* Chicago IL: CCH Inc. Publishing.

Welsh, Dianne, and Ilan Alon, Eds. (2001). *International Franchising in Emerging Markets: Central and Eastern Europe and Latin America.* Chicago IL: CCH Inc. Publishing.

Welsh, Dianne, and Ilan Alon, Eds. (2002). *International Franchising in Industrialized Markets: North America, Pacific Rim, and Other Developed Countries.* Chicago IL: CCH Inc. Publishing.

Part I

Franchising Approaches and Frameworks

1
Franchising in Emerging Markets

Ilan Alon, Dianne H.B. Welsh, and Cecilia M. Falbe

1.1 Introduction

In the U.S., Canada, and parts of Western Europe, retail franchising has reached domestic market saturation, while emerging markets remain relatively untapped. Retail franchises have been established in these markets primarily in the last 15 years through master franchises and corporate franchise agreements, and to a lesser extent joint venture franchising and conversion franchising (Alon and McKee, 1999; Connell, 1999; Doherty and Quinn, 1999; Hadjimarcou and Barnes, 1998; Hoffman and Preble, 2003). Emerging markets, which account for 80 percent of the world's population and 60 percent of the world's natural resources, present the most dynamic potential for long-term growth to businesses, in general, and to franchisors, specifically. The U.S. Department of Commerce estimated that over 75 percent of the expected growth in world trade over the next two decades will come from emerging countries, particularly Big Emerging Markets, which account for over half the world's population but only 25 percent of its GDP.

Emerging markets are among the fastest growing targets for investment by international franchisors. Several surveys conducted by industry experts showed that more and more franchisors are seeking opportunities in these markets. A recent article in *Franchising World* stated, "Franchises are springing up in the most unlikely, and for many of us unheard-of, places...Those franchisors who can establish a beach-head on these wilder shores could do very well, but the risks are great" (Amies, 1999: 27–28).

A number of authors, both industry analysts and academics, identified emerging markets as a topic that needs further research (Kaufmann and

Leibenstein, 1988). Researchers responded to this call. In 1990 Welsh conducted the first survey on franchising in Russia, when McDonald's opened its first franchise in Moscow to a tremendous welcome from the Russian people and press. An empirical study was subsequently published (Welsh and Swerdlow, 1991). Since the 1980s, franchising in emerging markets has grown dramatically. For example, by 1995, there were 26 more franchisors in Brazil alone than there were in all of South America in 1985 (International Franchise Research Centre, 2000). By 1997, the top 50 US food chains had $33.1 billion in international sales as a result of significant efforts by large U.S.-based food retail franchisors (Breuhaus, 1998).

The recent acceleration of franchising in emerging markets is now receiving greater attention in both the academic and practitioner literature. However, this literature is widely dispersed and, in some cases, a challenge to access. The first purpose of this paper is to provide a review and summary of the literature on retail franchising in emerging markets. In addition to the traditional literature searches generally targeted at the leading journals, we also accessed franchise-specific sources of information that have limited circulation among the academic public. The review includes journal articles, including all of the *Proceedings of the International Society of Franchising* from the initial publication in 1986 to 2002, contributions from *Franchising Research: An International Journal*, as well as articles in recently published books on international franchising in emerging markets. This paper integrates the research that has been conducted in emerging economies in order to help to understand international retail franchising opportunities and threats in emerging economies in the hope of expanding the research in this area in the future, as well as assisting the retail franchise industry.

The second purpose of this paper is to present a conceptual model of the stakeholders of international retail franchising including consumers, franchisees, franchisors, host country markets and home country markets. The model provides a means of examining the benefits/costs of international business format franchising from the perspective of the stakeholders and examines the impact of these complex relationships on developments in international franchising.

We begin with a brief overview of the development of the literature and a discussion of the characteristics of emerging markets. The article then presents a model of stakeholder relations in franchising and links the stakeholder approach to concepts of international retail franchising. We conclude with a review of the research on area markets and offer suggestions for future research.

1.2   An overview of the literature

Early studies of franchising were linked to the classic argument that economic organization follows two general forms, markets and firms (Coase, 1937). Theorists identified franchising as a hybrid manifestation of the two forms since it included both market-like and firm-like qualities (Brickley and Dark, 1987; Mathewson and Winter, 1985; Norton, 1988; Rubin, 1978). Franchising is seen as a means of obtaining scarce capital as the franchisee is generally required to make a substantial investment in the business. Franchisees share risk with the franchisor. Franchising is also identified as a way of addressing the agency problem, specifically, the issue of monitoring managers (Brickley and Dark, 1987; Mathewson and Winter, 1985). Franchisees with substantial investments are more motivated to maximize revenues through administrative efficiency and protection of the franchise brand while minimizing operational costs.

These earlier arguments also apply to franchising in emerging markets which offer even greater challenges in the areas of monitoring, resource scarcity, and risk reduction. The issues of monitoring and risk are greatly increased in international franchising by both geographical and cultural distance (Fladmore-Linquist and Jacque, 1995). The stakeholder model highlights the location of potential problems in monitoring and risk.

Useful reviews of the literature on international franchising were published by Elango and Fried (1997) and Young et al (2000). In their survey of franchising research published in journals, Elango and Fried discovered that "the manner in which franchise systems work to create value had been ignored" (76). They cited a lack of franchising case studies as contributing to this problem. Their point is especially applicable for international retail franchising and distribution systems worldwide. Young et al examined the content of articles that were published in the *International Society of Franchising Proceedings*. Out of approximately 70 articles published between 1987 and 1999, nine dealt with economies in transition and 14 others dealt with developing economies.

Hadjimarcou and Barnes (1998) found that international retail franchise expansion is not just done by the largest franchises, but by all kinds of franchisors who see international retail expansion as a profitable venture and logical extension of their home operations. For example, some well-known UK retailers, including the Body Shop and

Mothercare, have used franchising as the hallmark of their international activity (Doherty and Quinn, 1999).

In *The Internationalization of U.S. Franchising Systems*, Alon (1999) provides a comprehensive review of the international retail franchising literature and classifies the theories of international franchising into two research streams – one focuses on environmental variables, and the other on the organizational capabilities of the franchisor. Such theories include the seminal works of Hackett (1976) and Welch (1989). Hackett was one of the first franchising researchers to point out the trend of domestic market saturation in the franchising sector that has forced franchisors to seek alternative markets, especially abroad. Welch (1989) proposed that franchising follows a life cycle that begins with internationalization into industrial markets similar to the U.S. (such as Canada, the UK, and Australia), continues into dissimilar developed markets (such as Japan), and progresses into emerging markets that are culturally distinct and economically less developed. The cycle ends with franchisors from the latter countries entering the original home markets to compete with the founders of the concept.

Although academics and practitioners are beginning to answer the call for more research and evaluation of retail franchising in these new markets around the globe, it is clear that coverage is incomplete and additional research is needed.

1.3   Characteristics of emerging markets

While there is no consensus on the definition of the term "emerging market," Czinkota and Ronkainen (1997) identified three characteristics associated with an emerging economy: level of economic development, economic growth, and market governance.

1.3.1   Level of economic development

The level of economic development is typically measured in terms of GDP per capita. GDP per capita is a useful measure of economic development because it is related to the population's wealth, the extent of the middle class, and the level of development of the industrial and service sectors (Alon and McKee, 1999).

The use of the level of economic development as a demarcation criterion for distinguishing emerging markets equates with the anachronisms of the World Bank and the United Nations (UN), which include terms such as Less Developed Countries (LDCs), Third World Countries, and Developing Countries. The World Bank divides countries on the basis of GDP per capita into four classes. Three of the Big Emerging Markets (India, China, and Vietnam) fall into the lowest income class, but have seen a surge of growth in recent years particularly in the technology sector. According to the UN, only about 15 percent of the world's population resides in developed market economy countries (Czinkota and Ronkainen, 1997). When considering an emerging market, it is important to adjust GDP per capita to purchasing power parity in order to gauge income in relation to the "real" cost of living.

1.3.2 Economic growth

Economic growth is usually measured in terms of a country's GDP growth rate. The use of economic growth is consistent with the concept of "emerging." Most of the countries referred to as emerging markets enjoyed GDP growth rates exceeding 5 percent from 1990 to 1997, with some markets, particularly in East Asia, displaying double-digit growth rates (Czinkota and Ronkainen, 1997). In 1997, 1998, and 1999, East Asia, Brazil, and Russia encountered financial crises that set back their economies' growth. Such crises demonstrate that the often-touted high growth rates of emerging markets may not be sustainable over a long period of time.

The level of economic growth is among the most important considerations for international franchising expansion (Alon and McKee, 1999). When examining an emerging market's GDP growth rate, one must contrast it to the growth in the population. If population growth rates exceed GDP growth rates, then the standard of living in those countries will actually drop over time. The most useful measure that captures both these growth rates is that of GDP per capita growth rate.

1.3.3 Market governance

The third criterion for judging emerging markets is the country's market governance. Market governance includes the level of free market activity, government control of key resources, stability of the market system and the regulatory environment. Countries that are liberalizing their economic institutions and democratizing their political structures are often referred to as Transitional Economies/Countries. These transitions have been welcomed by Western economies and are regarded as opportunities for international retail franchising expansion.

Among the most important transitional elements with respect to international investors are the political and economic risks that are introduced by the reorganization of economic and political units in emerging marketplaces (Czinkota and Ronkainen, 1997). Such risks are systematically evaluated by Western institutions such as the Economist Intelligence Unit, Institutional Investor, and International Country Risk Guide (the ICRG is a business-venture risk rating system, whereby a numerical value is attached to a foreign country by an independent collaborative group after many determining factors are evaluated and weighed).

Market governance influences a wide range of country risk elements such as government regulation and red tape, political stability, bribery, ownership restrictions, controls of capital flows, and import restrictions. All these factors are important to international franchisors' evaluations of foreign market potential and essential to determinations of franchise expansion in the international retail arena (Alon and McKee, 1999).

1.4   A stakeholder model of international franchising

The stakeholder approach to management views the consumer holistically within the context of the environment. The company must take into account not only the shareholders and ultimate consumers, but also any group directly or indirectly affected by the firm's business maneuvers. The general public, for instance, may be interested in how the foreign company might promote or defeat the country's economic goals, or simply may inquire how much pollution is incurred. In either case, the company's decisions affect the public welfare, and possibly individual rights, and therefore a prudent corporation exploring new borders should attempt to take into account all possible scenarios, or it may suffer irreparable consequences.

Thus, this article proposes the stakeholder model which illustrates international retail franchising in emerging markets from the viewpoint of the franchisor, franchisee, host market, home market, and consumer. The perspective focuses on the key stakeholders of international retail franchising in emerging markets and discusses how they relate to each other according to current research on international retail franchising (see Figure 1.1).

1.4.1   Franchisors

Emerging markets offer a number of advantages to franchisors. They include, but are not limited to, an expanding middle class necessary for retail franchising to excel, relatively unsaturated markets, urbanized and highly populated cities for the most part, a growing youth market, free trade zones, relatively friendly business laws, liberalized markets

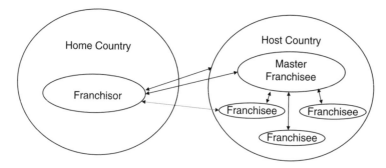

Figure 1.1 Global consumer markets

and transitioning economies, and a huge pent-up demand for Western-style goods and services.

In emerging markets, retail franchising allows companies to expand consumer offerings in geographical markets with relatively minimal financial investment and risk. Local franchisee ownership not only promotes political and cultural acceptability, but also decreases some of the negativity surrounding the purchasing of products not produced in the home country. In addition, it lowers much of the political risk surrounding foreign investment. The franchisor has the opportunity to acquire a broad base of knowledge concerning local customs and market conditions, economic networks, political affiliations, and the industry experience of the franchise partner, and this can greatly enhance the possibility of success for both the franchisor and franchisee(s). Brand-name recognition and customer loyalty are greatly enhanced through standardized customer service that leads to shared long-term success.

Stanworth, Price, and Purdy (2001) summarized the advantages of global franchising to the franchisor as fewer financial resources required; raw materials produced internally; reduced susceptibility to political, economic, and cultural risk;, and franchisees who are more familiar with local laws, language, culture, business norms, and practices. Risks to the franchisor included possible difficulties in repatriating royalties; protecting copyright and intellectual property; policing quality standards; understanding laws, regulations, language and business norms; servicing franchisees; and terminating contracts, as well as local imitations.

One downside of franchising in emerging markets from the perspective of the franchisor is capital controls that may inhibit repatriation of fees and royalties, which effectively may drastically reduce the economic benefits of the investment. Legal constraints, bureaucratic conditions, changes in the legal environment, unstable political leadership, limited infrastructure, and sporadic enforcement of established laws – particularly in regards to business ownership and operations – all have the effect of impeding international franchise expansion. In the area of intellectual property, legally protecting international copyrights, trademarks, and patents is difficult and expensive. Another perceived challenge involves the continuous training, monitoring, and controlling of international franchisees. This is exacerbated by differences in cultures that affect the franchisor-franchisee relationship.

1.4.2 Franchisees

The emerging market franchisee benefits from ongoing support in terms of periodic system-wide programs and promotions, new product innovations and development, superior market research, and advice. In some instances, because of the differences in host-country environments, various experiences of the franchisor may not be transferable from one country to another. This is particularly evidenced by the numerous examples of false starts and restarts that franchisors have made in some emerging markets. Overall, the chances of succeeding are greatly increased by the globalization of consumer markets and past successes in reproducing the business format in heterogeneous locations around the globe.

Kaufmann and Liebenstein (1988) discussed fringe franchisors that are not reputable. Although theory and research is based on the assumption that the franchisor is a respectable sound company with a proven concept, format, and history of support, this is not always true. Kaufmann and Leibenstein reiterate that disclosure statements are a must for governments to require when a retail franchise enters the country and the importance of such documentation in order to reduce a franchisee's risk.

1.4.3 Master franchisees

Indirect franchising, that is, use of a master franchisee to develop a territory or a whole country is a common strategy employed by franchisors in emerging markets. Nair (2001) noted that the advantages of this system include access to resources, knowledge of the local market, more adaptation, and the possibility of developing a successful franchise as a tool for selling to prospective franchisees. The indirect system also has disadvantages, including lower profits for franchisors and franchisees, and monitoring issues because of loss of control. There have been numerous examples of a master franchisee holding the sub-franchisees hostage to compete against the franchisor. Ultimately, success will be determined by the energy, capabilities and resources of the master franchisee.

1.4.4   Franchisor/franchisee relationships

New symbiotic relationships are created when retail franchising expands into developing countries. Retail franchising allows firms to achieve the expanded reach and efficiencies associated with internationalization more rapidly and effectively than the firms could accomplish on their own. Dana, Etemad, and Wright (2001) developed an Interdependence Paradigm to explain these franchise marketing networks using examples of firms in South Korea and the Philippines. In their paradigm, franchising involves a network of franchisees under the guidance of a parent firm, the franchisor. Franchisors that are well established can achieve greater efficiencies by incorporating smaller franchisees from emerging markets into international franchise networks. Importantly, the authors point out that franchising can help overcome local ownership requirements in regulated sectors. Therefore, franchising enhances the competitiveness of franchisors, while contributing to the development of emerging markets. A "symbiotic interdependence" forms between franchisors and franchisees in a network. Dana, Etemad, and Wright view the consequences of this paradigm shift from independence to interdependence to be far reaching and to have a major impact on the way business is handled internationally.

1.4.5   Host-home country markets and influences

Franchising in emerging markets also offers the host countries certain advantages. These benefits include obtaining foreign currency with little capital outlay, increases in employment, and thereby, growth in the franchisor's tax-base and gross domestic output. Also, franchise growth and development spawn entrepreneurial development comprised of small and medium enterprise networks. Certainly, "home grown" franchises are more likely to develop. There is a resulting increase in the knowledge base of the business population concerning product distribution, market management, and Western-style marketing techniques, all of which increase the skill base of local labor. There are increasing efficiencies that result from innovation and rationalization in all sectors of the economy – retail, wholesale, and manufacturing. This leads to further development of the host country's infrastructure, particularly in the areas of transportation and supplies. Alon (2004) examined the macro environmental impacts of franchising on the host and home markets and included in his analyses economic, political, and social ramifications, both positive and negative. He concluded that the probable overall impact, however, is positive in the long term.

Governments have increasingly become aware of the benefits to their country that franchising has to offer. As a result, many governments are in the process of improving their country's business environment in order to attract high quality franchises. The improvements have included positive legislation for franchise regulations and establishing support organizations, trade associations, and franchise education programs. In many cases, foreign governments have funded programs to encourage economic development through retail franchising in emerging economies, such as the USAID Programs in the former Soviet Republics.

On the other hand, retail franchising may have adverse effects on the host market. Retail franchising can sometimes supplant traditional and local cultural elements, which over time can lead to homogenization and westernization of preferences, especially among the youth population. The older generations and the political establishments often resist such cultural shifts.

International retail franchising often has the effect of displacing local industry, particularly "mom-and-pop" stores. These stores can not compete effectively with the distribution and marketing expertise of multinational franchisors. At the national level, franchising can negatively influence the host country's balance of payments over time because of the repatriation of fees and royalties by the franchisor.

1.4.6 Global consumers

Overall, franchising worldwide has had the effect of offering consumers lower prices through efficient distribution of goods and services, and consistent quality through standardization. This has been particularly true with the expansion of retail franchising. It is questionable it without retail franchising these two areas, higher quality and lower prices (that is, consumer value), would have improved at the rate that they have throughout the world market.

The efficiencies from the technological and digital revolution will probably lower costs even more for consumers. Increased retail franchising in the developing world will provide the data necessary for researchers and host-country governments to determine the impact of retail franchising on economic development. Such empirical research is badly needed.

1.5   A model of international retail franchising

1.5.1   Model development

Two major models have been developed in the area of retail franchising. In the first, Alon (1999) developed and tested a model of international franchising based on the literature of agency and resource-based theories that utilizes organizational characteristics – size, age growth, rate, fees, and royalties, combined with physical dispersion – to explain the internationalization of U.S. franchisors. The second approach examined marketing through a modular system as the standardization of the core elements ("absolutely must have modules") with the option to adapt peripheral elements ("menu modules"). Haueter (1983) was the first to develop this concept of core elements. Thompson and Merrilees (2001) apply this modular concept to three international retail franchise cases: McDonald's (U.S.), Cash Converters and CarLovers (both Australian). Through these case studies, the authors make a case for the applicability of this modular approach to international franchise research, regardless of the franchising system's origin. They argue that all franchisors contemplating internationalizing into emerging markets could benefit from having a system containing these three modular subsystems – marketing, branding, and operations. Each subsystem requires a "core" and also needs to contain "menu elements." The host country's culture is cited by the authors as a critical element for successful franchise development. Emerging markets are heterogeneous rather than homogenous in nature. The authors believe that culture itself will determine the way in which menu elements are determined because of this heterogeneity. They call for further research to include these key concepts in model development.

1.5.2   Practice and theory development

Authors have also examined why retail franchising has had such an impact internationally and what forms retail franchising has taken in different parts of the world. Grimaldi (1992) analyzed the opportunities for retail franchising in free trade zones. Kaufmann (2001) inspected issues of cultural and legal differences in the age of the Internet and the impact of retail franchising on host country development. Specifically, he investigated already proven concepts in retail franchising, modes of entry, cultural and legal differences, host country development, and technological advances. The purpose of the paper was to begin examining the benefits and costs of international business format franchising from the perspective of three major constituencies – the host country government, the local franchisee, and the international franchisor. Integral to this discussion was the adaptability of the franchise systems to the various cultures, legal frameworks, and economic issues in developing countries.

Stanworth, Price, and Purdy (2001) deemed retail franchising a means of technology-transfer for developing economies. Their article explored the background inherent in the internationalization of retail franchising, including favorable factors to growth, benefits to developing economies, other consequences to developing economies, advantages and risks to franchisors, as well as government action to encourage retail franchising. The authors recognized factors that are favorable to the growth of retail franchising as growing urbanization, rising disposable incomes, and expanding consumer markets. The benefits to developing countries were identified as managerial, marketing, and consumer know-how.

Other consequences to developing countries of the entry of retail franchising were cultural homogeneity by exposure to Western tastes, loss of economic diversity, possible displacement of existing local businesses, repatriation of fees and profits, and notions of control from a distance. Government action to encourage retail franchising was cited as the relaxation of legislation to allow foreign ownership and conformity with international codes of copyright protections, trademark rights, and other forms of intellectual property. The authors conferred special insight into Indonesia, China, and Brazil. The authors used the example of Indonesia and China to illustrate government action to encourage retail franchising. The paper closes with the call for development of models, theory, and research in emerging franchise markets.

1.6   World market areas

Table 1.1 summarizes international retail franchising articles by world market, year published, title of article, and author(s). These articles are reviewed below.

Central and Eastern Europe. Article, "The Use of Franchising as a Tool for SME Development in Developing Economies: A Case of Central European Economics," gave his personal perspective on the use of retail franchising as an economic development tool from his numerous experiences with those countries. He summarized the current state of retail franchising in Eastern Europe as compared to 1997 when he first looked at the topic (Sanghavi, 1997).

Table 1.1   Summary of U.S. published articles on franchising in emerging markets*

Year	Title	Author(s)
1988	Franchising in Asia	Justis, Neilson, and Yoo
1988	International business format franchising and retail entrepreneurship: A possible source of retail know-how for developing countries:	Kaufmann and Leibenstein
1990	Franchise management in East Asia	Chan and Justis
1991	Opportunities and challenges for franchisors in the U.S.S.R.: Preliminary results of a survey of Soviet university students	Welsh and Swerdlow
1992	The future of franchising in the U.S.S.R.: A statistical analysis of the opinions of Soviet university students	Swerdlow and Welsh
1992	Franchising opportunities in the free trade zones of developing countries	Grimaldi
1992	Pizzas in Mexico? Si!	Willems, English, and Ito
1992	Franchising entry and developmental strategies in the former Soviet Union	Christy and Haftel
1993	Pizza Hut in Moscow: Post-coup system development and expansion	Christy and Haftel
1993	A cross cultural study of American and Russian hotel employees: A preliminary review and its implications for franchisors	Welsh and Swerdlow
1994	A survey of franchising in Singapore	Chan, Foo, Quek, and Justis
1994	Franchising in China: A look at KFC and McDonald's	English and Xau
1994	Does business format management master Marxism in post-coup Russia?	Swerdlow and Bushmarin
1995	Franchising in Brazil	Josias and McIntryre
1995	Franchising in India: An introduction	Paswan and Dant
1995	Franchising in Indonesia	Chan and Justis
1996	Franchising in South Africa	Scholtz
1996	Franchising into Asia: An overview of selected target markets	McCosker
1996	Local franchising development in Singapore	Goh and Lee
1996	The case of the elegant shoplifter, Shuwaikh, Kuwait	Welsh, Raven, and Al-Bisher
1997	Franchising as a tool for SME development in transitional economies: The case of Central European countries	Sanghavi
1997	An overview of South African franchising	Scholtz
1998	NAFTA and franchising: A comparison of franchisor perceptions of characteristics associated with franchisee success and failure in Canada, Mexico, and the United States	Falbe and Welsh

Continued

Table 1.1 Continued

Year	Title	Author(s)
1998	Franchising in Slovenia: Support to the development of franchise systems in Central Europe	Pavlin
1998	Case Study: Strategic alliances in international franchising – the entry of Silver Streak Restaurant Corporation into Mexico	Hadjimarcou and Barnes
2000	New trends in Slovenian franchising	Pavlin
2000	International franchising: Evidence from US and Canadian franchisors in Mexico	Lafontaine and Oxley
2001	International Franchising in China: An Interview with Kodak	Alon
2002	American Franchising Competitiveness in China	Alon, Toncar, and Lu
2003	Exporting Retail Franchises to China	Frazer
2004	Brand country of origin knowledge and image: India	Paswan and Sharma
2005	The International Business Environments of Franchising in Russia	Anttonen, Tuunanen, and Alon
2005	Determinants of Monitoring Capabilities: East Asia	Choo
2005	Real Estate Franchising: The Case of Coldwell Banker Expansion into China	Alon and Ke
2007	The Selection of International Retail Franchisees in East Asia	Choo, Mazarol, and Soutar
2008	A Cross-Cultural Comparison of the Pluer Forms in Franchise: Brazil	Dant, Perrigot, and Cliquet
2008	Issues for International Franchising: Poland	Lee
2008	Using a Modular System Approach to International Franchising: Poland	Miller
2009	Impacts of US based Franchising in the Developing World: Middle East	Grunhagen, Witte, and Pryor

Note: For a complete citation, see the Reference list.
*The authors do not intend for this list to be comprehensive.

Swerdlow, Roehl, and Welsh (2001) and Alon and Banai (2001) in their respective articles "Hospitality Franchising in Russia for the 21st Century: Issues, Strategies, and Challenges," and "Franchising Opportunities and Threats in Russia," gave us a historical review of franchise development in Russia, as well as a current and future look at the prospects for retail franchise development in an area of the world that is barely realizing its full potential as an economic power. Both articles examined the postcommunist economy with a focus on environmental factors associated with international retail franchise development and entry strategies that those potential franchisors would find successful. The articles included some practical suggestions for those entering and maneuvering through this huge market. Skip Swerdlow and Dianne Welsh, along with coauthors, published a number of articles in the early 1990s examining franchising in the former U.S.S.R. that are summarized in the aforementioned article (Swerdlow and Bushmarin, 1994; Welsh and Swerdlow 1991, 1993). Christy and Haftel also summarized the early Russian market place in a 1992 article. The next year (1993), these authors published the only case study on franchising in Russia in the early era, on Pizza Hut entering the Moscow market. Today's Russia is very different, both politically and economically. Anttonen et al (2005) provide an up-to-date examination of the opportunities and threats in the Russian franchising market. Despite much liberalization, many obstacles remain in the market.

Aneta Nedialkova (2001) specifically examined franchising opportunities in Bulgaria, with a focus on the macroeconomic factors of the Bulgarian economy associated with retail franchising. While international investors have been developing franchises in Bulgaria for more than 25 years, the market has remained sluggish, given the government system and bureaucracy. However, the article described a number of positive elements and success stories that gave reasons to be optimistic concerning the future of retail franchise development in Bulgaria.

Ljiljana Viducic and Gordana Brcic (2001) described the two types of franchise arrangements that are prevalent in Croatia, using the examples of McDonald's and Diners Club. Primarily, retail franchising has taken the form of several corporate facilities in operation, where local interaction with the store is limited to employment, not ownership. The second form, where an entrepreneur is taken on as a franchise holder with the understanding that his capital involvement will increase over time as well as his ownership interest as a full franchisee. Additionally, the article elaborated on the current state of Croatian franchise activity and other forms of market expansion that have been successful in Croatia.

Pavlin (2001) analyzed empirically the current condition of Slovenian franchising. Using the definition of franchising adopted by the European Franchise Federation, there are currently more than 40 operating franchise systems in Slovenia. He compared these results to studies he conducted on Slovenian franchising that were published in 1998 and 2000. In 1998, there were 40 franchises operating in his country, of which 20 participated in his survey on the current state of franchising. The article included results from a recent survey of prospective

Slovenian franchisees, identifying their core attributes and offering a framework for profitable future development of the franchise industry in Slovenia.

Mexico and South America. Three articles focus on different aspects of Mexican franchising. Teegan (2001) examined foreign expansion and market entry from three different perspectives. The first perspective is the Mexican franchisee who might purchase the rights to an U.S.-based franchise. The second perspective is the U.S. franchisor that might sell the rights to its business format. The third perspective is that of the host government, namely Mexico, in terms of the economic impact and development within their country. The author shared the results of a survey of more than 70 Mexican franchisees of U.S.-based franchise systems. Results showed that the commonly held beliefs within both the United States and Mexico concerning the desirability of retail franchising as a mode of market entry and caution on the part of franchisees, franchisors, and the host governments are both warranted. The article gives a realistic view of the risks and rewards of retail franchising and a bountiful amount of information for those contemplating retail franchising in Mexico.

Hadjimarcou and Barnes (2001) explained the expansion process of a relatively new and small franchisor, Silver Streak Restaurant Corporation, into Mexico in a case study. Silver Streak Restaurant Corporation originally opened its first franchised restaurant in 1996 in Juarez, a city of 1.5 million on the border of the United States (Hadjimarcou and Barnes 1998). The authors explained the cultural challenges of entering Mexico, the company's efforts to identify a suitable partner in the host country, the adaptation of the concept to address differences in the new market, and the multitude of crucial decisions that must be made when going international. The authors discussed the recent changes in the law that favored franchising, as well as the role that strategic alliances played in the success of the corporation's international franchise efforts. Implications for both research and practitioners are explicated.

Welsh (2001) updated a study conducted by Falbe and Welsh from 1988 that was the first to examine the effect, if any, of the North American Free Trade Agreement (NAFTA) on franchisor perceptions of characteristics associated with franchisee success and failure in Canada, Mexico, and the United States. The original research addressed two key issues in franchising. The first was the extent of the franchisee study's success and failure, which they studied by analyzing franchise executives' perceptions of the importance of a number of characteristics associated with franchisee success and failure. The second was the differences among the executives' perceptions of these characteristics based on the location of the franchisor – Canada, Mexico, or the United States. Their study found that the respondents' perceptions of the importance of system quality, brand name, local environment and communication, and other scales of franchisor and franchisee activities differed by country of origin. Additionally, the study's results showed that neither business type nor franchise size had any effect on perceptions of success or failure. Welsh examined the research that had been conducted since the study appeared in 1998 and what was known as of 2001. In a similar study, Lafontaine and Oxley (2000) found that the majority of U.S. and Canadian franchisors employed the same contract terms in Mexico as in their home market. Their study discussed the operations of more than 200 U.S. and Canadian franchisors in Mexico.

In 1995 Josias and McIntyre published the first article examining franchising in Brazil. In 2001, McIntyre gave us an update on what is now the third largest franchising market in the world. Only the United States and Canada have more franchises than Brazil. The author covers the history of franchising in Brazil, describing what is unique about Brazilian franchising, and giving her view of the country's prospects for the future franchise market. McIntyre views Brazilian franchising as ripe for development, evidenced by the size of the domestic franchise industry, the demographics of the population, and current economic conditions.

Asia. Researchers began publishing articles on franchising in Asia during 1995. McCosker (1996) reported on a survey of foreign franchisors that wished to enter the Asian markets of Singapore, Malaysia, Hong Kong, and Indonesia. He gathered information from the existing literature as well as franchisors that had already entered these markets and interviews during visits to those countries. Chan, Foo, Quek, and Justis (1994) published an article that reported on a survey identifying the major franchises that existed, the different types of franchises, and the nature and characteristics of franchise agreements in Singapore. Subsequent to an earlier study that examined franchising in East Asia, in general (1990), Goh and Lee (1996) surveyed 62 franchisors in Singapore. They assessed the state of retail franchise development as well as franchise fee structures, the prevalence of homegrown franchises, and the effect of the government's efforts to promote franchising. Chiou, Hsieh, and Yang (2004) examined franchisee satisfaction and intention to remain in the franchise system in Taiwan. In 1995, Chan and Justis looked at franchising in Indonesia by investigating the climate for franchising and the perceptions of the Indonesian people on franchising.

English and Xau (1994) explored franchising in China by reporting on the entrance into and subsequent experiences of two U.S.-based franchises in that country: Kentucky Fried Chicken (KFC) and McDonald's. Recent relations between the U.S. and China have been anything but warm; however, the Chinese still love the retail franchising concept. In April of 2001, when a U.S. surveillance plane went down on Chinese soil, there was still a block-long line on a rainy evening to dine at Pizza Hut. There are 326 McDonald's, as well as several Starbucks Coffee, Kenny Rogers Roasters, Pizza Hut, and KFC franchises, among others, that were showing no sign of slow sales . Not unlike Russia, China has also changed markedly in the last number of years and the conditions vary by industry. Alon and his colleagues (2002, 2005) provide a review of the restaurant and professional services, respectively.

Other Areas. Franchising around the globe has been explored in a number of other emerging market countries, including India (Paswan and Dant 1995), Kuwait (Welsh, Raven, and Al-Bisher 1996), and South Africa (Scholtz 1996, 1997). Paswan and Dant (1995) published an exploratory study of franchising in India that looked at the definition of franchising and its meaning in the American markets as compared to the Indian markets. The authors also included a framework for understanding the franchise industry internationally. Kuwait is explored from a case study perspective of a Mercedes Benz retail franchise dealing with a shoplifter of spare parts (Welsh, Raven, and Al-Bisher 1996). Scholtz in his 1996 and subsequent 1997 articles described the state and penetration of franchising as a form of business in South Africa. He included an overview of the environment for franchising, the population, and the legal regulations concerning franchising. In 1997, he reported that there were 170 franchise systems and 6000 outlets operating in the country and that the market was ripe for more entry of international retail franchises.

1.7   Conclusion

We have attempted to summarize and explain the current state of research in the area of emerging franchise markets worldwide. We accomplished this by first discussing the nature and scope of emerging markets, then summarizing the research both from a theoretical and practical development perspective as well as by specific franchise studies by region of the world. In doing so, we hoped to have raised the level of understanding among franchisors, franchisees, franchise associations, consultants, and academics concerning franchising around the globe. To our knowledge, this is the first attempt at summarizing the research on a global basis, from both practitioner and academic viewpoints.

Emerging markets are becoming more important as opportunities for retail franchising in the U.S. diminish because of market saturation and increased competition. Many of the industries in which franchising prevails are mature and offer little economic profit in developed markets. Such industries include fast food, retailing, hotels and motels, and other service-based businesses.

On the other hand, emerging markets prefer markets that are unsaturated, poised for growth, and have pent-up demand for products and services embodying international standards and quality. Franchising allows local entrepreneurs to own and operate outlets that belong to multinational companies and that have well-known brand name awareness. Kodak Express outlets in China are a case in point. These outlets, owned and operated by Chinese entrepreneurs, distribute a variety of image-based internationally known products to local consumers in 50 cities around China. There are currently more then 5000 such outlets operating in China alone (Alon, 2001).

1.8   Future research

We hope this furthers the discussion of franchising in emerging markets and leads to a more comprehensive development of the international field of retail franchising. In particular, theory development as well as thorough empirical research need to be conducted on all aspects of franchising in emerging markets. Consideration should be given to the role of government in the franchise relationship. How this varies from country to country and region to region needs to be examined, as well as the climate toward the host country franchise and the culture of the country and region.

Future research should also concentrate on the role of information technology in franchising globally and the positive and negative aspects of the information age in franchising. For example, the Internet is a great way to disseminate training information worldwide but may also have the negative effect of a lack of personal contact during which to exchange vital information between the franchisee and the franchisor, such as cultural norms and behaviors that are better understood on a personal basis.

More research is also needed to identify the determinants of the modes of entry available for international retail franchisors. While there are many permutations for international retail franchising, such as licensing, area franchising, master franchising, direct franchising, etc. little research is available to explain why and how franchisors have used various modes of entry in penetrating emerging markets. Master international retail franchising, joint ventures, and wholly owned subsidiaries have all been used as methods of entering emerging markets. Master international retail franchising seems to be the preferred mode by many small and medium sized franchisors.

The need for adaptation vs. standardization needs to be explored further in emerging markets. While standardization allows a franchisor to ensure consistent quality which leads to brand awareness, emerging markets are often so different that significant modifications in operations or format of the original system are sorely needed. This area is ripe for research, as international retail franchising in emerging markets will continue to increase. Further model development needs to occur. We hope that this article will stimulate additional discussion and debate both in academic circles and by international retail franchising practitioners who seek a greater understanding of their global environment.

References

Alon, Ilan (1999). *The Internationalization of U.S. Franchising Systems*. New York, New York: Garland Publishing.

Alon, Ilan (2001). "International Franchising in China: An Interview with Kodak," *Proceedings of the International Society of Franchising.* Minneapolis, Minn.: University of St. Thomas Institute for Franchise Management.

Alon, Ilan (2004). "Global Franchising and Development in Emerging and Transitioning Markets," *Journal of Macromarketing*, 24 (2), 156–67.

Alon, Ilan, and Moshe Banai (2001). "Franchising Opportunities and Threats in Russia," in *International Franchising in Emerging Markets: Central and Eastern Europe and Latin America.* Eds. Dianne H.B. Welsh and Ilan Alon. Chicago, Ill.: CCH, Inc., 131–48.

Alon, Ilan, and Ke Bian (2005). "Real Estate Franchising: The Case of Coldwell Banker Expansion into China," *Business Horizons*, 48 (3), 223–31.

Alon, Ilan, and David I. McKee (1999). "Towards a Macro-Environmental Model of International Franchising," *Multinational Business Review* 7(1), 76–82.

Alon, Ilan, Mark Toncar, and Lu Le (2002). "American Franchising Competitiveness in China," *Journal of Global Competitiveness*, 10 (1), 65–83.

Amies, Michael (1999). "The Wilder Shores of Franchising," *Franchising World*, 27–28.

Anttonen, Noora, Mika Tuunanen, and Ilan Alon (2005). "The International Business Environments of Franchising in Russia," *Academy of Marketing Science Review*, (5), 1–18.

Arnold, David J., and John A. Quelch (1988). "New Strategies in Emerging Markets," *Sloan Management Review* 40 (1), 720.

Boyle, Emily (1999). "A Study of the Impact of Environment Uncertainty on Franchise Systems: The Case of Petrol Retailing in the UK," *Journal of Consumer Marketing* 16(2), 18195.

Brehaus, Brian (1998). "Risky Business?", *Restaurant Business* (November 1), 3542.

Brickley, James A. and Frederick Dark (1987). "The Choice of Organizational Form: The Case of Franchising," *Journal of Financial Economics* 18 (June): 40120.

Chan, Peng S., John K.S. Foo, George Quek, and Robert T. Justis (1994). "A Survey of Franchising in Singapore," *Proceedings of the International Society of Franchising*. Minneapolis, Minn.: University of St. Thomas Institute for Franchise Management.

Chan, Peng S., and Robert T. Justis (1990). "Franchise Management in East Asia," *Academy of Management Executive* 4 (2), 75–85.

Chan, Peng S., and Robert T. Justis (1995). "Franchising in Indonesia," *Proceedings of the International Society of Franchising*. Minneapolis, Minn.: University of St. Thomas Institute for Franchise Management.

Chiou, Jyh-Shen, Chia-Hung Hsieh, and Ching-Hsien Yang (2004). "The Effect of Franchisors' Communication, Service Assistance, and Competitive Advantage on Franchisees' Intentions to Remain in the Franchise System." *Journal of Small Business Management* 42 (1) 19–36.

Choo, Stephen (2005). "Determinants of Monitoring Capabilities in International Franchising: Foodservice Firms within East Asia." Asia Pacific Journal of Management, 22 (2), 159–77.

Choo, Stephen, Tim Mazzarol, and Geoff Soutar. (2007). The selection of international retail franchisees in East Asia. Asia Pacific Journal of Marketing and Logistics, 19 (4), 380–97.

Christy, Ronald, and Sandra M. Haftel (1992). "Franchising Entry and Developmental Strategies in the Former Soviet Union," *Proceedings of the International Society of Franchising*. Minneapolis, Minn.: University of St. Thomas Institute for Franchise Management.

Christy, Ronald, and Sandra M. Haftel (1993). "Pizza Hut in Moscow: Post-Coup System Development and Expansion," *Proceedings of the International Society of Franchising*. Minneapolis, Minn.: University of St. Thomas Institute for Franchise Management.

Clarke, Greg. (1997). *Buying Your First Franchise*, 2nd ed., London, England: Kogan Page.

Coase, Ronald H. (1937). "The Nature of the Firm," *Economica* 4 (November): 386–405.

Connell, John (1999). "Diversity in Large Firm International Franchise Strategy," *Journal of Consumer Marketing* 16 (1), 8695.

Czinkota, Michael R., and Ilkka A. Ronkainen (1997). "International Business and Trade in the Next Decade: Report from a Delphi Study," *Journal of International Business Studies* 28 (4), 82744.

Dana, Leo Paul, Hamid Etemad, and Richard W. Wright (2001). "Franchising in Emerging Markets: Symbiotic Interdependence within Marketing Networks," in *International Franchising in Emerging Markets: Central and Eastern Europe and*

Latin America. Eds. Dianne H.B. Welsh and Ilan Alon. Chicago, Ill.: CCH, Inc., 119–29.

Dant, R., Perrigot, R., and Cliquet,G. (2008). "A Cross-Cultural Comparison of the Plural Forms in Franchise Networks: United States, France, and Brazil," Journal of Small Business Management, 46 (2), 286–311.

Doherty, Anne Marie, and Barry Quinn (1999). "International Retail Franchising: An Agency Theory Perspective," *International Journal of Retail and Distribution Management* 27 (6), 224–36.

Elango, Balasubramanian, and Vance A. Fried (1997). "Franchise Research: A Literature Review and Synthesis," *Journal of Small Business Management* 35 (3), 68–81.

English, Wilke, and Chin Xau (1994). "Franchising in China: A Look at KFC and McDonald's," *Proceedings of the International Society of Franchising.* Minneapolis, Minn.: University of St. Thomas Institute for Franchise Management.

Etemad, Hamid, Richard W. Wright, and Leo Paul Dana (2001). "Symbiotic International Business Networks: Collaboration between Small and Large Firms," *Thunderbird International Business Review* 43 (4), 281–301.

Falbe, Cecilia M., and Dianne H.B. Welsh (1998). "NAFTA and Franchising: A Comparison of Franchisor Perceptions of Characteristics Associated with Franchisee Success and Failure in Canada, Mexico, and the United States," *Journal of Business Venturing* 13 (2), 151–71.

Frazer, Lorelle (2003). "Exporting Retail Franchises to China. Journal of Asia Pacific Marketing, 2 (1), 111

Goh, Mark, and Heng Lee (1996). "Local Franchising Development in Singapore," *Franchising Research: An International Journal* 1 (3), 8–20.

Grimaldi, Antonio (1992). "Franchising Opportunities in the Free Trade Zones of Developing Countries," *Proceedings of the International Society of Franchising.* Minneapolis, Minn.: University of St. Thomas Institute for Franchise Management.

Grünhagen, Marko, Carl L. Witte, and Susie Pryor (2009). "Impacts of U.S.-based Franchising in the Developing World: A Middle-Eastern Consumer Perspective," *Journal of Consumer Behaviour* (forthcoming).

Hackett, Donald W. (1976). "The International Expansion of US Franchise Systems: Status and Strategies," *Journal of International Business Studies* 7 (1), 65–75.

Hadjimarcou, John, and John W. Barnes (1998). "Case Study: Strategic Alliances in International Franchising- the Entry of Silver Streak Restaurant Corporation into Mexico," *Journal of Consumer Marketing* 15 (6), 598–607.

Hadjimarcou, John, and John W. Barnes. (2001). "Strategic Alliances in International Franchising: The Entry of Silver Streak Restaurant Corporation into Mexico," in *International Franchising in Emerging Markets: Central and Eastern Europe and Latin America.* Eds. Dianne H.B. Welsh and Ilan Alon. Chicago, Ill.: CCH, Inc., 293–306.

Haueter, Edward (1983). "Organizing for International Marketing," *Vital Speeches of the Day,* 49 (20), 620–24.

Hoffman, Richard, and John Preble (2003). "Convert to Compete: Competitive Advantage through Conversion Franchising." *Journal of Small Business Management,* 41 (2), 187–204.

International Franchise Research Centre (2000). "World Wide Franchising Statistics," Available (IFRC Web Site) http://www.wmin.ac.uk/~purdyd/

Josias, Allen, and Faye S. McIntyre (1995). "Franchising in Brazil," *Proceedings of the International Society of Franchising*. Minneapolis, Minn.: University of St. Thomas Institute for Franchise Management.

Justis, Robert T., Warren Nielson, and Sang J. Yoo (1988). "Franchising in Asia," *Proceedings of the International Society of Franchising*. Minneapolis, Minn.: University of St. Thomas Institute for Franchise Management.

Kaufmann, Patrick J. (2001). "International Business Format Franchising and Retail Entrepreneurship: A Possible Source of Retail Know-How for Developing Countries-Post-Script," in *International Franchising in Emerging Markets: Central and Eastern Europe and Latin America*. Eds. Dianne H.B. Welsh and Ilan Alon. Chicago, Ill.: CCH, Inc., 80–85.

Kaufmann, Patrick J. and Harvey Leibenstein (1988). "International Business Format Franchising and Retail Entrepreneurship: A Possible Source of Retail Know-How for Developing Countries," *Journal of Development Planning* 18, 165–79.

Lafontaine, Francine, and Joanne Oxley (2000). "International Franchising: Evidence from US and Canadian Franchisors in Mexico," *Proceedings of the International Society of Franchising*. Minneapolis, Minn.: University of St. Thomas Institute for Franchise Management.

Lee, K. (2008). Issues for International Franchising: Lessons from the Case of a Poland-Based Restaurant Operator. Cornell Hospitality Quarterly, 49 (4), 454. Retrieved August 6, 2009, from ABI/INFORM Global. (Document ID: 1596424091).

Mathewson, G. Frank and Ralph Winter (1985). The Economics of Franchise Contracts," *Journal of Law and Economics* 28 (October): 503–26.

McCosker, Colin F. (1996). "Franchising into Asia: An Overview of Selected Target Markets," *Proceedings of the International Society of Franchising*. Minneapolis, Minn.: University of St. Thomas Institute for Franchise Management.

McIntyre, Faye S. (2001). "World-Class Franchising: The Case of Brazil," in *International Franchising in Emerging Markets: Central and Eastern Europe and Latin America*. Eds. Dianne H.B. Welsh and Ilan Alon. Chicago, Ill.: CCH, Inc., 223–32.

Milbank, Dana (2001, April 21). "Protesters Disrupt Summit on Trade," *Washington Post*, 124 (137), A1, A16.

Miller, B. (2008). Using a Modular System Approach to International Franchising: Analyzing the Case Study of a Poland-Based Restaurant Operator. Cornell Hospitality Quarterly, 49 (4), 458. Retrieved August 6, 2009, from ABI/INFORM Global. (Document ID: 1596424101).

Nair, S.R. (2001). "Franchising Opportunities in China from the Perspective of a Franchisee," in *International Franchising in Emerging Markets: China, India, and other Asian Countries*. Eds. Ilan Alon and Dianne H.B. Welsh. Chicago, Ill.: CCH, Inc., 109–21.

Nedialkova, Aneta A. (2001). "Bulgaria-Economic Development and Franchising," in *International Franchising in Emerging Markets: Central and Eastern Europe and Latin America*. Eds. Dianne H.B. Welsh and Ilan Alon. Chicago, Ill.: CCH, Inc., 203–14.

Norton, Seth W. (1988). "An Empirical Look at Franchising as an Organizational Form," *Journal of Business* 61 (2): 197–218.

Paswan, Audhesh K., and Rajiv P. Dant (1995). "Franchising in India: An Introduction", *Proceedings of the International Society of Franchising.* Minneapolis, Minn.: University of St. Thomas Institute for Franchise Management.

Paswan, Audhesh K. and Dheeraj Sharma. (2004). "Brand-country of origin (COO) knowledge and COO image: investigation in an emerging franchise market," *The Journal of Product and Brand Management*, 13 (2/3), 144–55.

Pavlin, Igor (1998). "Franchising in Slovenia: Support to the Development of Franchise Systems in Central Europe," *Proceedings of the International Society of Franchising.* Minneapolis, Minn.: University of St. Thomas Institute for Franchise Management.

Pavlin, Igor (2000). "New Trends in Slovenian franchising," *Proceedings of the International Society of Franchising.* Minneapolis, Minn.: University of St. Thomas Institute for Franchise Management.

Pavlin, Igor (2001). "Central Europe: Franchising in Slovenia," in *International Franchising in Emerging Markets: Central and Eastern Europe and Latin America.* Eds. Dianne H.B. Welsh and Ilan Alon. Chicago, Ill.: CCH, Inc., 189–201.

Rubin, Paul (1978). "The Theory of the Firm and the Structure of the Franchise Contract," *Journal of Law and Economics* 21 (April): 223–33.

Sanghavi, Nitin (1997). "Franchising as a Tool for SME Development in Transitional Economies: The Case of Central European Countries," *Proceedings of the International Society of Franchising.* Minneapolis, Minn.: University of St. Thomas Institute for Franchise Management.

Scholtz, Gert J. (1996). "Franchising in South Africa," *Proceedings of the International Society of Franchising.* Minneapolis, Minn.: University of St. Thomas Institute for Franchise Management.

Scholtz, Gert J. (1997). "An Overview of South African Franchising," *Franchising Research: An International Journal* 2 (4), 145–51.

Stanworth, John, Price Staurt, and David Purdy (2001). "Franchising as a Source of Technology Transfer to Developing Countries," *International Franchising in Emerging Markets: Central and Eastern Europe and Latin America.* Eds. Dianne H.B. Welsh and Ilan Alon. Chicago, Ill.: CCH, Inc., 87–103.

Swartz, Leonard N. (2001). "Franchising Successfully Circles the Globe," in *International Franchising in Emerging Markets: Central and Eastern Europe and Latin America.* Eds. Dianne H.B. Welsh and Ilan Alon. Chicago, Ill.: CCH, Inc., 43–61.

Swerdlow, Skip, and Nicholas Bushamarin (1994). "Does Business Format Management Master Marxism in Post-Coup Russia? Franchise System Mentality Creeps into the Lodging Industry," *Proceedings of the International Society of Franchising.* Minneapolis, Minn.: University of St. Thomas Institute for Franchise Management.

Swerdlow, Skip, Wesley S. Roehl, and Dianne H.B. Welsh (2001). "Hospitality Franchising in Russia for the 21st Century: Issues, Strategies, and Challenges," in *International Franchising in Emerging Markets: Central and Eastern Europe and Latin America.* Eds. Dianne H.B. Welsh and Ilan Alon. Chicago, Ill.: CCH, Inc., 149–70.

Swerdlow, Skip, and Dianne H.B. Welsh (1992). "The Future of Franchising in the U.S.S.R.: A Statistical Analysis of the Opinions of Soviet University

Students," *Proceedings of the International Society of Franchising.* Minneapolis, Minn.: University of St. Thomas Institute for Franchise Management.

Teegan, Hildy (2001). "Strategic and Economic Development Implications of Globalizing through Franchising: Evidence from the Case of Mexico," in *International Franchising in Emerging Markets: Central and Eastern Europe and Latin America.* Eds. Dianne H.B. Welsh and Ilan Alon. Chicago, Ill.: CCH, Inc., 265–92.

Thompson, Megan, and Bill Merrilees (2001). "A Modular Approach to Branding and Operations for International Franchising Systems in Emerging Markets," in *International Franchising in Emerging Markets: Central and Eastern Europe and Latin America.* Eds. Dianne H.B. Welsh and Ilan Alon. Chicago, Ill.: CCH, Inc., 105–18.

Viducic, Ljiljana and Gordana Brcic (2001). "The Role of Franchising in Establishing and Internationalization of Business with Special Reference to Croatia," in *International Franchising in Emerging Markets: Central and Eastern Europe and Latin America.* Eds. Dianne H.B. Welsh and Ilan Alon. Chicago, Ill.: CCH, Inc., 215–22.

Welch, Lawrence S. (1989). "Diffusion of Franchise Systems Use in International Operations," *International Marketing Review* 6 (5), 7–19.

Welsh, Dianne H.B. (2001). "NAFTA and Franchising: A Post-Script," in *International Franchising in Emerging Markets: Central and Eastern Europe and Latin America.* Eds Dianne H.B. Welsh and Ilan Alon. Chicago, Ill: CCH, Inc.

Welsh, Dianne H.B. and Cecilia M. Falbe (2001). "Multiple Uses of the Internet in Franchising," Symposium presented at the 15th Conference of the International Society of Franchising, Las Vegas, Nev.

Welsh, Dianne H.B., Peter Raven, and Faisel Al-Bisher (1996). "The Case of the Elegant Shoplifter, Shuwaikh, Kuwait," *Franchising Research: An International Journal* 11 (3), 43–45.

Welsh, Dianne H.B., and Skip Swerdlow (1991). "Opportunities and Challenges for Franchisors in the U.S.S.R.: Preliminary Results of a Survey of Soviet University Students," *Proceedings of the International Society of Franchising.* Minneapolis, Minn.: University of St. Thomas Institute for Franchise Management.

Welsh, Dianne H.B., and Skip Swerdlow (1993). "A Cross-Cultural Study of American and Russian Hotel Employees: A Preliminary Review and Its Implications for Franchisors," *Proceedings of the International Society of Franchising.* Minneapolis, Minn.: University of St. Thomas Institute for Franchise Management.

Willems, Jo, Wilke English, and Victor Ito (1992). "Pizzas in Mexico? Si!," *Proceedings of the International Society of Franchising.* Minneapolis, Minn.: University of St. Thomas Institute for Franchise Management.

Young, Joyce A., Faye S. McIntryre, and Robert D. Green (2000). "The International Society of Franchising Proceedings: A Thirteen-Year Review," *Proceedings of the International Society of Franchising.* Minneapolis, Minn.: University of St. Thomas Institute for Franchise.

2
Franchising as an Entrepreneurial Form

Ilan Alon and Marc Sardy

2.1 Introduction

This study makes a singular contribution to the literature by being the first to analyze the differences between nascent entrepreneurs and franchisees using the Panel Study of Entrepreneurial Dynamics (PSED) national database of the United States of America. The PSED, developed through the entrepreneurship research consortium, was one of the most comprehensive studies ever completed on nascent entrepreneurs.

Entrepreneurs and franchisees are often considered different types of people when considering risky start-up ventures. The image of an entrepreneur is a person who is willing to take large risks on uncertain ventures on the chance that they will create something original and sustainable. Franchisees have a slightly different image as they become partners in an already established business model and attempt to develop it to sustainability through the institutional wisdom of the franchisor. In short, franchises are arrangements that let a person or team start a business using the name and standards of a parent corporation. Franchises combine the advantages of a large corporation with those of a sole proprietorship or partnership. Therefore, franchisees can be said to be a type of entrepreneur. There are multiple entrepreneurial types (Williams, 1999). They range from solo self-employed individuals to corporate entrepreneurs. Franchisees are positioned somewhere between them (Knight, 1984).

According to Kaufmann and Dant (1999), franchisees meet several definitional frameworks of entrepreneurship: Liebenstein's (1968) framework through risk taking, leadership, motivation, and ability to meet crises; Knight's (1984) framework through their uncertainty of investment and their uncertainty aversion; Low and MacMillan's (1988) and Gartner's (1985) framework through creation of new enterprises; and Cole's (1968) framework through initiation and development of profit-oriented business. Franchisees receive training in how to operate the business and pay a fee and a percentage of their income or profit to the parent corporation.

Very few studies have examined the differences between nascent entrepreneurs and franchisees. Knight (1984) examined the differences between Canadian franchisees and independent entrepreneurs with respect to personal characteristics, management skills, financing required, and support services and found that differences exist, in part, because franchisees are less independent than other entrepreneurs. We examined many variables that enabled us to make comparisons between Knight's study and (PSED) data.

Section 2.2 will discuss the model, the variables used, and the reasoning for using them. Section 2.3 will discuss the methodology in our comparison of Knight (1984) to the PSED data. Section 2.4 will discuss the results of our comparison between the PSED and Knight. In Section 2.5 we will show a logistic model that we have developed to differentiate nascent entrepreneurs from franchisees. We will conclude with Section 2.6.

2.2 The model

Our model breaks the differences and similarities between entrepreneurs and franchisees into three functional areas: prior experience; growth objectives; and motivation and risk. Prior experience plays a role in the differences between franchisees and nascent entrepreneurs as they may have different values regarding previous experience and the skills and abilities that will be required for the success of their venture. Growth objectives may also differ between nascent entrepreneurs and franchisees as the franchisee should have an established business model that requires a certain level of staffing for an effective, approved business unit, while entrepreneurs are more likely to depend on their start-up team and may have different ideas of the overall growth objectives. In our analysis we also considered the start-up size as well as the ultimate size objective of the functional firm – whether they wanted the firm small and manageable or as large as possible. The final dimension had more to do with motivation and risk. We considered the level of risk which both groups considered, the effort they were willing to put into the venture, and the level of confidence that they exhibited in the prospects of their future venture.

While there may be more aspects of the "start-up decision," three dimensions of the attitudes and desires of the nascent businessperson seem to differentiate them: prior experience, objectives for growth, and motivation and risk. These dimensions account for much of the variation among start-ups; there is much in the literature that concurs with the importance of these variables, for example, Cliff et al (2006) and McCarthy and Leavy (1998/1999) discuss the value of previous experience, Greenbank (2006) and Sage (2003) discuss motivation and risk as well, and Baum, et al (1998) and Stevenson and Jarrillo-Mossi (1986) discuss objectives a driver for success in entrepreneurial firms. We accept Hunter's (2005) notion that there is a life cycle to entrepreneurship, common to both nascent entrepreneurs and franchisees. However, Price (1999) suggests that differences between nascent entrepreneurs and franchisees may be come from the audience that results from the way franchises are marketed.

Prior experience: We hypothesized that our two groups (nascent entrepreneurs and franchisees) based much of their decisionmaking on the values they hold about experience, their position on skills and abilities, and the importance of education. There is little agreement in the literature on value of prior experience, with Basu (1998) arguing the merit and Birley and Westhead (1993) arguing the opposite. Jo and Lee (1996) take the position that lack of education related to prior experience leads to the inconsequential merit associated with it. Wilkerson (1993) makes a case for the need for better training of franchisees.

Previous comparisons of the prior experience of our two groups have been displayed in minute detail in the work of others such as Stoner and Fry (1982) However, there are limitations to using the PSED data to mirror the original study. The PSED was primarily created to examine the attitudes and motivations of nascent entrepreneurs. In the course of the survey data on franchisees were also collected. The nature and direction of the questions were somewhat different from Stoner and Fry's original study. However we have identified several survey questions that capture similar information.

The PSED questionnaires also identified prior experience as the pragmatic skills and abilities the subjects believe that they already posses at start-up. Emphasis on what they already have is in striking contrast to what they may actually need to acquire for a successful venture. These skills and abilities are also distinct from those achieved through formal education, defined operationally by the PSED as the specific elements of education and various types of training measured by length of time of exposure and credentials acquired.

Objectives for growth: A second component of our model is the specific goals groups of nascent entrepreneurs and franchisees have for their objectives regarding growth. We hypothesize that these goals are seen in a continuous time frame in which we can identify both start-up and eventuality, with its essential ingredient of vision or futurity. The vision or futurity aspect is illusionary and, according to Ottesen and Gronhaug (2005), is a key element of innovation which is essential to new ventures. The goals of nascent entrepreneurs and franchisees were operationalized in our dataset by responses to questions in which nascent entrepreneurs envisioned the size of the start-up team and its long-term growth. Kamm et al (1990) discuss these size objectives of the team and the importance of defining the dimensions of the venture before expanding the team. Specifically, the size of the team might be seen as continuously small and manageable in future operations or it might be envisioned that the team would grow the venture into a very large organization. This projection of future vision may conflict with an analytical approach used by larger firms, such as searching for diminishing returns or increasing returns to scale or even one that utilizes a more realistic vision that considers competitors, financing, or other more objective measures.

Motivation and risk: The third and final component of our model is motivation and risk. There is a rich and controversial literature on motivation and risk at start-up. Recent publications by both Cressy (2006) and Kincaid (2005) point out that risk is a major determinant of start-up decisions. However, failure rates for nascent entrepreneurs and franchisees are in dispute. Castrogiovanni et al (1993) argue that the failure rate for and franchisees is lower than entrepreneurs, while Stanworth et al (1998) argue there are no differences. Levesque and Minniti (2006) point out that age, wealth, and risk aversion are critical to the start-up decision. Michael (1996) argues that risk undermines effective use of human capital, which is fundamental to motivation and risk. Norton and Moore (2006) make the case that it is information and not risk aversion which is fundamental to a venture's growth. Williams (1999) suggests that the gains from trade that are available to entrepreneurs are not available to franchisees and this increases franchisee risk.

Our PSED assessment of motivation and risk used a number of subjectively based questions that were not analytical (i.e. risk vs. return) and were extended to include effort and confidence as other elements of motivation and risk. Corman et al (1988) identified entrepreneurial motivation and risk-taking behavior, and a training program established at Glamorgan business school focused on building student confidence and motivating through exposure to entrepreneurial risk.[1] The concept of effort was defined globally as "if I work hard enough it will be difficult to fail, in contrast to a more specific appraisal of effort that would include hours of work, labor intensity, benefits, etc. Thus, confidence is seen as an element of motivation and risk. A high degree of confidence shapes and modifies this element."

These three components of our model are considered to be hierarchical, with all being at the same level, but with the elements considered as substates of the components. A flow chart of the model appears as Figure 2.1.

2.3   Methodology

We used the PSED dataset to because of its comprehensiveness and because it can be compared to other studies of nascent entrepreneurs and franchisees such as Knight (1984) and Stoner and Fry (1982). Although, the PSED study had also been conducted in several countries in Europe, Australia, and Latin America, a large part of that data remains unconsolidated with the data collected in the United States. Nevertheless, the PSED study remains the most comprehensive study of nascent entrepreneurs in existence today (Gartner et al, 2004).[2]

The PSED initially screened 64,622 respondents and contacted 830 nascent entrepreneurs and 431 comparison group members. Among the nascent entrepreneurs were 52 franchisees. Once respondents had agreed to be part of the survey they were sent mail surveys over a period of three years and ultimately contacted by phone to complete a phone survey. The combined surveys generated more than 5000 data items that follow respondents over a period of three years. For our study we have focused mainly on the results in the first year of the PSED. For a more in-depth coverage see Gartner et al (2004). We also compare results from the seminal study by Knight (1984) with the results from the PSED: this allows us to contrast Canadian data with the PSED data for the U.S. We use the results of our findings to offer models that may prove useful in differentiating these nascent individuals.

Until now the PSED dataset has been used solely to explore the attitudes and motivation of nascent entrepreneurs. However we found a great opportunity also to explore relationships and differences between nascent entrepreneurs and franchisees.[3] The dataset is quite robust and

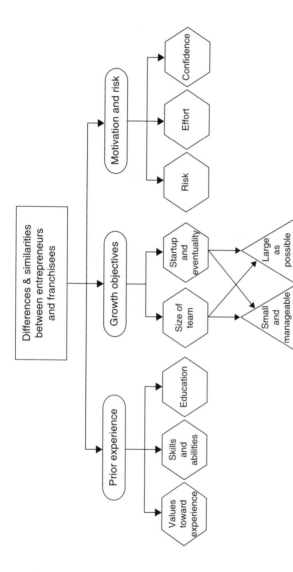

Figure 2.1 Nascent entrepreneur vs. franchisee components of differences and similarities

gathers information in several ways. For example, more than 41 question/response modes address the topic of experience. In the following analysis, a variety of statistical techniques was used with the result that the data range from categorical responses to continuous numerical data. As much of the data we used is categorical we used the "Chi-Square" test to examine differences in expected and observed values. We did not wish to start with assumptions of normality so the nonparametric Jonckheere-Terpstra comparison Test (J-T) was used to compare our findings to those of Knight.

2.4 Results

When we compared our findings with those of Knight, we found directionally similar results but PSED showed some significant differences. In Table 2.1 the directional agreement between several of our model variables is shown. In most cases we observe similar results in both studies. However, when we did a statistical analysis of comparison between both studies several of our comparison variables differed in the magnitude of their results between the two studies; skills and abilities, preference for future firm size, the confidence in the level of effort, and the expected first-year firm income (summaries of PSED variables are shown in Appendix 2.1).

Both studies found that the entrepreneurial group put more weight on previous experience. The Knight study put the independent (nascent

Table 2.1 Comparison of PSED findings with Knight (1984)

	PSED	Knight	
Past experience very valuable	Nascent entrepreneurs	Independents	Previous management experience in same industry very important
Skills and abilities will help	Nascent entrepreneurs	Independents	Management ability is very important
Team size	Similar	Similar	Team size of one
Confident I can put in effort	Nascent entrepreneurs	Independents	Willingness to work hard is very important
Experience of one year or less	Franchisees	Franchisee	No previous experience

entrepreneurs) group at 64 percent vs. 11 for franchisees. We found the PSED data showed that 67 percent for nascent entrepreneurs vs. 37 of the franchisee group agreed very strongly with the value of previous experience. Start-up team size was also similar with Knight (1984) showing roughly the same number of sole owner operated firms for both independent and franchisee groups: 35 percent for independents vs. 33 for franchisees. PSED data show similar results with nascent entrepreneurs at 47 percent vs. franchisees at 52. Both Knight (1984) and PSED data agreed on the entrepreneurial groups as being more confident that they could put in the effort required to make the start-up successful. Knight showed that there was a similar response by independents and franchisees with a slight edge to independents at 97 percent vs. 92 for franchisees in their willingness to work hard. While the PSED study asked whether they were confident that they could put in the required effort, 49 percent of nascent entrepreneurs vs. 9.7 of franchisees completely agreed with this statement. So, there was some differentiation in the level of confidence between the two groups. Finally, both Knight and the PSED data agreed that franchisees were the most common group to have less than one year of experience in the industry of their new business. According to Knight franchisees were 72 percent more likely to have no experience while PSED data showed that 65 percent of franchisees had less than one year of experience in their current industry. On the entrepreneurial side only 18 percent of the independents and 27 percent of the nascent entrepreneurs had little experience. In Table 2.2 we point out the differences in the opinions expressed in Knight (1984) and the current PSED study.

Past experience: Data from the PSED show 40 percent of franchisees will start a business with less than one year of experience in an industry.

Table 2.2 Summary of findings

Jonckheere-Terpstra Test	Std. J-T Statistic	2 Tailed p-values
Value of tangible assets of owners	−0.420	0.674
Past experience very valuable	−3.371	0.001
Skills and abilities will help	−3.590	0.000
Education	0.182	0.856
Team size	−1.337	0.181
Preference for future firm size	−3.001	0.003
Confident I can put in effort	−1.901	0.057
Expected first year firm income	−2.540	0.011

This stands in stark contrast with entrepreneurs where less than 10 percent of entrepreneurs will start business with less than one year of experience. In fact, 90 percent of franchisees will have less than five years of industry experience before starting a franchise. Among the nascent entrepreneurs only 20 percent would have started a business with less than five years of industry experience. One possible explanation for this contrast is that franchisees depend more heavily on the institutional expertise of the franchiser. In the 1984 study, independent experience by nascent entrepreneurs was a prerequisite to success while the franchisee needed to have little experience. When we tested the null hypotheses comparing Knight's data with the current study, the Jonckheere-Terpstra (J-T) statistic rejected the null at the .001 level of significance.

Skills and abilities: Both groups were asked whether their skills and abilities would help them with their start-up. The nascent entrepreneurs agreed strongly that their skills and abilities would be critical 90 percent of the time. Franchisees only responded this way 70 percent of the time and were more likely to disagree that their skills and abilities were critical to success of their venture. This may be interpreted a number of different ways. Considering the position of the nascent entrepreneurs, the uniqueness of their business model might require some level of expertise prior to the launch of their business. Franchisees, as stated earlier, might be relying on the institutional expertise of the franchisor. The franchisee's initial up-front investment is not just financing a location and equipment but it is financing know-how. Here again when we tested the null hypotheses of no difference when comparing Knight's data with the current study, the Jonckheere-Terpstra (J-T) statistic rejected the null at the .0001 level of significance.

Preference for future firm size: When we examine the vision of the future for the enterprises, some interesting differences emerge between nascent entrepreneurs and franchisees. Franchisees, as a group, envision that their firms will grow to be as large as possible. Nascent entrepreneurs see themselves in enterprises they will self-manage or that will remain relatively small. Given the nascent entrepreneurs' objectives for a management team of between four and eight, these would be relatively small firms. There is a statistically significant difference between the two groups, with Chi-Square significant at p < .003. Not only do these differences show themselves to be significant but very few entrepreneurs see themselves as managing firms that are as "large as possible." This is also consistent with the findings of Ucbasaran et al (2003), who found the size of the founding team was significantly negatively associated with subsequent team member entry. So, there is a negative relationship between increasing the size of entrepreneurial start-up and the size of the existing management team. It would appear that nascent entrepreneurs seek to exercise personal control over a large proportion of the details and decisions of the firms they start up. While the findings of the current study corroborate Knight's findings they disagree on the magnitude at the $p > .003$ level of significance.

The confidence in the level of effort: This element was measured by the statement "I am confident that I can put in the effort." In the questionnaire this indicates that effort is regarded as important to the success of the enterprise. The differences between nascent entrepreneurs and franchisees are statistically significant at $p < .000$. In new start-ups it is common for the business owner to assert that they can make the business succeed by effort alone. It is also consistent with the small firm size, since the franchisee or entrepreneur must be able to work on their own if the firm's size is to remain small. In each category of response to this question (shown in Figure 2.1) the franchisees agree more than the nascent entrepreneurs. However, in the last category which indicates, "total agreement" with the statement, the entrepreneurial and franchisees groups reverse. Franchisees seem to be in less than complete agreement with the statement while nascent entrepreneurs surge to the highest level of agreement with the statement. It would stand to reason that those putting more assets at risk would do so only if they believed they were committed to the project. Here again this seems to be a given, since our J-T results between PSED and Knight (1984) were significantly different at the $p > 0.057$ level.

The expected first-year firm income: A key aspect of motivation is confidence of success. We measured confidence with a question from the PSED instrument. The question surveyed their level of confidence by asking their expected income in the first year. The mean income expected by nascent entrepreneurs (more than $358,000) was compared to that of the franchisees (more than $386,000). These means were not significantly different. While the mean expected incomes were relatively similar, their spread was quite different. The dispersion of expected incomes for franchisees was much smaller than for nascent entrepreneurs. An "F" test indicates that the differences in the dispersion of the two groups were statistically significant at $p < .000$. This could mean entrepreneurs have more uncertainty about the timing and size of early year income but very high expectations. Franchisees may consider that the investment will pay off quickly, but that the average payout will be lower and more consistent then those of the nascent entrepreneurs.

2.5   Logistic model

While the differences between the two studies raise some interesting issues; some might be explained to the passage of time since Knight's (1984) original study and others might be explained by the difference between the two countries concerned (U.S. and Canada). A more fundamental question begs to be answered; what are the differences between the franchisees and entrepreneurs? For further analysis we consider the logistic model that would incorporate the differences on the dimensions we raised in our earlier model. In Table 2.3 a logistic comparison is made between franchisees and nascent entrepreneurs.

Table 2.3   Logistic differences between nascent entrepreneurs and franchisees

Logistic regression results of attitudinal differences	Franchisee		Nascent Entrepreneur
Maximum size of the business (Q322) β_1	B Coefficient Sig Exp (B)	−1.364 (.002) .256	.848 (.009) 2.335
Dollar amount of expected Income (Q317) β_2	B Coefficient Sig Exp (B)	0.000 (.145) 1.00	_____ _____ _____
If I work hard, I can successfully start a business (Q1KA) β_3	B Coefficient Sig Exp (B)	_____ _____ _____	.286 (.004) 1.331
Overall my skills and abilities will help me start a business (Q1KD) β_4	B Coefficient Sig Exp (B)	_____ _____ _____	.322 (.056) 1.394
My past experience will be very valuable in starting a business (Q1KE) β_5	B Coefficient Sig Exp (B)	−.622 (.001) 5.37	_____ _____ _____
Constant α	B Coefficient Sig Exp (B)	2.578 (.013) 13.169	−2.228 (.033) .108

In this analysis a backward stepwise binary logistic regression was run for franchisees and then another logistic regression was run for nascent entrepreneurs. Since we had earlier established the relevance of these variables as part of our initial model, which was also consistent with Knight (1984), the rationale of using these variables is strong. In the table, the logistic beta coefficients associated with each variable are displayed above their significance levels, which are in turn displayed above the exponentially the beta a proxy for the odds ratio. What is most interesting is the almost complete lack of overlap between the two groups, and that the one variable where there is overlap, the maximum size of the business, has directionally different betas. Ultimately to logistic models can be derived from these results:

For nascent entrepreneurs the logistic model takes the form:

$$Ln(E) = \alpha + \beta_1 X_1 \beta_3 X_3 + \beta_4 X_4 \tag{1}$$

where the odds of the respondent being a nascent entrepreneur may be evaluated through:

$$E = e^{\alpha + \beta_1 X_1 + \beta_3 X_3 + \beta_4 X_4} \tag{2}$$

For franchisees the logistic model takes the form:

$$Ln(\Gamma) = \alpha + \beta_1 X_1 + \beta_2 X_2 + \beta_5 X_5 \tag{3}$$

where the odds of the respondent being a franchisee may be evaluated through:

$$\Gamma = e^{\alpha + \beta_1 X_1 + \beta_2 X_2 + \beta_5 X_5} \tag{4}$$

In the case of the nascent entrepreneur our results in Table 2.3 show that nascent entrepreneurs are 1.3 times more likely than franchisees to believe in their skills and abilities ($p > .056$) and confidence ($p > .044$) being relevant to their success. Again this is consistent with the empirical findings earlier. It seems they are also 2.3 times more likely than franchisees to want to grow their business into a much larger business ($p > .009$). This is consistent with the limits to growth that may be part of the contractual obligation of a franchisee versus the unlimited growth potential of an entrepreneurial venture. The franchisees, in contrast, were much more pragmatic regarding the significant variables related to the size of the firm ($p > .002$) and the expected income (p > .000). However, the negative coefficient of experience suggests franchisees placed much less value on previous experience; it could be said that the franchisee group placed 5.3 times less significance than the nascent entrenpreneurs on the value of previous experience (p > .001). These variables are the result of the known income potential associated with a franchise. Interestingly experience seems to be significant for the franchisees but it agrees directionally with the empirical evidence that franchisees have less experience in the industry they are entering.

2.6 Conclusion

The purpose of this paper was to use the PSED dataset for deriving a better understanding of the nature of entrepreneurs and, more specifically, to explore the nature of the differences between nascent entrepreneurs and franchisees. The three dimensions of our exploration showed differences. There are a number of conclusions we can draw:

1. Franchisees have less industry experience, one year compared to four years.
2. Franchisees are less confident that their skills are critical to success.
3. Education is comparable, although franchisees education seemed skewed higher.
4. Franchisees value their previous experience less.
5. There is no significant difference in team size at start-up, but nascent entrepreneurs show twice the propensity to have a team size of three to five members.
6. Franchisees have a vision of a larger organization
7. Franchisees are less well capitalized (assets).
8. Reputation capital (via experience) is less important to franchisees.
9. Franchisees are less confident that they can make the business a success
10. Franchisees expect first year income to be less variable than do nascent entrepreneurs.

Many of these conclusions are also presented in Table 2.2 where they are compared with Knight's (1984) study. Our study's results agree with Knight's with respect to directionality, but are different in terms of magnitude. Our study shows that the franchisees have less experience, fewer skills and abilities, a greater desire to be larger, more confidence, and higher expected income as compared to independent/nascent entrepreneurs. Knight's sample, methodology, conceptualization, country of origin, and year of analysis are different to ours. Despite these differences, our study confirms many of the characteristics of franchisees identified by Knight. More research is needed to examine these variables further in order to be able to profile nascent/independent entrepreneurs and franchisees better. Such efforts will help policymakers interested in developing their franchising sector, franchisors in need of identifying qualified franchisees, and entrepreneurs wishing to know if franchising is right for them.

Appendix 2.1   Summary of results of critical variables

Number of years of previous experience

	≤1	1<Y≤2	2<Y≤3	3<Y≤4	Y>4	Chi-Square	Chi-Square (Sig)
Nascent entrepreneurs	0.151	0.05	0.035	0.047	0.717	–	–
Franchisees	0.517	0.103	0.069	0.069	0.241	34.5	0.000

Current team size

	1	2	3	4	≥5	Chi-Square	Chi-Square (Sig)
Nascent entrepreneurs	0.48	0.38	0.06	0.04	0.03	–	–
Franchisees	0.54	0.44	0.02	0	0	0.192	0.996

Confident that I can put in the effort

	Completely disagree	Generally disagree	Neutral	Generally agree	Completely agree	Chi-Square	Chi-Square (Sig)
Nascent entrepreneurs	0.003	0.022	0.068	0.416	0.492	–	–
Franchisees	0.032	0.129	0.194	0.548	0.097	32.462	0.000

Goals for future size of business

	As large as possible	Size to manage by self	Chi-Square	Chi-Square (Sig)
Nascent entrepreneurs	21.10%	78.90%	–	–
Franchisees	39.20%	60.80%	9.005	0.003

My industry experience was important in starting this business

	Yes	N/A	Chi-Square	Chi-Square (Sig)
Nascent entrepreneurs	56.30%	43.70%	–	–
Franchisees	21.10%	78.90%	17.606	0.000

Value of tangible assets

Dollars ($)	Nascent entrepreneurs (%)	Franchisees (%)
1000	4.60	0.00
5000	6.60	13.60
10000	11.20	6.80
50000	47.90	47.70
100000	16.30	22.70
500000	10.90	9.10
1000000	2.10	0.00
>1000000	0.50	0.00
Mean	81115.39	47818.18
SD	1383678	196305.1
N	608	44
F-Value		49.68
Sig		0

Expected income in first year

Dollars ($)	Nascent entrepreneurs (%)	Franchisees (%)
<0	0.40	0.00
0	1.50	0.00
500	1.90	4.30
1000	2.10	4.30
5000	5.70	10.90
10000	10.60	10.90
50000	41.10	54.30
100000	17.10	6.50
500000	16.50	8.70
1000000	1.50	0.00
5000000	1.50	0.00
Mean	358354.3	38682.59
SD	2209565	1231356
N	581	46
F-Value		3.231
Sig		0

Notes

1. Anonymous (2001). "Preparing the small-firm entrepreneurs of tomorrow," *Training Strategies for Tomorrow*. Bradford: Jan/Feb 2001. Vol. 15, No. 1, 15–18.
2. There are several idiosyncrasies in the data as a result of oversamples included in the initial analysis and used to answer some very specific research questions regarding gender and ethnicity. Any research on the data which involves examining the ethnicity or gender of respondents must include weightings to readjust the dataset to reflect more accurately the universe of nascent entrepreneurs (Gartner et al 2004). Since our study does not focus on gender or race there is no need to adjust for the oversample.
3. There are several problems that are a result of not having direct input into the original questionnaires; questions were asked with a specific purpose in mind and we are using the data for a different analysis. While this might present some problems, the dataset is quite robust and offers many different question items to address these issues.

References

Basu, A. (1998). An exploration of entrepreneurial activity among Asian small business in Britain, *Small Business Economics* 10 (4), 313–26.
Baum, J. R., E. A. Locke, and S. A. Kirkpatrick (1998). "A longitudinal study of the relation of vision and vision communication to venture growth in entrepreneurial firms," *Journal of Applied Psychology*, 83(1), 43–54.
Birley, S., and P. Westhead (1993). "A comparison of new businesses established by 'novice' and 'Habitual' Founders in Great Britain," *International Small Business Journal* 12 (1), 38–60.
Castrogiovanni, G., R. Justis, and S. Julian (1993). "Franchise failure rates: An assessment of magnitude and influencing factors," *Journal of Small Business Management* 31 (2), 105–14.
Cliff, J. E., P. D. Jennings, and R. Greenwood (2006). "New to the game and questioning the rules: The experiences and beliefs of founders who start imitative versus innovative firms," *Journal of Business Venturing*, 21(5), 633.
Cole, A. H. (1968). "The entrepreneur: Introductory remarks," *American Economic Review*, 58(2), 60–63.
Corman, J., B. Perles, P. Yancini (1988). "Motivational factors influencing high-technology entrepreneurship," *Journal of Small Business Management*, 26(1), 36–43.
Cressy, R, (2006). "Why do Most Firms Die Young?" *Small Business Economics* 26 (2), 103–16.
Gartner, W. B. (1985). "A conceptual framework for describing the phenomenon of new venture creation," Academy of Management Review, 10, 696–707.
Gartner, W.B., K.G. Shaver, N.M. Carter, and P.D. Reynolds, , Eds. (2004). *Handbook Of Entrepreneurial Dynamics The Process of Business Creation*. Thousand Oaks, CA: SAGE Publications.
Greenbank, P. (2006). "Starting up in business: an examination of the decision-making process," *International Journal of Entrepreneurship and Innovation*, 7(3), 149.

Hunter, I. (2005). "Risk, persistence and focus: a life cycle of the entrepreneur," *Australian Economic History Review* 45 (3), 244–95.

Jo, H., and J. Lee (1996). "The relationship between an entrepreneur's background and performance in a new venture," *Technovation* 16 (6), 161–71.

Kaufmann, P.J., and R.P. Dant (1999). "Franchising and the domain of entrepreneurship research," *Journal of Business Venturing*, 14(1), 5–17.

Kincaid, S. (2005). "Entrepreneurship about taking risks," *Knight Ridder Tribune Business News* (November 2), 1.

Knight, R. (1984). "The independence of the franchisee entrepreneur," *Journal of Small Business Management* 22 (2), 53–61.

Levesque, M. and M. Minniti (2006). "The effect of aging on entrepreneurial behavior," *Journal of Business Venturing* 21 (2), 177–94.

Liebenstein, H. (1968). "Entrepreneurship and development," *American Economic Review*, 58(2), 72–83.

Low, M. B. and I.C. MacMillan (1988). "Entrepreneurship: Past research and future challenges," *Journal of Management*, 14(2), 139–61.

McCarthy, B. and B. Leavy (1998/1999). "The entrepreneur, risk-perception and change over time: A typology approach," *Irish Journal of Management*, IBAR, 19/20(1), 126–141.

Michael, S. (1996). "To franchise or not to franchise: An analysis of decision rights and organizational form shares," *Journal of Business Venturing* 11 (1), 57–71.

Norton, W., and W. Moore (2006). "The influence of entrepreneurial risk assessment on venture launch or growth decisions," *Small Business Economics* 26 (3), 213–26.

Ottesen, G., and K. Gronhaug (2005). "Positive illusions and new Venture creation: Conceptual issues and an empirical illustration," *Creativity and Innovation Management* 14 (4), 405–12.

Price, R. (1999). "Who reports earnings when reporting is optional? The market for new franchises," *Journal of Accounting and Economics* 28 (3), 391–413.

Sage, G. (2003). "Entrepreneurship as an economic development strategy," *Economic Development Review*, 11(2), 66–68.

Stanworth, J., D. Purdy, and S. Price (1998). "Franchise versus conventional small business failure rates in the US and UK: More similarities than differences," *International Small Business Journal*, 16 (3: April), 56–69.

Stevenson, H. H. and J. C. Jarillo-Mossi (1986). "Preserving entrepreneurship as companies grow," *Journal of Business Strategy*, 7(1), 10–23.

Stoner, C., and F. Fry (1982). "The entrepreneurial decision: Dissatisfaction or opportunity," *Journal of Small Business Management* 20 (2), 39–44.

Ucbasaran, D., A. Lockett, M. Wright, and P. Westhead, (2003),."Entrepreneurial Founder Teams: Factors Associated with Member Entry and Exit," *Entrepreneurship Theory and Practice* 28 (2), 107–28.

Wilkerson, J. (1993). "A growing need for franchising pros," *Franchising World* 25 (4), 1.

Williams, D. (1999). "Why do entrepreneurs become franchisees? An empirical analysis of organizational choice," *Journal of Business Venturing* 14 (1), 103–24.

3
Internationalization of Franchising

Ilan Alon, Liqiang Ni, and Raymond (Youcheng) Wang

3.1 Introduction

In the U.S. economy, the service sector has witnessed a tremendous growth in the past several decades, and the hospitality industry is one of the major components of this fast growth (Ketchen et al 2006). Different to most of the other service sectors, the hotel industry is usually capital intensive and its logistics and supply chain can be as complex as those of manufacturing operations (Chen and Dimou, 2005). For hotel companies, this can be a great obstacle to equity-based expansion models in various markets, particularly in the international market. This also raises the issue of the importance of the internationalization process through franchising for hotel companies.

Hotel chains prefer to use nonequity forms of organization for their international expansion and operation mainly out of cost efficiency concerns. Nonequity-based agreements, such as franchising, are the most common forms of organizational structure in market entry (Contractor and Kundu, 1998) among hotel and motel chains partly because setting up a hotel requires a large amount of financial capital. In other words, the hotel and motel industry is capital intensive, requiring a large financial outlay upfront for establishing the facilities. Franchising provides an opportunity for hotels to lower the risk and the level of investment in expansion. Franchising allows hotel and motel franchisors to share the cost of expansion with the franchisees, who typically pay the startup costs, initial fees, and ongoing royalties. In return, the franchisees obtain brand name recognition, economies of scale, and managerial expertise from the franchisors. Contractor and Kundu (1998) proposed that competitive advantage can be derived by separating knowledge-based expertise from capital ownership. A franchise is a way of transferring tangible and intangible expertise with limited risk of capital.

However, internationalization through franchising can be a complex process since the decision can be affected by a multitude of forces, particularly organizational factors and market conditions. Although previous research has examined factors contributing to internationalization through franchising as an entry mode, most of the research outputs generated are mainly applicable to the manufacturing industry (e.g. Baker and Dant 2008; Gatignon and Anderson, 1988), providing limited practical guidelines and market implications to the hotel industry's efforts at internationalization. Alon and McKee (1999a) proposed that the effect of organizational factors on the decision to internationalize is industry specific. This study intends to narrow this research gap by explaining the internationalization of franchising systems in the hotel industry. In particular, the study attempts to identify and understand the impacts of organizational factors and market condition variables on the decisions of hotel companies to enter international markets through franchising, within a framework of agency-based theory.

This study uses the Burton and Cross definition of international franchising. They defined international franchising as "a foreign market entry mode that involves a relationship between the entrant (the franchisor) and a host country entity, in which the former transfers, under contract, a business package (or format), which it developed and owns, to the latter" (Burton and Cross, 1995: 36). This definition is suitable because this study does not differentiate between the various modes of international franchising. It focuses on the decision to internationalize, regardless of the mode of entry chosen. According to the Burton and Cross definition, the host country entity can be either a franchisee, a master franchisor, or an entity which is partly owned by the franchisor itself, for example, a joint venture.

3.2 Theoretical background

The internationalization of hotel and motel chains started in the 1950s and 1960s with firms such as Hilton, Sheraton, Holiday Inn, Marriott, and Ramada Inn. Franchising systems in the hotel industry are among the most mature of the franchised services, and therefore, further along the product life cycle. They also face stiffer domestic and global competition and declining profit margins, which together contribute to a greater awareness of the need to think of the world in global terms

(Huszagh et al 1992). In fact, plural forms are becoming the norm among franchising systems across the hotel industry (Baker and Dant, 2008; Perrigot, 2006). That is, franchising hotel companies use franchised outlets and various master and area development agreements all at the same time. In recent years, multiunit franchising has become a popular method for expansion, particularly in international hotel markets (Altinay, 2003; Cho, 2005).

A review of the literature indicates that the growth of the hotel franchise sector through international franchising in various markets around the world is based on the following organizational and market condition factors: 1) level of domestic saturation; 2) competition in the home market; 3) potential in emerging countries, in particular in Asia and Latin America; 4) regional trade agreements, such as the European Union and the North American Free Trade Agreement; and 5) liberalization of the formerly communist countries (Johnson and Vanetti, 2005; Kostecka 1988; Lashley and Morrison, 2000; Tucker and Sundberg 1988). American hotel companies tend to use franchising as a business strategy to expand their brand (sometimes globally) with limited risk (Dunning et al 2007).

Using the competitive theory of the firm literature, Huszagh et al (1992) found that time in operation (age), number of units (size), and to a lesser extent equity capital and headquarters location, are significant factors differentiating between domestic and international franchisors. Shane (1996) built on Huszagh et al's research and concentrated on the agency costs associated with internationalization. His findings revealed that the price structure of franchises and the monitoring capabilities contribute to internationalization. Eroglu (1992) developed a conceptual model of internationalization which used organizational determinants such as the firm's size and operating experience, as well as top management's international orientation, tolerance of risk, and perception of competitive advantage.

Fladmoe-Lindquist (1996) built on the aforementioned research and developed a conceptual framework for international franchising based on resource-based and agency theories. He did not test his model since it had a normative or managerial orientation. But Alon and McKee (1999a) took the opportunity to test a model combining resource-based and agency variables on the professional business service industry and found size to be the only a significant variable influencing franchisors' decision to internationalize. The number of outlets a franchisor has is among the most common predictors of internationalization. Alon (1999) suggested that the effect of resources and monitoring skills (often measured as the number of outlets) on internationalization is common across industries, but its impact may be industry specific.

The internationalization of hospitality firms and hotel chains is multidimensional. Using a single embedded case study, Altinay (2007) showed that internationalization of hospitality firms is often based on shareholders' pressure, the desire to extend the core competencies of the firm, and demand by international customers. Contractor and Kundu (1998) suggested that reservation systems and hotel brands allow franchises to thrive in foreign markets because they act as barriers against partner opportunism.

Much of the research on international franchising in the hotel sector has focused on explanations of modal choices. Alon (2005), for example, suggested that cultural distance between the host and home market of the firm would favor a nonequity-based mode of entry, such as franchising or management contracts. Management quality concerns, on the other hand, may favor the use of owned properties (Contractor and Kundu, 1998). While the debate on the exact specification of mode of entry model is still ongoing, our focus here is on the decisions of franchise hotels to go global through franchising within the framework of agency-based theory.

Agency theory is a dominant paradigm explaining franchising, particularly in the U.S. (Baker and Dant, 2008). The theory suggests that an agency relationship exists between a franchisor (the principal) and the franchisee (the agent). Since the parties may have divergent goals, agency costs arise along with the risk of opportunism. Principals can reduce agency costs and opportunism through direct observation and monitoring or through a system of aligned incentives (Eisenhardt, 1989; Jensen and Mckling, 1976).

Rubin (1978) applied agency theory to explain franchising relationships. Franchising reduced monitoring needs by aligning the incentives of the agent (franchisee) and the principal (the franchisor) through making the franchisee a residual claimant on revenues. In the hotel industry, franchising is, thus, a substitute for direct observation when monitoring costs are high or when distance separates the principal from the agent (Brickley and Dark, 1987; Fladmoe-Lindquist and Jacque, 1995; Norton, 1988).

Hotel franchising, in turn, has its own set of monitoring needs. Intangible assets can be appropriated, income can be misreported, and quality can deteriorate in the absence of controls. Monitoring skills are a key to successful franchising, especially when crossing borders, cultures, and marketing environments.

Some agency explanations of the internationalization of franchising systems using agency theory were originally developed by Shane (1996). To minimize agency costs, franchisors charge their international franchisees higher initial fees in relation to royalties, in comparison to what they charge their domestic counterparts. This pricing structure creates high bonding between the franchisor and the international franchisee since the latter has much at stake. The initial fee the franchisee pays accounts for about one-half of the total investment, often representing a major portion of the franchisee's wealth. The cost of termination is, therefore, higher because the franchisee can lose the initial fee if he/she does not follow the strict format of the franchisor. Therefore, it is hypothesized that

H1: *The greater the price bonding the hotel franchisor uses in its contracts, the more likely it will seek international franchisees.*

Opportunistic behavior by the franchisees can also be controlled through effective monitoring (Fladmoe-Lindquist, 1996). Hotel franchisors' monitoring skills are in increasing demand as they cross borders. New risks are introduced by the changing environment, different key success factors, and the local socioeconomic and political environment. Since monitoring skills are not directly observable, various proxies were used in past research. Shane (1996) found support that *monitoring* – measured as a multiplicative composite index consisting of the number of franchised units – the percentage of franchised outlets and the age of the franchise system is positively related with the internationalization of franchising. Elango (2007) captures monitoring skills through the experiences of franchisors, namely the percentage of franchised units and number of years franchised. Hotel franchisors which have franchised for a while and achieved a high degree of franchise ownership in their system are also more likely to possess the monitoring skills required to succeed across heterogeneous locations.

Hotel franchisors with dispersed units are more likely to seek international franchisees since they are used to operating at arm's length in distant locations, which are subjected to slightly different conditions. Franchisors with many franchisees in heterogeneous locations across the U.S. are better positioned to take advantage of economies of scale in promotion and monitoring because such locations incorporate differing levels of return and risk (Huszagh et al 1992).

From the above discussion we can postulate three interrelated hypotheses tied to the ability of franchisors to monitor international franchisees.

H2: *Hotel franchisors with strong franchising monitoring skills are more likely to seek international franchisees.*

H2a: *The greater the domestic geographical scope of the hotel franchisor, the more likely it will seek international franchisees.*

H2b: *The higher the franchising experience of the hotel franchisor, the more likely it will seek international franchisees.*

H2c: *The greater the proportion of franchising in the hotel franchisor's system, the more likely it will seek international franchisees.*

In franchising, size matters. Size is often measured by the scale of the operations or the number of outlets in a franchising system. It is often assumed that a hotel franchisor must reach a certain size before it can venture abroad. It must demonstrate that it is successful in the variety of local environments before it is ready to be tested in global environments. Scale infers financial capital, brand name recognition, managerial and routine-processing know-how, and monitoring skills. It is very risky to internationalize prematurely because international franchising systems in the hotel industry often incur great expenses long before they receive any return, even if the initial fee is substantially low (Mendelsohn, 1994).

Fladmoe-Lindquist (1996) emphasized the need for distance, cultural, and host country management skills for the successful process of internationalization. As the franchising hotel grows, it develops additional franchised units, which allow it to acquire the resources necessary for expansion overseas. As such, the franchising hotel's scale (measured in terms of the number of domestic outlets) may be decisive in seeking international opportunities. If domestic opportunities are high and the franchisor has not saturated its market, then additional domestic franchises can be built and the opportunity cost of seeking more distant, risky locations may be less attractive. In short, the number of outlets in the hotel franchisor's domestic system should positively influence the franchisor's decision to internationalize. The bigger the franchising hotel company, the greater the economies of scale (Huszagh et al 1992), financial capital, brand name recognition (Aydin and Kacker, 1990), market power (Huszagh et al 1992), and market saturation (Shane

1996). The more outlets there are in the hotel franchisor's system, the more likely it is that the franchisor can lower the operating cost per outlet. There are also economies of scale in purchasing, promotion, R&D, monitoring, and quality controls. Some services such as advertising, product development, and reservation can be centralized, adding to the cost savings and to the consistency of the marketing program.

Finding international franchisees should also be easier for big hotel franchisors because of brand name recognition (Aydin and Kacker, 1990). The success of McDonald's overseas expansion was partly a result of its highly recognized trade name. McDonald's has the second most recognized trade mark in the world following Coca-Cola (Fullerton et al 2007). It is also easier for large hotel franchisors to raise capital in foreign markets through their market power and perceived credibility (Huszagh et al 1992). There is also a greater possibility that the bigger the franchisor, the more likely it will saturate the domestic market (Shane, 1996). Thus, hotel international franchising can be seen as an avenue of growth in light of limited opportunities at the home market.

H3: *The greater the scale of domestic operations, the more likely a hotel franchisor will seek international franchisees.*

The expansion of franchisors into emerging and developing markets also corresponded with the increased use of multiunit franchising. Plural forms of ownership and franchising have been well documented in the franchising and hotel management literature (e.g. Vianelli and Alon, 2008). Garg and Rasheed (2006) suggested that 1) multiunit franchising is growing in popularity in the international context where geographic and cultural distance exist, and that 2) agency-theorety explanations are especially well suited to explain this growth. Multiunit franchising is different from single-unit franchising in that franchisees own, operate, and control more than one unit (Kaufmann and Dant, 1996). Several permutations of multiunit franchising exist: 1) franchisors can allow area development agreements which give the franchisee a defined territory in which they can develop units, 2) franchisors can choose to use subfranchising contracts (often called master franchising) that allow the franchisee to be both the agent to the franchisor and the principal to others (subfranchisees), and/or 3) franchisors can allow franchisees to establish additional units in a given territory (consecutive franchising). The use of multiunit franchising was shown to be positive to system growth (Kaufmann and Dant, 1996).

Multiunit franchising reduces agency costs (including shirking, adverse selection, inefficient risk bearing, free riding, and quasi-rent appropriation) and promotes internationalization (Garg and Rasheed, 2006). Shirking is reduced at the subsystem level because multiunit franchisees detect cheating in their local context, are able to compare same-store sales in a given geographical context, and are delegated the monitoring needs of the franchisor. Adverse selection is reduced because the multiunit franchisee can collect more relevant local information, and franchisors can economize on recruiting, screening, and training. Information flow is increased because multiunit franchisees often reside in proximity to subfranchisees allowing more and better monitoring, know the local market conditions, and can apply necessary adjustments. Inefficient risk bearing is reduced because multiunit franchisees put a large part of their assets into the venture, and are owners of a more diversified portfolio spreading fixed costs against a greater number of outlets. Free riding is minimized because the brand name capital is captured over a greater number of units. Quasi-rent appropriation is lessened because multiunit franchisees can earn an acceptable return on investment in the chain.

H4: *Hotel companies that use multi-unit franchising are more likely to seek international franchisees.*

H4a: *Hotel companies that use area development in expansion are more likely to seek out international franchisees.*

H4b: *Hotel companies that allow franchisees to add more franchising units are more likely to seek out international franchisees.*

3.3   Methodology

This study employs logistic regression analysis to examine the effect of the four hypotheses. Using seven independent variables (listed in Table 7.1) to measure the constructs, we specified and tested an agency-theory model of international franchising with 120 observations for 18 US-based hotels chains (i.e. AmericInn, Baymont, BestInn, Candlewood, Country Inns, Doubletree, Embassy, Hampton, Hawthorn, Hilton, Hilton Garden, Homewood Hospitality, Microtel, Motel 6, Radisson, Ramada, Red Roof, and Studio 6). These companies may not necessarily be a fair representation of U.S.-based hotels, but they do provide a reasonable platform for research. Logistical regression is used because the decision to internationalize is modeled as dichotomous (go/no go). The binary dependent variable IE (international expansion) is the indicator of whether the company seeks for overseas expansion. The dependent variable was conceptualized as per past research on the topic of international franchising (Alon and McKee, 1999b; Eroglu, 1992; Shane, 1996).

Data were obtained from *Franchisor Questionnaire 2001–2008, Bond's Franchise Guide*. These data were previously used by past researchers (Hendrikse and Jiang, 2005). The data are comparable to the one collected by *Entrepreneur*, but are more detailed and extensive. Table 3.1 summarizes the predictive variables and their definition and relationship to the hypotheses. In addition to the independent variables in Table 3.1, we also use the minimum total investment in U.S.\$ millions (Tinv) to take into account the capital intensive nature of the industry. Table 3.2 provides some descriptive statistics on the variables, while Table 3.3 shows the correlation table. Logistical regression analysis requires that there would be no problem of multicollinearity. An examination of the correlation table shows no significant problem of multicollinearity among the predictors.

It should be recognized that one salient feature of the data is the longitudinal nature of the observations. On the average, each company has about 6.32 observations during eight years. We do not expect that the responses for the same company are uncorrelated, which suggests that we might consider a mixed-effects logistic regression with fixed effects for the predictive variables aforementioned and a company-

Table 3.1   The hypotheses, variables, and definitions

Hypothesis	Variable	Relation	Definition
H1	FRratio	Positive	the ratio of franchising fee over royalty rate (\$k/percentage).
H2a	Disper	Positive	the number of U.S. states where the company has presence.
H2b	Fexp	Positive	the number of years the company has been franchising.
H2c	FranPer	Positive	the percentage of franchised units among total number of units.
H3	USscale	Positive	the number of U.S. units.
H4a	AreaDev	Positive	the indicator whether area development agreements exist.
H4b	AddUnits	Positive	the indicator if the additional outlets within the area can be added.

Table 3.2 Summary statistics of variables in data analysis

	min	max	mean	Sd
IE	0.000	1.000	0.675	0.470
FRratio	83.300	2500.000	973.700	502.559
Disper	11.000	50.000	36.250	9.651
Fexp	3.000	41.000	15.242	8.146
FranPer	0.054	1.731	0.742	0.338
U.S.scale	33.000	1382.000	323.992	318.056
AreaDev	0.000	1.000	0.100	0.301
AddUnits	0.000	1.000	0.650	0.479
Tinv	0.200	33.000	6.138	7.236

Table 3.3 Sample correlation coefficient matrix

	IE	Frratio	Disper	Fexp	FranPer	U.S.scale	AreaDev	AddUnits	Tinv
IE	1.000								
Frratio	0.353	1.000							
Disper	0.086	0.258	1.000						
Fexp	0.472	0.337	0.127	1.000					
FranPer	0.571	0.086	0.186	0.263	1.000				
U.S.scale	−0.117	−0.067	0.521	0.141	0.029	1.000			
AreaDev	−0.153	0.135	0.042	−0.075	−0.197	−0.019	1.000		
AddUnits	0.542	0.552	0.118	0.215	0.417	−0.104	−0.056	1.000	
Tinv	0.267	0.694	0.146	0.471	−0.046	−0.145	0.218	0.379	1.000

specific random effect. Meanwhile, to deal with possible temporal pattern, we may include the time and its interaction with other predictive variables in the model. Lafontaine and Shaw (1999) investigate the pattern of the royalty rate using a mixed-effect linear model with the time as the only fixed-effect variable and a company-specific random component. However, in this paper, with relatively moderate sample size of 120 data points, it is bound to encounter numerical problems if we pursue that direction. We leave this interesting topic for future study.

Data triangulation was then used to enhance the credibility and external validity of the study results of the quantitative data analysis. Triangulation is an approach to data analysis that synthesizes data from multiple sources (Creswell, 2009). Triangulation seeks to examine existing data quickly to strengthen interpretations and improve practical implications based on additional evidence available. By examining information collected by different methods, findings can be corroborated across data sources, reducing the impact of potential biases that can exist in a single dataset. One approach of triangulation is to combine information from quantitative and qualitative studies by making use of expert judgment (Yin, 2003).

Data triangulation was achieved in this study through first sharing the data analysis results with three industry executives and then conducting personal interviews to solicit their feedbacks and insights based on their professional experiences. All the three informants have tremendous working experience in the hotel industry and are knowledgable about hotel internationalization and franchising strategies and practices both in the hotel industry in general and the specific hotel companies they work for in particular. Informant A is Executive Vice President of Global Brands, Hilton Hotels Corporation. Informant B is Vice President of the Ritz Carlton Club, and informant C is Executive Vice President of Portfolio Management and Administration for CNL Hotels & Resorts. The interview results of the three informants were integrated into the conclusions and discussions section.

3.4   Results

The fitted model and the coefficient estimations are shown in Table 3.4. The fit has a residual deviance of 47.375 on 106 degrees of freedom and a pseudo R-square 0.6607. Figure 3.1 shows the plot of international expansion (IE) versus the single index (the linear combination of

Table 3.4   Coefficient estimation of the logistic regression model

	Coefficient	Std. error	z-value	p-value
Intercept	−10.323	3.196	−3.231	0.001
FRratio	0.004	0.002	2.241	0.025
Disper	0.032	0.053	0.595	0.552
Fexp	0.656	0.173	3.780	0.000
FranPer	−0.630	1.500	−0.420	0.674
U.S.scale	−0.007	0.002	−2.978	0.003
AreaDev	−4.176	1.841	−2.268	0.023
AddUnits	3.398	1.316	2.581	0.010
Tinv	−0.147	0.135	−1.083	0.279

Notes: Null deviance: 139.641 on 114 degrees of freedom
Residual deviance: 47.375 on 106 degrees of freedom
(5 observations deleted due to incompleteness)
AIC: 65.375
Pseudo R^2 = (139.641−47.375)/139.641 = 0.6607

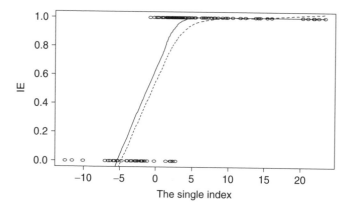

Figure 3.1 IE vs the single index

predictive variables identified by the model fit in Table 3.4) where the lowess smoothing curve of the fitted probability (dashed line) and that of observed IE (solid line) are superimposed for visual enhancement. We test the predictive capacity of the fitted model on the available data. The closeness of two curves in Figure 3.1 and high prediction accuracy indicate that the model fits the data very well. This model is also quite robust without any conspicuous influential data points. If we adopt a naïve rule that we predict IE = 1 if the fitted probability is larger than 0.5 and predict IE = 1 otherwise, we would correctly predict IE 93.0 percent of the time.

Based on the sign and significance of the estimated coefficients, we may test the hypotheses postulated in literature review. The sign of coefficient of FRratio is positive as expected in H_1, with a p-value of 0.025. There is strong evidence supporting H_{2b} that the higher the franchising experience of the franchisor, the more likely it will seek international franchisees. Meanwhile, the evidence for H_{2a} and H_{2c} is not strong. The biggest surprise perhaps is that the data are strongly against H_3 partially as a result of the fact that companies of smaller size are also actively seeking international expansion or of the lack of middle-size samples as shown in Figure 3.2. It is interesting to see that the impacts of area development agreements and allowing additional units in the franchisee's area are significant and in the opposite direction. The companies using area development agreements are less likely to seek international expansion, while the companies that allow additional units are more likely to seek international franchisees.

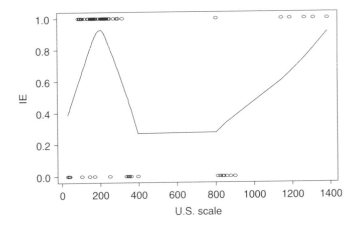

Figure 3.2   IE vs U.S. scale with a lowess smoothing curve

3.5   Conclusion and discussions

Within the framework of agency theory, the current study proposes and tests an agency-based organizational model of international franchising in the hotel sector. This study contributes to the extant literature of international franchising by examining the role of the use of multiunit franchising in international hotel franchising. It also tests other agency-theory hypotheses linking franchising to hotel internationalization. On the practical side, the article highlights franchising factors associated with hotel internationalization and provides guidance as to when international hotel franchising is often sought. The results of the data analyses support most of the hypotheses proposed, demonstrating a strong normative validity of the study. There are several interesting and intriguing findings, which will be highlighted in the following section.

The study results indicate that franchise experience is positively related to hotel franchisors' decisions to internationalize. This is by and large consistent with previous research which reveals that a lack of franchising experience causes high organizational uncertainty, which makes the monitoring of performance challenging and costly, thus hampering the internationalization endeavor. This international experience is especially important for hotel companies since franchising in the hotel sector presupposes a heavy investment in sunk costs in the process of developing the franchise package. It is also possible that a hotel company with limited international experience may find it more difficult to attract and select qualified franchisees in the first place. This finding was observed and supported by informant B who believes that without an established base of franchising, international franchising may pose incremental hurdles in comparison to domestic franchising. One the contrary, with an established domestic franchise base, the challenges of international franchising may be diluted.

Relating to the positive impact of franchise experience, the study results also indicate that hotel franchisors with strong franchising monitoring skills are more likely to seek international franchisees. Although this hypothesis was supported by the empirical data tested in this study, both informants B and C pointed out that, though franchising can be a strategy for expansion during specific times for hotel companies possessing high monitoring skills, the "high degree of franchising" may be more reflective of the brand strength, the company's strategy, and the hotel operator's needs at the time, more so than the monitoring skills. Often, franchising is a method of expanding the brand in areas that it has not been able to expand on into its own. Citing Marriott as an example, informant B does not believe that the arm's-length relationship and slightly different locations are the drivers as much as the specific locations or the expansion strategy of the company. For example, the Marriott's expansion plan has been to establish the brand in gateway cities and then expand beyond based on the feasibility of the market, be it through franchising or ownership for the business and brand growth. In Europe, because of relatively low brand recognition, Marriott has not used franchising as an expansion strategy; rather, it has acquired established international brands to achieve the strategy of international growth and expansion.

The results reveal that the hotel company's decision to go international is negatively related to size (operationalized as the scale of the U.S. operations), which is contradictory to the mainstream research findings in this area. In the hotel internationalization process, size is usually regarded as having positive effect on franchising practices, mainly because large hotel companies have more resources to allocate to facilitate the franchising process and a higher resilience to failure should the system fail. Presumably, this may also have an impact on management risk perception in that larger hotel companies will experience less impact in financial risk which is often reflected by the franchising cost. However, previous research findings on the relationship between firm size and the decision to expand is not consistent, and sometimes even contradictory (Azevedo and Silva, 2001). It might be the case that it is not the hotel size per se that determines whether to internationalize; it is the characteristics of a particular transaction that influence the decision. This has to be taken into consideration when different hotel market segments representing different levels of asset specificity go international (Rodriguez, 2002). As a result, hotel companies choose to use various entry strategies in expanding their international markets.

For example, Chen and Dimou (2005) argue that service is usually more basic in budget and midscale hotels. In this case, services provided and the required skills from management and staff are limited and can be reduced to standard operating procedures and transferred to a third party via a franchise package. However for high end luxury hotels, the provision of services requires highly skilled employees to guarantee the level of service and meet the expectation of the brand. In this process, the transfer of knowledge is more complicated and difficult since this type of know-how cannot easily be translated into standard operating procedures. As a result, regardless of size, franchising is not a commonly sought after entry mode in upper hotel market segments compared with, for example, management contracts.

The decision can also be affected for the sake of quality assurance and free-riding control. For example, high control modes of expansion are considered to be less risky regarding quality depreciation. Furthermore, free riding by the franchisees is more likely to happen when the value of a brand name is high, which requires higher degrees of control. Again, regardless of size, higher quality brand hotels will be more likely to choose a high control, high integrated entry mode rather than a franchising arrangement should they decide to go international.

The study results also indicate that hotel companies that allow franchisees to add more franchising units are more likely to seek out international franchising, thus providing evidence to support H_{4b}. This adds more evidence to the argument that the current size and/or the pro-growth strategy of a hotel company may have a positive impact on the company's decision to internationalize. For the franchisor, this might be an effective and sustainable growth strategy, since growth by international franchising based on the existing sizable operation can take advantage of economies of scale (Huszagh et al, 1992), financial capital (Alon et al 2004), brand name recognition (Aydin and Kacker, 1990), market power (Huszagh et al, 1992), and market saturation (Shane, 1996). Specifically, expanding the current franchise system will be more cost effective since the cost per outlet can be substantially lower as the number of outlets increases. Financially, because of the centralization of the system, the savings for each additional outlet can be huge in the areas of marketing and promotion, quality control, product development, and day-to-day operation. In addition, large franchising systems tend to have a better brand recognition, which can be attractive in international markets, especially when the domestic market is saturated.

It is noted from the interviews with the three industry informants that above all the factors identified in the model testing as affecting a hotel company's likelihood of going international, brand might play an important role in determining what strategies they adopt in doing so. Informant A cited Hilton Hotel Corporation's franchising strategies with their economy brand Hampton Inns in international markets as an example. Despite the fact that the brand (i.e. Hampton Inns) has more than 1400 hotels and nearly 172,000 rooms under the Hilton brand umbrella, it is largely unknown outside of the U.S. The Hilton's management decided to arm the economy brand (along with Doubletree and Embassy Suites) with the full equity of the Hilton name itself, and renamed the brand Hampton by Hilton outside the U.S. He justified this strategy by commenting that: "while all three brands are well known within the United States, the Hilton name – one of the most recognized in the hospitality industry worldwide – is far better known in Canada and Latin America, representing a supreme opportunity for Doubletree, Embassy Suites and Hampton Inns to be better recognized in those areas by virtue of their Hilton affiliation." As a result, they have added "by Hilton" to certain brands that are rapidly expanding into new markets abroad. This strategy was adopted in their merger with Hilton International and enhances their goal to become the premier global hotel franchising company. These strategies will afford Hilton a great opportunity to diversify its income further with the internationalization of its highly successful portfolio of brands, through franchising and multiunit area development agreements.

The limitation of the study can be reflected by the fact that the study only focuses on key organizational and market factors in predicting hotel internationalization through franchising, without taking into consideration other factors that might create different dynamics in the process of international franchising, such as market specific characteristics and other situational factors. It is easily conceivable that the franchising process is market sensitive and that, as a result, various market characteristics will play important roles in affecting the franchising operation. These factors may include, but not be limited to, the market segment in which franchising is considered, the degree of control enforced by either the hotel industry sector or government policy, the risks and costs of entry, and similarities of cultural norms and business. In addition, other situational factors can also be potentially important in affecting how hotel franchising is practiced in a certain market, such as the maturity and stability of the financial market of the host country, the level of technology infrastructure development in the market, and the overall economic and financial condition in the target market. Although anecdotal evidence is revealed in multiple case studies in different markets (e.g. Vianelli and Alon, 2008), no systematic studies have been conducted to examine the impact of market-specific dynamics and other situational factors on international hotel franchising. Efforts toward this direction will certainly be worthwhile and rewarding in future research.

References

Alon, I. (1999). *The Internationalization of US Franchising Systems*. New York: Garland Publishing.
Alon, Ilan (2005). *Service Franchising: A Global Perspective*, New York: Springer.
Alon, I., and D. McKee (1999a). "The Internationalization of Professional Business Service Franchises," *Journal of Consumer Marketing* 6(1), 74–85.
Alon, Ilan, and D. McKee (1999b). "Towards a Macro Environmental Model of International Franchising," *Multinational Business Review* 7 (1), 76–82.
Alon, I., R. Perrigot, and G. Cliquet (2004). "The Internationalization of French and American Franchisors in the Hotel Sector," *Sasin Journal of Management* 10, 4–18.
Altinay, L. (2003). "How Will Growth Be Financed by the International Hotel Companies?" *International Journal of Contemporary Hospitality Management* 15 (5), 274–82.
Altinay, L. (2007). "The Internationalization of Hospitality Firms: Factors Influencing a Franchise Decision-making Process," *Journal of Service Marketing* 21 (6), 398–409.
Aydin, N., and M. Kacker (1990). "International Outlook on US-Based Franchisors," *International Marketing Review* 7 (2), 206–19.
Azevedo, P., and V. Silva (2001). "Contractual Mix Analysis in the Brazilain Franchising," Proceedings of the 5th Annual Meeting of the International Society of New Institutional Economics, Berkley, USA: 13–15.
Baker, Brent L., and Rajiv P. Dant (2008). "Stable Plural Forms in Franchise Systems: An Examination of the Evolution of Ownership Redirection Research," in George W.J. Hendrikse, Mika Tuunanen, Josef Windsperger, and Gerard Cliquet, Eds. *Strategy and Governance of Networks: Cooperatives, Franchising and Strategic Alliances*. Heidelberg: Physica-Verlag, a Springer Company, 87–112.
Brickley, J.A., and F.H. Dark (1987. "The Choice of Organizational Form. The case of Franchising," *Journal of Financial Economics* 18, 401–420.
Burton, F.N., and A.R. Cross (1995). "Franchising and Foreign Market Entry," in S. J. Paliwoda and J. K. Ryans, Eds., *International Marketing Reader*. London: Routledge, 35–48.
Chen, J., and I. Dimou (2005). "Expansion Strategy of International Hotel Firms," *Journal of Business Research*, 58, 1730–40.

Cho, M. (2005). "Transaction Costs Influencing International Hotel Franchise Agreements: The Case of the Holiday Inn Seoul," *Journal of Vacation Marketing* 11 (2), 121.

Contractor, F. J., and S.K. Kundu (1998). "Model Choice in a World of Alliances: Analyzing Organization Forms in the International Hotel Sector," *Journal of International Business Studies* 29 (2), 325–357.

Creswell, J.W. (2009). *Research Design: Qualitative, Quantitative, and Mixed Methods Approaches*. London: Sage Publications.

Dunning, J. H., Y. S. Pak, and S. Beldona (2007). "Foreign Ownership Strategies of UK and US international franchisors: An Exploratory Application of Dunning's Envelope Paradigm," *International Business Review* 16, 531–548.

Eisenhardt (1989). " Agency Theory: An Assessment and Review," Academy of Management Review 14(1), 57–74.

Elango, B. (2007). "Are Franchisors with International Operations Different from Those Who are Domestic Market-Oriented?," *Journal of Small Business Management* 45(2), 179–193.

Entrepreneur (1990–1997). "Franchise 500," January Editions.

Eroglu, S. (1992). "The Internationalization Process of Franchise Systems: A Conceptual Model," *International Marketing Review* 9, 19–30.

Fladmoe-Lindquist, K. (1996). "International Franchising: Capabilities and Development," *Journal of Business Venturing* 11, 419–38.

Fladmoe-Lindquist, Karin, and Laurent L. Jacque (1995). "Control Modes in International Service Operations: The Propensity to Franchise," *Management Science* 41 (July), 1238–49.

Fullerton, J.A., A. Kendrick, K. Chan, M. Hamilton, and G. Kerr (2007). "Attitudes towards American Brands and Brand America." *Place Branding and Public Diplomacy* 3, 205–12.

Garg, V.K., and A. Rasheed (2006). "An Explanation of International Franchisors' Preference for Multiunit Franchising," *International Journal of Entrepreneurship* 10, 1–20.

Gatignon, H. and E. Anderson (1988). "The Multinational Corporation's Degree of Control Over Foreign Subsidiaries: An Empirical Test of a Transaction Cost Explanation," *Journal of Law, Economics and Organization* (Fall), 305–66.

Huszagh, S.M., F.W. Huszagh, and F. McIntyre (1992). "International Franchising in the Context of Competitive Strategy and the Theory of the Firm," *International Marketing Review* 9, 5–18.

Jensen, M.C., and W.H. Meckling (1976), "Theory of the Firm: Managerial Behavior, Aagency Costs and Ownership Structure," *Journal of Financial Economics* 3, 305–360.

Johnson, C., and M. Vanetti (2005). "Locational Strategies of International Hotel Chains," *Annals of Tourism Research* 32 (4), 1077–99.

Kaufmann, Patrick J., and Rajiv Dant (1996). "Multi-Unit Franchising: Growth and Management Issues," *Journal of Business Venturing* 11 (5), 343–58.

Ketchen, D., J. Combs,, and J. Upson, (2006). "When Does Franchising Help Restaurant Chain Performance?" *Cornell Hotel and Restaurant Administrative Quarterly* 47 (1), 14–26.

Kostecka, A. (1988). *Franchising in the Economy*. Washington DC: US Department of Commerce.

Lafontaine, F., and K. Shaw (1999). "The Dynamics of Franchise Contracting: Evidence from Panel Data," *Journal of Political Economy* 107, 1041–80.

Lashley, C., and A.J. Morrison (2000). *Franchising Hospitality Services*. London: Butterworth-Heinemann.

Mendelsohn, M. (1994). *The Guide to Franchising* (5th edition) London: Cassel.

Norton, S. (1988). "An Empirical Look at Franchising as an Organizational Form," *Journal of Business* 61(2), 197–218.

Perrigot, R. (2006). "Services vs Retail Chains: Are There Any Differences?: Evidence from the French Franchising Industry," *International Journal of Retail & Distribution Management* 34 (12), 918–30.

Rodriguez, A. R. (2002). "Determining Factors in Entry Choice for international expansion: The Case of the Spanish Hotel Industry," *Tourism Management*, 23, 597–607.

Rubin, P.H. (1978). "The Theory of the Firm and the Structure of the Franchise Contract," *Journal of Law and Economics* 21, 223–33.

Shane, S. (1996). "Why Franchise Companies Expand Overseas," *Journal of Business Venturing* 11 (2), 73–88.

Tucker, K., and M. Sundberg M.(1988) *International Trade in Services*. Worcester: Billing and Sons Ltd.

Vianelli, D., and I. Alon, (2008). "Opportunities and Risks of International Franchising in the Italian Hotel Sector," *Mercati e Competitività* 3, 73–98.

Yin, R. (2003). *Case Study Research: Design and Methods*. London: Sage Publications.

4
Clustering for International Market Selection

Ilan Alon and Amir Shoham

4.1 Introduction

International franchising research has advanced in recent years and, with it, the state of knowledge on why and how franchising companies expand into new markets. Initial research into the emerging field of international franchising has focused on both organizational and environmental determinants. Organizational determinants, which are among the causes of internationalization (Dunning, 1981), included size, age, growth, franchise fee and royalties, and dispersion (Alon, 1999; Elango, 2007; Fladmoe-Lindquist et al 1995; McIntyre et al 2006).

The international franchising sector has become a major player in the development of countries, particularly Anglo-Saxon ones. But franchising development has been uneven. One of the factors that impact the type and quantity of the international franchising is the local environment of the host country. Currently there are no studies which categorize countries according to factors that are important to franchising decisions. Categorizing countries by cluster analysis is a common method in the international business field (Ronen and Shenkar, 1985). The innovation of this research lies in finding the relevant environmental variables for international franchising and using these variables in the formation of national clusters that can help in franchising analysis.

Building upon a variety of franchising studies including survey (Arthur Andersen, 1996; McIntyre et al 2006), empirical (Elango, 2007; Yavas, 1988), and conceptual (Alon and McKee, 1999; Burton and Cross, 1995; Eroglu, 1992) research in international franchising, previous studies examined several location-specific characteristics relating to franchising firms. Among the environmental determinants are economic, demographic, social, and political factors affecting international franchising. We use these variables to cluster countries for international franchising market entry and selection.

Understanding international franchising market clusters has both research and practical implications. Clusters are needed for a variety of reasons as suggested by Haritgan (1975): **Naming** – clusters can be named and thus identified for further analysis; **summarizing** – each cluster helps to described nations by using both cultural and socioeconomic variables related to franchising; and **explaining** – grouping suggests similar variables that impact franchising.

From a research perspective, inferences can be made from environmentally similar clusters. International franchising of clusters allows for more robust analysis of contextual and environmental differences affecting franchising. Franchisors can use these clusters to understand commonalities among markets better, leading, for example, to selection of new markets for expansion, organization of markets for the purpose of control, and/or the establishment of regional offices, to mention a few uses.

For the purpose of this study, we define international franchising as "a foreign market entry mode that involves a relationship between the entrant (the franchisor) and a host country entity, in which the former transfers, under contract, a business package (or format), which it developed and owns, to the latter" (Burton and Cross, 1995: 36). The host country entity can be a master franchisor, a domestic franchisee, or the franchisor itself. International franchising is a unique method of entry into a host country that is different from licensing, exporting, and foreign direct investment because the franchisor can change the ownership structure over the life of the franchise system (Burton and Cross, 1995). International franchising is, thus, a unique form of international business involving both contractual rights and obligations along with varying levels of financial investment (Shane, 1996). Differences between international franchising and other forms of international market entry were explored in Alon (2005).

In summary, this paper contributes to the literature of international franchising by delineating the relevant environmental variables for international franchising and, then, using these variables in the formation of relevant clusters for franchising analysis. We first discuss the literature of franchising in the context of environmental variables. We then construct a database from available variables and apply cluster analysis to the data. Finally, the resultant clusters are discussed and analyzed.

4.2 Literature: Environmental determinants of international franchising

In general, the more favorable the environment of the host country, the more likely international franchisors will select this host country for international expansion (Eroglu, 1992). Therefore, in the aggregate, it is expected that countries with more favorable conditions will have more international franchisors. But, what are the market conditions that make international franchising investment attractive?

In an empirical article, Yavas (1988) found that among the economic factors market size (typically measured in GDP) was positively associated with international franchising, while among the demographic variables the ratio of female workers to the total labor force was positively related to international franchising. Markets that are more developed, with greater proportions of female labor participation, are more likely to be attractive to international franchisors. He did not, however, examine the effect of political and cultural variables on international franchising.

In a survey study, Arthur Andersen (1996) found that international franchisors considered economic and demographic, as well as political and cultural dimensions of a host country in order to assess the chances of success in the foreign market. Other studies noted the influences of political (Burton and Cross, 1995), economic, cultural and demographic environments (Alon and McKee, 1999; Eroglu, 1992) on franchising expansion. We will first delineate the economic, demographic, social, and political factors affecting international franchising expansion and then use these variables in the construction of relevant market clusters.

4.2.1 Economic factors

Among the economic factors, the effect of per capita GDP on the receptivity of a foreign market to a new franchise concept was identified in several studies as an important factor of international franchising (Alon and McKee, 1999; Arthur Andersen, 1996; Aydin and Kacker, 1990; Yavas, 1988). Arthur Andersen (1996) reported that the average income of the population is an important determinant to international expansion, and Yavas (1988) found that per capita income was significant and positively correlated to the number of international franchisors in a host country.

Income distribution was also identified as an important determinant for a franchising market. In a study attempting to rank in order the franchising market size of emerging markets, Alon (2006) used the income distribution in addition to the total income to determine the real potential. Taken together, these variables embody the wealth of the population, the general level of economic development, and the size of the middle class.

Because franchising is primarily in the service sector, Alon (2006) also uses the extent of the service sector in evaluating the market potential for franchising in emerging markets. The research suggests that Mexico and Russia have greater market potential then China, for example, because of their larger service economies.

4.2.2   Demographic factors

The three demographic variables that were discussed in the literature of international franchising include: 1) the level of the population (Arthur Andersen, 1996), 2) the level of urbanization (Arthur Andersen, 1996; Yavas, 1988), and 3) the proportion of female workers (Arthur Andersen, 1996; Yavas, 1988). These variables sum up many of the population dynamics that are important to international franchisors.

The level of population is seen as an important predictor of franchise viability. This is because even in countries with a relatively small middle class, a situation which characterizes many developing countries, there is a percentage of the population which is affluent, and able and willing to spend substantial amounts of money on discretionary products. In countries with a larger population, this relatively small percentage can be a sizable number that can support the expansion of international franchisors. Furthermore, franchisors often think in the long term when they enter an impoverished but highly populated country, such as Brazil, Russia, India, or China (BRIC). The potential of franchising in Russia, for example, has been expressed by one top executive of McDonald's who said: "we know the pay-off is a long way off. But it's an investment in our future" (Love, 1995: 465). Thus, both the level of population and income distribution affect the viability of international franchising in a given country.

The level of urbanization is another demographic factor influencing international franchisors. It was ranked as the fifth most important factor of the acceptance of the franchise system in a foreign market with 73 percent of respondents reporting it as either important or very important (Arthur Andersen, 1996). Urban life puts time pressures on the affected individuals, raising the opportunity cost of time. Many individuals, therefore, need to purchase services previously produced at home, increasing the chances of success of franchise systems tailored to fulfill this need.

A highly concentrated market is more efficiently served than a market that is geographically dispersed. This is because a viable market for both the factors of production and output exists in a densely populated area. With this in mind, it would seem that highly urbanized countries would represent more attractive opportunities for international franchisors.

In nearly all countries of the world, men and women have traditionally assumed different duties. Men have traditionally been the primary breadwinners of the family, while women have traditionally been expected to maintain the household. Women have entered the workforce in increasing numbers, making the dual income family a widespread phenomenon worldwide. However, as women have entered the workforce, they, by and large, have continued to carry their domestic responsibilities as well. Pressed for time, women around the world have increasingly adopted new products that are faster, easier, more convenient to use, and reflect the scarcity of free time in their working lives. Yavas (1988) found a positive association between female labor participation and the occurrence of international franchisors in a host country. We would expect that as the percentage of women in the workforce increases, so would the popularity of franchise systems, many of which provide products which specifically address the shortage of time of working women.

4.2.3   Cultural factors

Cultural variables influence the feasibility and acceptance of a franchising system (Alon and McKee, 1999; Alon et al 2000). Cross-cultural research in franchising has employed the cultural dimensions of Hofstede (Falbe and Welsh, 1998). According to Hofstede, cultures vary along four dimensions: 1) individualism/collectivism, 2) power distance, 3) uncertainty avoidance, and 4) sex role differentiation (Hofstede, 1991). Updates to Hofstede's dimensions were carried out by the GLOBE research team.

Arthur Andersen (1996) found that an entrepreneurial culture is highly regarded by international franchisors seeking to expand abroad. A total of 65 percent of the respondents reported that an entrepreneurial culture is either an important or a very important consideration in choosing a host country. This is because franchisees need to be entrepreneurial, possessing the skills needed to start and run a business. Highly entrepreneurial cultures are more likely to have a qualified market of potential franchisees, a necessary ingredient in developing a successful franchising system (Alon and McKee, 1999). Entrepreneurial culture is highly correlated with an individualist culture in the national society (Morris et al 1993; 1994).

Individualism/collectivism dimension has to do with the extent to which the self or, alternatively, the group, is the prime social identifier (Hofstede, 1997). The GLOBE research distinguishes between "institutionalism collectivism" and "in-group collectivism," the former focusing on the societal and organizational levels and the latter at the individual level (House and Javidan, 2004). As described by de Mooij (1998), individualist cultures are "I-conscious" while collectivist cultures are "we-conscious." It seems that highly individualist cultures would represent much more fertile ground for franchise development than highly collectivist ones. Cultures that are highly individualistic would be more likely to search out business arrangements that allow them to express their individuality as well as give maximum opportunity for individual achievement and success (Hofstede, 1991).

Power distance (PD), a dimension identified by both GLOBE and Hofstede, is the degree to which people expect power and authority to be distributed and expressed equitably or inequitably (Carl et al, 2004; Hofstede, 1980; 1983). The term was coined by Mulder (1977), who wrote about the degree of inequality in power between a less powerful individual and a more powerful individual, where both belong to the same social system. In the GLOBE project, PD was defined as "the degree to which members of an organization or society expect and agree that power should be shared unequally" (House et al, 2004: 517). High PD cultures are hierarchical with strong dependence between a principal and an agent. Since an agency relationship is necessary between the franchisor and the franchisee, high PD cultures would tend to be conducive to international franchising. On the other hand, high PD cultures also tend to experience periods of stability followed by periods of upheavals and disturbances. Crises in Russia (1999, 2008), Brazil (1998), and Asia (1997) provide examples of such upheavals. Such periods lessen the attractiveness of these foreign markets for international franchising investments. Therefore, it is not clear how power distance will affect international franchising.

Uncertainty avoidance, also common to GLOBE and Hofstede, assesses the degree to which a society's members are able to cope with the unpredictability of the future and the resulting ambiguity (de Luque and Javidan, 2004; Hofstede, 1980). This relates to the extent to which individuals are made uncomfortable by the absence of structures, rules, and conformity. Countries with high uncertainty avoidance cultures tend to generate more rules and have lower tolerance for deviance. Conformity to rules and the strong legal structure that these societies generate seems to be favorable to franchisors. However, cultures high in uncertainty avoidance also tend to reject foreign ideas. Since international franchisors often introduce foreign ideas to a host country, high uncertainty avoidance, therefore, can be unfavorable to international franchising.

Sex role differentiation (also referred to as Masculinity/femininity index) refers to the culture's use of gender differences to discriminate between social roles. Cultures that are masculine, and high in sex role differentiation, tend to be more ambitious, assertive, and aggressive pursuing material wealth. Masculine cultures are, therefore, more likely to attract international franchisors who seek these characteristics in franchisees (Hofstede 1991). Hofstede (1980) claimed that one of the most fundamental ways in which societies differ is in the extent to which each prescribes and proscribes different roles for women and men.

Clustering nations and countries by using cultural variables is a well developed method (Cattell, 1950; Gupta et al 2002; Ronen and Shenkar 1985; Toynbee, 1947). Previous research, from the early work of Cattell (1950) to the contemporary study of Gupta et al (2002), used data for cultural clusters that included variables other than culture, including economic and demographic variables. On the basis of the economic, social, and political variables mentioned above we conducted the cluster analysis contained in the next section.

4.2.4 Political factors

The effect of political factors on the expansion of international franchising has been discussed in the literature. Some researchers, such as Aydin and Kacker (1990) and Hoffman and Preble (1991), suggested that political risk is not an important factor. This is because local franchisees usually assume the risk and exchange risk is relatively low since most of the inputs are local. Other researchers, such as Alon and McKee (1999) and Eroglu (1992), disagreed because political risk may deter international expansion and because political factors such as red tape, monetary and exchange controls, corruption, import restrictions, and ownership restrictions can significantly increase the cost of doing business in the host country. Furthermore, exchange rate fluctuations caused by political risk affect royalties payments measured in domestic currency (Eroglu, 1992). Political risk factors have the potential to raise the price of, and complicate, business transactions.

4.3 Method

4.3.1 Sample

Based on the literature in the previous section, we gathered a sample of countries that had cultural scores as well as other available factors. We used the GLOBE study as our source for culture scores (as it is a more recent framework for cultural scores than Hofsetede, but uses roughly the same categories). In total, we used 56 out of the 62 societies of the GLOBE study. We mainly excluded from our sample countries that had two scores in the GLOBE study, e.g. Germany, which had a cultural score for the former East and another cultural score for the former West. Table 4.1 presents the 56 countries in our empirical study.

Table 4.1 Countries by cluster

Country	Cluster
Albania	
Egypt	
Georgia	1
Indonesia	
Kazakhstan	
Costa Rica	
Greece	
Hungary	
Israel	
Italy	
Poland	2
Portugal	
Slovenia	
South Korea	
Spain	
Taiwan	
Australia	
Austria	
Canada	
Denmark	
Finland	3
France	
Netherlands	
Sweden	
Switzerland	

Continued

Table 4.1 Continued

Country	Cluster
England	
Hong Kong	
Ireland	
Japan	4
New Zealand	
Singapore	
United States	
Argentina	
Bolivia	
Brazil	5
Mexico	
Namibia	
Kuwait	
Malaysia	6
Qatar	
Colombia	
Ecuador	
El Salvador	
Guatemala	
Iran	
Morocco	
Nigeria	
Philippines	7
Russia	
Thailand	
Turkey	
Venezuela	
Zambia	
Zimbabwe	
China	
India	8

4.3.2 Variables

Based on the literature presented above, we used variables that should help us to distinguish between different types of countries from a franchising point of view. In total we have 14 variables. The variables include three types: demographic, economic, and cultural. A short description of each of the variables and its corresponding measure follows.

Growth Domestic Product per capita purchasing power parity [GDPPC (PPP)] = the value of all final goods and services produced within a nation in 2006 divided by population as of 7/1/2006. The nation's purchasing power parity (PPP) exchange rate is the sum value of all goods and services produced in the country valued at prices prevailing in the U.S. This is the measure most economists prefer when looking at per capita welfare and when comparing living conditions or use of resources across countries. We used the CIA *World Fact Book* (2006).

Gini = measures economic inequality, which assesses the extent to which the distribution of income among households within a country deviates from a perfectly equal distribution. If income were distributed with perfect equality, the index would be zero; if income were distributed with perfect inequality, the index would be 1. We used the CIA *World Fact Book* (2006).

Service percentage of the economy = the percentage distribution of the labor force in the service sector. Economies with a strong service orientation are more likely to attract franchising since most franchises are in the service sector (Alon, 2005; 2006).

Corruption Perception Index (CPI) = The definition of corruption is "the abuse of entrusted power for private gain" that means the degree to which corruption is perceived to exist among public officials and politicians. A higher score means less (perceived) corruption. The scores are between 0 and 10. We used Transparency International (2006).

Population = the number of inhabitants a nation had in 2006. Larger societies have more demand for all sort of products, including ones offered by franchising. Source: CIA *World Fact Book* 2006.

Ease of doing business index = is a world bank's index. A high score on the ease of doing business index means the regulatory environment is conducive to the operation of business. That indicates better, usually simpler, regulations for businesses and stronger protections of property rights. This index uses ten topics, made up of a variety of indicators like: starting a business – procedures, time, cost, and minimum capital to open a new business; and dealing with licenses – procedures, time and cost of business inspections, and licensing.

Percentage upper- middle class = We used the Senauer and Goetz (2004) method to calculate the percentage of the upper-middle class. The size of the emerging middle class is estimated with a cutoff level of U.S.$6000 GNI per capita. We used the World Bank data in for GNI per capita, converted into U.S. dollars using PPP and the percentage shares of income or consumption by 10 percent of the population (see Senauer and Goetz, 2004 for a more detailed explanation). Currie and Alon (2005) underscored the importance of income distribution in franchising.

Urbanization = the percentage of the urban population out of the total population. The source is *World Population Prospects* by the United Nations Population Division.

Economic Freedom = We used the *Index of Economic Freedom* of The Heritage Foundation.[1]

Political risk = describes the risks companies and investors face as a result of the exercise of political power. These include potential losses from nationalization, regulatory changes, and potential risk of a government or government agency not honoring a contract, as well as potential losses due to riots, civil war, or terrorism.[2]

Culture uses four culture variables that were primarily estimated using variables from the House et al (2004) GLOBE study of 62 societies, which has been called "probably the most sophisticated project undertaken in international business research". We used four out of the nine culture dimensions in the GLOBE study. The four culture dimensions are equivalent to those of Hofstede (1980; 1983) and are More Up Power Distance Index, Gender Egalitarianism, Uncertainty Avoidance, and Individualism/collectivism.

4.3.3 Analyses

We clustered the 56 countries using the 14 variables described above. We used a squared Euclidean distance in the cluster process. The main problem with this method is that if the variables are measured in units that are not comparable, the procedure will give more weight to variables with large variances. Therefore, we standardized the variables so they were measured on the same scale. All the variable scores during the statistical process were normalized with a mean of 50 and a standard deviation of 10. In a squared Euclidean distance one places progressively greater weight on objects that are farther apart. For example, a cluster with China and India is formed mainly because the population of those countries is so much larger than the population of the other countries in the sample.

4.4 Results

Using cluster analysis methods on the variables presented above, we received eight different clusters for franchising. Table 4.1 shows the countries that are included in each cluster. Table 4.2 shows the non-standardized mean for each variable of each cluster for meaningful comparisons.

Each cluster is different from the other clusters, but how different? Table 4.3 helps us to understand in a statistical and visual way the differences between the clusters. The table is a result of normalized variables (mean 50, s.d 10): the higher the score, the greater the difference between the clusters.

As can be seen in Table 4.2, the biggest difference exists between clusters three and eight. Cluster three contains Australia, Austria, Canada, Denmark, Finland, France, Netherlands, Sweden, and Switzerland. Cluster eight contains China and India. The difference is quite clear between the clusters and it is well presented in Table 4.2.

4.5 Discussions

From our data and empirical research we received eight different clusters (see Table 4.1) of host countries regarding to franchising. As mentioned earlier, we used a squared Euclidean distance in our empirical tests, which gives greater weight in formulating the clusters to objects that are farther apart. According to the method, we named the eight clusters by the main characteristic of the countries in the cluster, and provided some descriptive explanations for each of the clusters (as per Table 4.2).

Group 1: Modernizing Islamic nations includes some of the modernizing Islamic states: Albania, Egypt, Georgia, Kazakhstan, and Indonesia. Interestingly, these states are from geographically diverse areas. Their average GDP per capita is considered "developing" with about U.S.$5400 PPP GDP per capita. The economies, however, are becoming increasingly liberal, service-based, and only mildly politically risky. With a population of about 68 million people and urbanization rates reaching about half of the population, these countries provide a large "emerging" market for international franchisors. But for franchisors from Western countries, a challenge exists in understanding and operating within the cultures of these countries, which are relatively more power distant and more collectivistic.

Group 2: Latin European PIGS and newly industrialized includes a diverse group of developed and "emerged" markets, both static and dynamic. The PIGS (Portugal, Italy, Greece, Spain) are the static EU powers, while Slovenia, Hungary, and Poland are the "emerging" and

Table 4.2 Clusters mean

	1	2	3	4	5	6	7	8
GDPPC (PPP)U.S.$	5400	22,727	33,733	35,471	9080	21,933	5964	5750
GINI (between 0 and 100)	33.08	35.24	29.46	40.97	58.18	46.10	48.57	38.25
Economic freedom	1.62	2.42	3.00	3.21	2.18	2.42	1.68	1.48
Service percent of the economy	51.24	65.45	70.42	71.43	57.70	39.17	54.38	50.35
Political risk	66.25	75.68	85.39	83.64	69.20	75.83	59.21	64.75
CPI	2.74	5.36	8.81	8.31	3.26	5.27	2.90	3.30
Ease of doing business	111.80	49.55	18.00	6.14	82.60	34.00	97.00	103.50
Urbanization	48.20	68.40	77.44	81.83	67.80	82.33	57.57	32.50
Population	67.66	22.95	18.70	72.69	70.04	9.40	43.40	1225.80
GE	3.04	3.65	3.19	3.52	2.89	3.23	3.55	3.24
PD	5.05	5.28	4.71	5.02	5.20	5.01	5.57	5.26
UA	3.99	3.75	4.91	4.51	3.80	4.33	3.70	4.55
CII	5.70	5.32	4.06	4.68	5.28	5.34	5.75	4.55
% upper-middle class	0.32	0.89	0.95	0.94	0.44	0.59	0.33	0.33

Table 4.3   Distances between cluster centers

Clusters	1	2	3	4	5	6	7	8
1	0							
2	39.7	0						
3	62.7	39.9	0					
4	61.6	30.2	20.1	0				
5	30.3	37.1	58.5	52.1	0			
6	37.2	30.5	43.7	39.2	32.3	0		
7	26.4	36.7	69.1	61.2	26.8	39.9	0	
8	52.8	67.5	83.9	80.6	61.1	66.7	57.4	0

dynamic EU powers. South Korea, Chinese Taipei, and Israel are the newly industrialized countries in the group from Asia and the Middle East, respectively. Costa Rica is the Latin equivalent. The PPP GDP per capita for this group is around U.S.$23,000, which is "developed" in economic terms. These economies are service driven, and relatively safe politically. Income is more equitably distributed compared to group 1.

Group 3: Middle mowers, a term borrowed from political science, include the "developed" countries that are not superpowers, but that have a strong regional and economic influence. They include mostly European countries, such as Denmark, Finland, France, Sweden, Switzerland, Netherlands, and Austria, but also others, such as Australia and Canada, which have started to diverge from their original Anglo-inspired origins. These countries all have high incomes, with relatively low income inequality. They are free, service oriented, and safe, and doing business there is relatively easy. Because a large portion of the population can afford products and services offered by franchising, these markets are good candidates for franchising development.

Group 4: Anglo-Saxon inspired countries are mostly ex-colonies of the UK: Hong Kong, Ireland, New Zealand, Singapore, and the U.S., but also include Japan whose culture and development were largely influence by the U.S. after World War II. This set of countries is quintessential for global franchising development, including the following characteristics: service oriented, large populations with high incomes, politically stable, and urbanized. The consumers in these countries are relatively rich and willing to engage in franchising-based consumption. Franchising has thrived in these environments.

Group 5: Emerging Latin markets with the exception of Namibia, countries in Latin America and including Brazil, Argentina, Mexico, and Bolivia. While these countries are mostly "developing" and "emerging" their PPP GDP per capita, on average, is above U.S.$9000, but their income is unequally distributed, political risk exists, economic freedom is limited, and doing business there is not easy. Thus, while the potential is high, global franchising was slow in gaining a footing.

Group 6: Gateways to the Muslim world consists of only three countries: Malaysia, Qatar, and Kuwait. All of these are Muslim countries, with a high level of economic development, a PPP GDP per capita approaching U.S.$22,000, and relatively stable political system. The challenge for franchisors is that only a small part of their economy is based in services, and that large adaptation may be needed to adjust to the local culture.

Group 7: Untapped developing countries consists of mostly developing countries from around the world: Latin America (Colombia, Ecuador, El Salvador, Guatemala, and Venezuela), MENA (Iran, Morocco, and Turkey), Africa (Nigeria, Zambia, and Zimbabwe), Asia (Philippines, and Thailand), and Eastern Europe (Russia). While these countries' level of development is low with a GDP per capita below U.S.$6,000, on average, these countries suffer from lack of economic freedom, low level of service economy, high political risk, and difficulties in doing business. Great potential is, thus, mired by franchising underdevelopment.

Group 8: The biggest emerging markets, the world's most populous nations: China and India. While the level of economic development is low, the emergence of these countries' economies is undisputable. Given their large populations, the multinational company cannot ignore these markets in their global product portfolio, despite difficulties in doing business there.

4.6 Conclusion

This research's main innovation is by clustering the global environment by using variables that previous literature recognizes as the main ones that should impact international franchising activities. We have 56 countries in our database; the GLOBE scores for culture limited our sample to those specific countries. The statistical tests resulted in eight different clusters of countries with regards to international franchising. We used data from four different categories that previous literature has as the main factors that impact international franchising decisions:

1. Economic Factors
2. Demographic Factors

3. Cultural Factors
4. Political Factors

Clustering countries in relation to international franchising is important because the research in the field has advanced in recent years and the international franchising sector has become a major player in the development of countries. But previous research did not cluster the countries into different types of countries in view of the opportunities and threats in the local environment. The countries in each of our clusters, presented above, have a common unique characteristic. Knowing the characteristic that separates one cluster from the the other clusters can help in understanding the special factors that impact one's local environment.

Notes

1. See http://www.heritage.org/Index/countries.cfm for a more detailed explanation.
2. See http://www.prsgroup.com/PRS_Methodology.aspx for a more detailed explanation.

References

Alon, Ilan (1999). *The Internationalization of U.S. Franchising Systems*. New York: Garland Publishing.

Alon, Ilan (2005). *Service Franchising: A Global Perspective*. New York: Springer.

Alon, Ilan (2006) "Executive Insight: Evaluating the Market Size for Service Franchising in Emerging Markets," *International Journal of Emerging Markets* 1 (1), 9–20.

Alon, Ilan, and David McKee (1999). "Toward a Macro Environmental Model of International Franchising," *Multinational Business Review* 7 (1), 76–82.

Alon, Ilan, and Dianne Welsh, Eds. (2001). *International Franchising in Emerging Markets: China, India and Other Asian Countries*, Chicago IL: CCH Inc. Publishing.

Alon, Ilan, Mark Toncar, and David McKee (2000). "Evaluating Foreign-Market Environments for International Franchising Expansion," *Foreign Trade Review*, 35 (1), 1–11.

Arthur Andersen (1996). *International Expansion by U.S. Franchisors*. Chicago/ Washington, DC:, Il. ArthurAndersen LLP, in cooperation with the International Franchise Association.

Aydin, N., and M. Kacker (1990). "International Outlook on US-Based Franchisors," *International Marketing Review* 7 (2), 206–19.

Burton, F.N., and A.R. Cross (1995). "Franchising and Foreign Market Entry," in S.J. Paliwoda and J.K. Ryans, (Eds.), *International Marketing Reader*. London: Routledge, 35–48.

Carl, D., V. Gupta, and M. Javidan (2004). "Power distance," in, R.J. House, P.J. Hanges, M. Javidan, P.W. Dorfman, and V. Gupta (Eds). *Leadership, culture, and organizations: The GLOBE study of 62 societies*. Thousand Oaks, CA: Sage Publications, 513–63.

Cattell, R. (1950). "The Principal Culture Patterns Discoverable in the Syntax Dimensions of Existing Nations," *Journal of Social Psychology* 32, 215–53.

CIA World Fact Book (2006). https://www.cia.gov/library/publications/the-world-factbook/internet link; last accessed on 13 December 2009

Currie, David M., and Ilan Alon (2005). "Estimating Demand for Kodak Film (with a Teaching Note)," Toronto: Ivey Publishing House (9B04D015, TN 8B04D15).

de Luque, M.S., and M. Javidan (2004). Uncertainty Avoidance. in, R.J. House, P.J. Hanges, M. Javidan, P.W. Dorfman, and V. Gupta (Eds). *Leadership, culture, and organizations: The GLOBE study of 62 societies*. Thousand Oaks, CA: Sage Publications, 602–53.

de Mooij, Marieke (1998). *Global Marketing and Advertising: Understanding Cultural Paradoxes*. Thousand Oaks, CA: Sage Publications.

Dunning, J.H. (1981). *International Production and the Multinational Enterprise*. London: Allen and Unwin.

Elango, B. (2007). "Are Franchisors with International Operations Different from Those Who Are Domestic Market Oriented?" *Journal of Small Business Management* 45 (2), 170–93.

Eroglu, Sevgin (1992). "The Internationalization Process of Franchise Systems: A Conceptual Model," *International Marketing Review*, 9 (5), 19–30.

Falbe, Cecilia M., and Dianne H.B. Welsh (1998). "NAFTA and Franchising: A Comparison of Franchisor Perceptions of Characteristics Associated with Franchisee Success and Failure in Canada, Mexico, and the United States," *Journal of Business Venturing* 13, 151–71.

Fladmoe-Lindquist, Karin, and Laurent L. Jacque (1995). "Control Modes in International Service Operations: The Propensity to Franchise," *Management Science* 41 (July), 1238–49.

Gupta, V., P.J. Hanges, and P. Dorfman (2002). "Cultural clusters: Methodology and findings," *Journal of World business* 37, 11–15.

Hartigan, J.A. (1975). *Clustering algorithms-Wiley series in probability and mathematical statistics* New York: Wiley.

Hoffman, Richard C., and John F. Preble (1991). "Franchising: Selecting a Strategy for Rapid Growth," *Long Range Planning* 24 (4), 74–85.

Hofstede, G. (1980). *Culture's consequences: International differences in work-related values*. Newbury Park, CA: Sage.

Hofstede, G. (1983). "Dimensions of National Cultures in Fifty Countries and Three Region," in J.B. Deregowski, S. Dziurawiec & R.C. Annis (Eds), *Expiscations in Cross-Cultural Psychology*, Lisse: Swets and Zeitlinger, 335–55.

Hofstede, Geert (1991). *Culture and Organizations: Software of the Mind*. London: McGraw Hill.

Hofstede, G. (1997). *Culture and Organization: Software of the Mind*. New York: McGraw Hill.

House, R. J., and M. Javidan (2004). "Overview of GLOBE," in, R.J. House, P.J. Hanges, M. Javidan, P.W. Dorfman, and V. Gupta (Eds). *Leadership, culture, and organizations: The GLOBE study of 62 societies*. Thousand Oaks, CA: Sage Publications, 9–28.

House, R. J., P.J. Hanges, M. Javidan, P.W. Dorfman, and V. Gupta (Eds) (2004). *Leadership, culture, and organizations: The GLOBE study of 62 societies.* Thousand Oaks, CA: Sage Publications.

Love, John F. (1995). *McDonald's Behind the Arches*, New York: Bantam Books.

McIntyre, Faye S., Faye W. Gilbert, and Joyce A. Young (2006). "US-Based Franchise Systems: A Comparison of Domestic versus International Operations," *Journal of Marketing Channels*, 13 (4), 5–21.

Morris, M.H., R.A. Avila, and J. Allen (1993). "Individualism and the Modern Corporation: Implications for Innovation and Entrepreneurship," *Journal of Management* 19 (3), 595–612.

Morris, Michael H., Duane L. Davis, and Jeffrey W. Allen (1994). "Fostering Corporate Entrepreneurship: Cross-Cultural Comparisons of the Importance of Individualism Versus Collectivism," *Journal of International Business Studies* 25 (1), 65–89.

Mulder, M. (1977). *The Daily Power Game*, Leiden, Netherlands: Martinus Nijhoff.

Ronen, S., and O. Shenkar (1985) "Clustering Countries on Attitudinal Dimensions: A Review and Synthesis," *Academy of Management Review* 10 (3), 435–54.

Shane, S. (1996). "Why Franchise Companies Expand Overseas," *Journal of Business Venturing* 11 (2), 73–88.

Statistical Yearbook (1994). 41st Issue, New York: United Nations.

Toynbee, A. (1947). *A Study of History,* New York: Oxford.

Transparency International (2006). http://www.transparency.org/

World Resource Institute, the, United Nations Environment Programme, United Nations Development Programme, and World Bank (1996). *World Resources, A Guide to the Global Environment: The Urban Environment.* Oxford: Oxford University Press.

Yavas, Burhan F. (1988). "The Role of Economic-Demographic Factors in US International Restaurant Franchising: An Empirical Investigation," *Journal of Global Marketing* 2 (1), 57–72.

Part II
Area Studies of Franchising

5
Franchising in Italy

Ilan Alon and Donata Vianelli

5.1   Introduction

Every year Italy provides millions of visitors with distinctive experiences, thanks to the natural, cultural, and social resources that characterize the country. An analysis of the role of the tourism industry – an important component of the Italian economy – is therefore appropriate and timely. Franchising can contribute greatly to a host market environment and to specific service industries in particular (Alon, 2004). Weaknesses in the Italian hospitality market could be compensated for and reduced by the development of the franchising concept, which is seldom used by Italian hotel chains as they seek to expand in the local market. The low level of franchising in the Italian hospitality sector stands in stark contrast to countries like the U.S., and to other countries where franchising represents as much as 65 percent of the total bed offer (Pine et al 2000). As Altinay (2004) points out, the implementation of franchising is a very difficult organizational activity, and this is particularly true in markets such as Italy, Spain, and Greece, where family-run companies resist the logic of franchising. Considering the data provided by Assofranchising (2005), in a positive overview which reveals a constant growth of franchising during recent years (during 2005 the increase in total turnover was 6.9 percent), the presence of franchising in the hotel sector is still insignificant: with a total turnover of €41.35 million, it represents only 0.2 percent of overall franchising activity in the country. And only about 10 percent of the hotels of the main hospitality groups in Italy are franchised.

The aim of this paper is to give an overview of the current situation related to the development of franchising in Italy, trying to find out 1) why in certain cases franchising is seen as a risk and/or an unfavorable organizational mode, and 2) what opportunities and/or advantages can be identified. More specifically, information derived from the research develops a better understanding of the main opportunities for franchising in the Italian hospitality sector, especially from a marketing perspective, and identifies the main limits related to the singularity of the business in its social, political, and economic contexts.

This paper makes a unique contribution to the development of franchising in Italy, particularly as it relates to the hospitality sector, by 1) examining franchising as an international mode of business entry and expansion, 2) focusing on the Italian franchising market, and 3) developing recommendations and approaches to the development of franchising practice and theory in the Italian context based on interviews with franchising industry leaders. As such, the paper helps to identify which kind of competencies should be strengthened among Italian entrepreneurs in order to stimulate the development of franchising. Based upon the limited amount of research dealing with hotel franchising as a mode of entry into foreign markets and a growth strategy at a national level, and the sparse academic contributions related to hotel franchising in Europe and even more so in the Italian market where this topic has been only marginally explored in the literature, this paper reviews the most recent trends for international franchising in the hotel business, and discusses the challenges and opportunities in the Italian market.

The paper begins by reviewing franchising and other modes of entry in the context of the hotel sector and the Italian marketplace. Particular emphasis is given to the cultural factors associated with a country, as described by Hofstede (1991), because these were shown to have an influence on the development of franchising around the world, and the attractiveness of a host market – in our example, Italy – to international franchising activities (Alon, 2005). A description of the research process follows. Last, the findings are discussed with regard to country/firm specific factors that explain the propensity to franchise in the Italian market.

5.2   Franchising as a modal choice in the global hotel sector

Since the 1990s research has been conducted on the internationalization of the hotel industry, although little of it focuses on franchising as a mode of entry into foreign markets and/or as a growth strategy at a national level. An overview of the research conducted in the last ten years is presented in Table 5.1. Coherently with the objectives of the present research, after a synthetic presentation of the various

Table 5.1 The internationalization of hotel groups: Selected research studies in the last decade

Author/s	Methodology	Sample of analysis	Main topic	Country focus
Connell (1997)	Qualitative	Single hotel group	Analysis of the franchise relationship in a global context	UK
Litteljohn (1997)	Qualitative, based on secondary data	Large hotel chains	Analysis of trends and issues in hospitality internationalization	World
Gannon and Johnson (1997)	Qualitative, based on secondary data and personal interviews	Large hotel chains	Analysis of the dimensions of control and coordination of managerial resources in the international hotel industry	Europe, North America, Asia
Zhao and Olsen (1997)	Qualitative, based on secondary data and personal interviews	Five international hotel chains	Analysis of entry strategies by international hotel chains	U.S. companies expanding abroad
Alon (1999)	Quantitative, based on secondary data	Franchised hotel chains	Organizational explanations for franchising hotel internationalization	U.S. companies expanding abroad
Contractor and Kundu (1998a, 1998b)	Quantitative, based on secondary data	1131 hotel properties in 112 nations (IHG Dir.)	Analysis of organizational forms in the hotel industry, with a focus on international franchising	World
Olsen and Roper (1998)	Qualitative, based on secondary data	Hospitality industry	Internationalization in the hospitality industry	World
Hong et al (2000)	Qualitative, based on secondary data	International hotel chains	Analysis of entry strategies by international hotel chains	Southeast Asia and Indo-China
Dev, et al (2002)	Quantitative	530 hotels (Global Hoteliers Club)	Analysis of the advantages/ disadvantages of franchising vs. management contracts for entering foreign markets	China, Australia, Singapore, Thailand, Indonesia, U.S., Canada, Germany
Altinay (2004)	Qualitative interviews and secondary data	Single hotel group	The role of entrepreneurs in the international franchise process of an organization	Europe
Alon et al (2004b)	Quantitative, based on secondary data	Franchised hotel chains	Comparative analysis of France and the U.S.	France, U.S.

organizational forms, it is appropriate to focus on 1) the advantages/ disadvantages of franchising as categorized by the literature and 2) the country specific variables influencing the development of franchising in a specific geographical area.

5.2.1   Market entry modes of international hotel chains

The main alternative organizational forms for expansion in the global hotel sector can be summarized as follows (see Contractor and Kundu, 1998b; Gannon and Johnson, 1997; Ista, 2005):

– wholly owned investments
– joint ventures and lease agreements
– company managed outlets
– management contracts
– consortium arrangements
– franchising modes

The different types of entry modes correspond to different levels of risk and return. Other models of expansion include hybrids, such as the ones employed by Best Western (Alon et al 2004a).

Full ownership gives the company complete control of the operations, which is shared in the case of partial ownership through joint ventures. Control is exercised over the level of quality of day to day operations, physical assets (including real estate), the tacit expertise embedded in the routines of the firm, and over codified assets such as the global reservation system and the firm's internationally recognized brand name.

In a joint venture, control is related only to codified assets, while other activities are shared with the partner. Moreover, the lease arrangement, where the hotel company provides initial working capital and certain inventories (Davé, 1984), can be identified as a form of partial equity investment. In fact, under most of these agreements the lease payments are considered a form of long-term debt, thus transferring the potential future debts of the hotel to the leasing company.

The managed hotel can be defined as an organizational form where the property is owned by a third party owner; the company which is in charge of managing the hotel – in all its dimensions – may or may not have an interest. The managing company pays a rental fee to the owner, and is fully responsible for the profit(s) and loss(es) of the hospitality activity.

A management contract is an agreement where the legal owners of a hotel make a contract with a hospitality company whose name is internationally recognized. In this way the hospitality group, in return for a fee paid by the local company, runs and manages the hotel as if it were owned by the chain under its well-known brand name. The hospitality group exercises a high degree of control over all operations with the exception of the ownership risks: in fact, it is the owner who is responsible for the profits and losses of the hotel. Nevertheless, the main risk of such a contract is that the owner could be interested in being more active in managing the hotel and, having acquired over the years an expertise in management, could decide to go it alone when the contract expires. From this perspective, a management contract appears to be less stable than a joint venture.

A consortium is an agreement between different hospitality organizations to group different hotels under one corporate brand. The definition of a consortium is quite broad, since it combines hotels that can have something in common: for example, technology, image, design, etc. It is a formula which allows for varying levels of local independence, but at the same time benefits individual hotels in the consortium by providing brand benefits and strong marketing by the consortium that enable small hotels to compete with corporate brands (Scoviak and Wolchuk, 2004).

Finally, in a franchising agreement the franchisee maintains full control of daily management and service quality, together with the ownership risk related to physical assets and the real estate. The franchisor, in return for a fee and royalties, generally provides a package of operational know-how which includes an operational system tied to the product, design, and décor of the physical properties (ambiance and atmosphere), the brand, the corporate image, and the reservations system. Less obvious, though potentially more important, the franchisor also assists in finding locations, financing, preopening and training activity, and all the guidelines related to increasing a franchisee's business know-how.

5.2.2 Characteristics of franchising in the global hotel sector

Franchising as a mode of entry by hotel companies has been analyzed mainly in the British and American literature, which has pointed out the numerous advantages and disadvantages from the point of view of both franchisor and franchisee. This focus on the American literature is obviously the result of the powerful role of American hotel groups in a global context and the prevalence of franchising in the American context (see Table 5.2).

The advantages and disadvantages to franchisors and franchisees in the hospitality industry have been discussed in detail by others (Alon

Table 5.2   Largest (20) hotel groups in the world by number of hotels/number of rooms (2003)

	Group	Number of hotels	Number of rooms	Nationality
1	InterContinental Hotel Group	3520	536,318	UK
2	Cendant Corp.	6402	518,747	U.S.
3	Marriott International	2718	490,564	U.S.
4	Accor	3894	453,403	France
5	Choice Hotel International	4810	388,618	U.S.
6	Hilton Hotels Corp.	2173	348,483	U.S.
7	Best Western International	4110	310,245	U.S.
8	Starwood Hotels & Resorts WorldWide	738	229,247	U.S.
9	Carlson Hospitality World Worldwide	881	147,624	U.S.
10	Hilton Group plc	392	98,689	UK
11	Hyatt Hotels/ Hyatt International	208	89,602	U.S.
12	Sol Melià, SA	331	80,494	Spain
13	TUI AG/TUI Hotels & Resorts	290	76,000	Germany
14	Sociètè du Louvre	896	66,356	France
15	Interstate Hotels & Resorts	295	65,250	U.S.
16	Wyndam International	190	50,980	U.S.
17	Extended Stay America	472	50,240	U.S.
18	FelCor Lodging Trust	161	45,000	U.S.
19	La Quinta Corp.	363	43,457	U.S.
20	Westmont Hospitality Group	332	40,000	U.S.

Source: Ista (2005).

2004; Contractor, Kundu, 1998a; Hollensen, 2004; Kotler, Bowen, Makens, 2003), but they are worth summarizing here. First, franchising guarantees a greater degree of control to the franchisor when compared to the growth strategies that derive from other contractual arrangements. Franchising, therefore, can be said to influence future investment by allowing franchisors to test the market with minimal upfront risk.

Control is additionally guaranteed through technical advances in global reservations systems, which create a constant link between far-flung hotels and administrative offices. This "connectedness" allows for the efficient development of strong marketing activities adapted to the different needs of local markets; uncooperative franchises and inefficient local organizations can also be weeded out more efficiently before negative effects impact on the brand name. Global connectedness has a further, unintended, positive effect: prospective franchisees can be attracted more easily, as would-be hoteliers are able to research information about business trends at a global and national level.

A second group of variables – also related to franchisee development – is franchising's relatively low risk and the low cost of entry. Franchisees invest in necessary equipment and know-how; thus, they have a stake in preserving the business, maximizing outlet profits, and indirectly enriching the chain. The investment incentives offered to franchisees generally outweigh any incentives that could be offered to salaried managers of company-owned outlets (Hoover et al 2003). From the franchisor's perspective, if on one side the creation of strong brand equity and a global reservation system represent a huge sunk cost, on the other side the cost of increasing the number of affiliates is low. Of course, success in the franchising format requires that the franchisor can confirm that the franchisee has not just the appropriate financial capabilities but also local market knowledge and relevant experience. Careful vetting of potential franchisees can lead to more rapid local expansion in the target market – if that expansion is desirable.

Finally, a significant advantage for the franchisor is the possibility of generating economies of scale not only in contracting with international customers but also in areas such as logistics, supply, and uniform design (Dev et al 2002). Standardization is a significant determiner in the reduction of transaction costs, attainable through a codification of management routines and knowledge, especially those activities related to training and staff development (Kaufmann and Eroglu, 1998).

A positive aspect of expanding the franchise network through local partners is that it also gives the possibility of negotiating support for national contracts with suppliers and the opportunity, as previously pointed out, to improve marketing strategies through the continuous exchange of marketing data and strategic information within the system.

Numerous, too, are the advantages that accrue to franchisees. One of the most important benefits is related to consumers' brand awareness of the hotel chain. Brand reputation is continuously monitored and reinforced by the franchisor, giving a strong competitive advantage to its franchisees who, on their side, contribute to brand awareness (and customer loyalty) by way of their operational activities and relations with clients (Michael, 1999). Brand image and access to a global reservation system represent two of the most important intangible assets a franchisee receives. The net result of affiliation with an established chain is quicker, more profitable growth – and a decreased risk of business failure in the crucial first years.

Furthermore, the franchisor does not take just a passive role in the hotel business. In return for royalties, franchisors contribute continuous injections of innovation, expertise, technology, product development, and high-quality daily-use supplies. In addition, especially in the beginning of the franchise relationship, the chain's know-how in relation to decisions on items such as site selection, architectural planning, and financing is invaluable to franchisees. And the franchisor tends to stay involved by providing a continuous consulting activity related to the operational system and the software that support oversight management and reservations.

Inevitably, there are also disadvantages to both the franchisor and the franchisee that are worth mentioning. First, the identification of the right partner and the negotiation of the agreement can be an expensive and time consuming activity for a franchisor. The possible difficulties, analyzed in the hotel context from a transaction cost theory perspective (Contractor and Kundu, 1998a; Williamson, 1979), can be mainly related to the selection of the right partner, especially abroad; the ability to specify in a contract those aspects that can negatively alter the business relationship; or the refusal to make investments specific or dedicated to a contract; the possible opportunism of the business partner, who sometimes requests continuous (inappropriate) monitoring of the business. Some obstacles can be recognized and overcome in the beginning, but it is not unusual for hurdles to appear later on, sometimes with reference to restrictions imposed by local legislation regarding payments, transfers of money, etc.

A second group of disadvantages is related to a franchisor's relatively weak control over the franchisee's activities, resulting in problems of communication and cooperation affecting the partnership; such problems can have a cascade effect, casting a pall on the goodwill and the brand name of the hotel chain, especially if the franchisee underperforms.

In addition, if it is proved that a continuous transfer of a firm's tangible and intangible resources is essential to maintaining consistency of the brand image and operations, the costs of creating and marketing a unique package of products and services that will still be recognized internationally can be significantly high (Dev, Erramilli, and Agarwal, 2002).

The would-be franchisee must also take into account some potential disadvantages (Kotler et al 2003). Apart from the fees and royalties due to the franchisor, the franchisee has to follow a strict and strongly codified standard in managing the hotel. Furthermore, if the performance of the franchisor is poor, this can affect the profitability of the franchisee's entire network. Finally, not all franchisees will benefit equally from top-down (franchisor determined) marketing/advertising plans, and this can lead to conflict.

5.2.3 The influence of country-specific variables on the development of hotel franchising

Basically, the analysis of international expansion and the developing strategies of major hotel chains makes the issue clear: while in some locations franchising is recommended, in other places companies choose either to run their own establishments or to choose other expansion strategies. Corporate decisionmaking tends to focus on country characteristics specific to the target location and a consequent evaluation of organizational alternatives.

The country specific factors that affect the adoption of franchising in the hospitality sector as an international entry mode are numerous. Of particular importance, especially with reference to some countries of entry, are political and economic risks (Contractor and Kundu, 1998a; Zhao and Olsen, 1997). In fact, if the country is not stable, a firm will try to reduce its equity involvement, preferring contractual agreements such as franchising. This choice contrasts, however, with another aspect: the degree of economic development, which has been demonstrated to be positively correlated to the expansion of franchising. There are two main motives related to this focus. First, the high level of competitiveness characterizing modern economies tends to force a reduction in return on investment, causing a given hospitality company to prefer a fixed franchising fee. The second reason is related to the necessity in franchising to transfer knowledge and organizational, technical, and marketing expertise. Not only does this process (i.e. franchising) require high adaptation costs, but it also forces the company, when considering underdeveloped economies, to face the problem of weaker protection of intellectual property and brand names – core assets in the hotel business. The combined effect is a reduced interest in franchising in those countries with relatively low degrees of economic development.

Alon and McKee (1999) have shown that international franchising systems are dependent on social structure and the resultant environment. Cultural distance is a variable which has to be taken into consideration when considering franchising as a development opportunity in a foreign country. Among the studies which have introduced different methods of analysis of the cultural dimensions of a target country (including Hall, 1990; Hofstede, 1980; Trompenaars, 1993), the model proposed by Hofstede appears to be more suitable to analyses of international franchising. Its indices are continuously updated (Hofstede, 2001), but it is an appropriate model, especially because many researchers have already tested its application in a franchising context (see, for example: Alon, Kellerman, 1999; Falbe and Welsh, 1998; Toncar, Alon, McKee, 1999).

The *power distance index* reflects the degree of inequality between less powerful individuals and more powerful ones in to the same social system. In particular, in high power distance cultures, subordinates expect to be told their tasks and accept authoritative leadership as they act under close supervision. This cultural dimension is important to franchisors who need franchisees willing to implement company procedures and policies (Toncar et al 1999).

The *individualism/collectivism index* describes the relationship between the individual and the collectivism that prevails in a given society. In an individualist country the most important subject is the individual. On the contrary, in a collectivist society more importance is given to the group. As a consequence, while individualist countries are characterized by cultural norms like autonomy, hedonism, self-initiated activities, and modernity, collectivist countries are traditional in form: private life is informed by institutional and organizational affiliations, activities are imposed by context, and security is provided by those organizations. As a result, franchising is more widely accepted in individualist countries.

The third dimension is *masculinity* opposed to *femininity*. This index identifies characteristics of a given society that are typical of the two sexes: although simplistic, in this indexical analysis, women attach more importance to social goals such as relationships, helping others, and the physical environment (feminine societies); men attach more importance to ego-driven (individualistic) goals such as career and money (masculine societies). As a consequence, in a country that rates high on the "masculinity scale," managers are very competitive, aggressive, and ambitious. They prefer large companies to small ones, and value higher pay over the fewer work hours expected in "feminine" societies. These characteristics make high masculinity countries a fertile ground for the development of franchising.

The *uncertainty avoidance index* points out ways in which different societies cope with uncertainty. More specifically, when considering a working environment, high uncertainty avoidance cultures are characterized by (worker) values such as company loyalty, a preference for larger organizations, lower ambition for advancement, more resistance to change, a tendency to take only known risks, etc. This dimension can be highly related to franchising in that it is known to be a low-risk investment both for the franchisor and the franchisees when compared to other entry modes.

Finally, the *long term orientation index* contrasts, as the name would suggest, long-term to short-term cultural orientations. Countries with a cultural predisposition to long-term arcs of action emphasize persistence, personal stability, respect for tradition, saving, and investing. Since international franchising is a long-term investment in foreign markets, a high value on this index can determine a positive reception of the contractual formulas inherent to franchising.

Furthermore, since each index of the model proposed by Hofstede (1980) captures only a specific dimension of the country's culture, Kogut and Singh (1988) developed an index which analyzes the overall cultural distance between different countries.[1]

The cultural characteristics of a given country favor or hamper the development of franchising, and indices with differing foci point out advantages and disadvantages of franchising vs. other growth strategies (Burgess et al 1995). Considering the relation between the propensity to franchise and cultural distance, some studies have pointed out that international franchising is mainly used by companies willing to internationalize in countries geographically or culturally similar to the national market of the franchisor (see, e.g. Hopkins, 1996). In the hotel sector this relationship does not seem to hold as Contractor and Kundu (1998a) show. They found that cultural diversity (between domestic and international markets) actually decreases the propensity to make equity investments such as greenfield ventures, acquisitions, or joint ventures.

5.3 Franchising in the Italian hospitality industry

Although individual circumstances and objectives can create a preference for one entry mode over another, international hospitality companies usually diversify their organizational modes using different entry strategies (Connell, 1997). Although franchising first boomed in other sectors of activity, it soon extended to the international hospitality industry. But from a geographical point of view, its diffusion was not homogeneous. An example is represented by the Italian market (Table 5.3).

Table 5.3 presents data on Italy, which has more total presences than any other European destination: 344,414 tourists. Italy is second only

Table 5.3 Tourism destinations in Europe: Italy and its main competitors

	Italy	France	Greece	Spain
Total arrivals	82,725	116,022	12,004	79,898
– *National*	47,719	76,667	5366	43,254
– *International*	35,006	39,355	6638	36,644
Degree of internationaliz. (internat. arr/total arr.)	42.3%	33.9%	55.3%	45.9%
Main nationalities	1. Germany	1. UK	1. Germany	1. UK
	2. UK	2. Germany	2. UK	2. Germany
	3. U.S.	3. Italy	3. France	3. France
	4. France	4. U.S.	4. Italy	4. Italy
Total presences	344,414	283,096	54,502	342,540
– *National*	204,760	179,352	14,094	124,689
– *International*	139,654	103,744	40,408	217,851
No of hosp. structures	113,344	28,649	9,022	30,868
– *Hotels*	33,480	18,217	8,689	17,102
– *Complementary structures*	79,864	10,432	333	13,766

Source: Adapted from Tci (2006).

to France in terms of total arrivals: 82,725. The degree of internationalization is high; Italy is one of the most visited tourist destinations in the world (the fifth, after France, Spain, the U.S., and China), and the hospitality industry as a whole is significantly developed: there is a very high number of hospitality structures (hotels and other complementary units, such as holiday camps and tourist villages, rental apartments, farm holidays, etc.), especially when compared to other European countries.

5.3.1 The research methodology

Considering the research methodology, it was decided to employ a qualitative research style, which seems to be particularly indicated when there is the necessity to provide insights into an area in which theory is limited. The final results of the research will be based on the discussion of the different variables pointed out through the literature review and analyzed in the study. This approach is also supported by Olsen and Roper (1998), who emphasize the importance of using less prescriptive and more qualitative research methods designed to reach deep into the internal workings of hospitality organizations. The result is then a more authentic and real-world view of strategies relevant to the contemporary marketplace.

In order to provide an analysis of the Italian market, the first part of the research was based on country-specific data, collected and adapted from the main Italian tourism associations, institutions, and journals. Furthermore, empirical research has been conducted through a series of in-depth, semistructured interviews covering the strategic intent and preferences of the main international hotel chains operating in the Italian market. More precisely, the qualitative approach was based on 16 semistructured interviews conducted between November 2005 and April 2006 with relevant organizational managers of some hotel chains responsible for the Italian market, franchise managers, sales and marketing managers of hotel chains, and consultancy companies specializing in the Italian hospitality industry.

The study sample includes companies that have chosen to develop through franchising in the Italian market (such as Accor, Intercontinental, Starwood, etc.), as well as companies that have chosen other models of expansion (Sol Melià, Tivigest, Hyatt, etc.). Hotel chains considered in the sample have been identified through the Ista Directory. Because this research is exploratory in nature: the interview guide consisted of open-ended questions; the conversation involved the subjects/questions detailed in Table 5.4. Descriptive variables related to the hospitality groups analyzed have also been investigated.

Documentary analysis was also used as a complementary data collection method. In fact, primary data have been integrated with

Table 5.4 The research questionnaire

Question	Based on your experience and on the experience of your company, which are *a)* the main risks/obstacles and/or vice versa *b)* the main opportunities/advantages of the development of franchising in the Italian hospitality industry, in relation to the following
1	Characteristics of the Italian hospitality industry
2	Entrepreneurial culture in the Italian tourism sector
3	Managerial knowledge in hospitality
4	Financial aspects
5	Technological issues (reservation systems, etc)
6	Demand characteristics
7	Image/Branding/Marketing of the hospitality company
8	Other

documentary analysis used as a complementary data collection method. In particular, publications about the organizations considered in the analysis include reports from different investment and research organizations, publications of trade journals and newspaper articles, and a wide number of publications and press releases related to the hotel industry (among the most important secondary sources: TCI, Ista, Federalberghi, Assofranchising, TTG, and Turistica). These data have been compared and analyzed in conjunction with interviews and observations. Based on the literature review previously provided, a framework of analysis is presented in Figure 5.1.

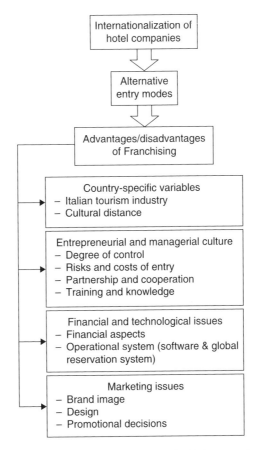

Figure 5.1 Franchising as a mode of entry in the Italian market: An analysis framework

5.3.2 Findings

5.3.2.1 The diffusion of hotel franchising in the Italian tourism industry

With reference to the specific reality of the hospitality industry in Italy, franchising is seldom used as an organizational mode by national and international hotel groups in the Italian market (Table 5.5). An analysis of the reports provided by Ista (2005) reveal a preference for the hotel ownership (59.40 percent) and the managed company (28.12 percent). Only 15.60 percent of the hotels in Italy are in franchises, followed by the lease, the consortium, and the management contract. In terms of numbers of hotels, the consortium is prevalent with 46.06 percent.

Regarding the internationalization of the few Italian franchising networks, the situation is even worse: consistent with the trend of Italian franchisors abroad – which is weak even in those sectors that could benefit from a positive "made in Italy" effect (Vianelli, 2003) – no Italian hotel chain uses international franchising to expand in foreign markets. This can be easily explained not only by the overall limited presence of Italian hotel groups abroad (Table 5.6), but also by the scarce use of franchising in the national context; in fact, franchising researchers have long been aware (Petersen and Welch, 2000; Welch, 1990) that experience of running a network of associates at the national level represents a background factor to internationalization. In other words, before venturing abroad, a company needs to have acquired the skill sets and knowledge necessary to initiate international expansion.

But what explains the limited use of franchising in Italy? Are there variables that represent real obstacles to the diffusion of franchising?

Table 5.5 Organizational modes of the main hotel groups in Italy

	Hotel groups (n = 64)		Number of hotels (n = 1005)	
Ownership	38	59.40%	224	22.30%
Lease	9	14.06%	58	5.79%
Managed company	18	28.12%	161	16.00%
Franchising	10	15.60%	85	8.45%
Management contract	6	9.30%	14	1.40%
Consortium	6	9.30%	463	46.06%
Total (%)		*135.78%**		*100%*

Note: *Some hotel groups present multiple organizational modes.
Source: Data elaboration on Ista (2005).

Table 5.6 Internationalization of Italian hotel groups

Hotel groups	Number of hotels	Internationalization targets
Baglioni	4	France
Blu Hotels	1	Austria
Boscolo	5	France, Czech Republic
Domina	17	Austria, Poland, Egypt, Estonia, Germany, Greece, Kenya, Lithuania, Tunisia, Uzbekistan, Slovenia, Hungary
Iti Hotels	9	Antigua, Brazil, U.S.
Jolly	7	Belgium, France, Germany, Netherlands, U.S., UK
Orovacanze	2	Cuba, Egypt

Source: Ista (2005).

Which of these variables are perceived as most critical by the international hospitality groups considered in the sample and willing to enter and grow in the Italian market? Alternatively, can some opportunities be pointed out? Different answers to these questions will be provided, analyzing the impact on franchising of the following aspects.

– characteristics of the country in terms of tourism industry and culture in general
– entrepreneurial and managerial culture in the Italian tourism industry
– financial and technological issues
– demand characteristics and brand perception

5.3.2.2   Characteristics of the country and of the Italian tourism industry

The Italian tourism industry is very attractive, even if in the last year the market has declined while, in the overall European market level, the value has remained stable. Estimates provided by Datamonitor (2005) are positive: the European hotel industry, which was characterized by a compound annual growth rate of 2.4 percent for the five-year period spanning 2001–2005, is set to expand by an additional 3.7 percent by 2010, accelerating its current performance. This trend speaks of an increasing competitiveness in the contextual market, and for this reason franchising could be interesting since it provides a constant fee.

Table 5.7   Main international hotel chains operating in the Italian market

	Group	Country	Hotel 2004	2005	Var.9(%)	Rooms 2004	2005	Var.(%)
1	Accor	Fra	2098	2159	2.9	226,272	235,205	3.9
2	Best Western	U.S.	1106	1126	1.8	71,497	73,455	2.7
3	Intercontinental H. G.	UK	462	469	1.5	72,882	72,273	−0.8
4	Louvre Hotels	Fra	858	861	0.3	60,529	60,730	0.3
5	Hilton Int.	UK	245	252	2.9	52,827	53,154	0.6
6	Sol Melià	Spa	207	205	−1.0	42,240	43,083	2.0
7	Tui	Ger	168	170	1.2	40,661	40,377	−0.7
8	Choice	U.S.	433	404	−6.7	35,681	34,794	−2.5
9	Marriott Int.	U.S.	280	144	−48.6	45,801	29,722	−35.1
10	NH Hoteles	Spa	195	200	2.6	27,228	28,037	3.0

Source: Adapted from Tci (2006).

Those considering the characteristics of the Italian hospitality industry speak of the predominance of family-run businesses. Although the main international groups have invested increasingly in the Italian market, especially in the last few years (Table 5.7), they still represent only a small percentage of the total. Ista (2005) and TCI (2006) point out that the international top ten chains represent just 3.4 percent of the total rooms; the same is true of Italian hospitality chains, whose top ten hotel companies represent a 3.2 percent of the total rooms. Our interviews show that the hospitality sector exhibits a high level of fragmentation together with a profound consciousness of the fact that the different forms of current alliances are not sufficient to reduce this pulverization. In addition, especially with reference to large groups, interviewees confirm a lack of interest in the reality of microhotels, and they point out the difficulty of finding a partner whose size is suitable and appealing to the larger hotel-franchising networks.

Based on the calculation of the cultural index proposed by Kogut and Singh (1998) using the Hofstede (2001) data, the cultural distance between Italy and the nationality of the main international hotel chains willing to expand in the country seems to be quite limited (Table 5.8). This aspect can justify the fact that, with a limited cultural distance, the main hospitality companies prefer and/or can choose to enter the country directly (mostly through direct ownership or managed companies) instead of using franchising. In contrast, with regards to the observations previously provided by the theory, analysis of the single indices reveals that Italy is a fertile field for franchising; in fact, apart from the long term orientation index – which is significantly low in comparison

Table 5.8   Cultural indices and cultural distance from Italy

Country	Power distance	Uncertainty avoidance	Individualism/ collectivism	Masculinity/ femininity	Long-term Orientation	Cultural Distance Index
Italy	50	75	76	70	34	0.000
France	68	86	71	43	39	0.737
Spain	57	86	51	42	19	0.898
U.S.	40	46	91	62	29	0.573
Germany	35	65	67	66	31	0.212
UK	35	35	89	66	25	0.921

Source: Elaboration based on Hofstede (2001) and Kogut and Singh (1988)

to similar countries – almost all other indices are significantly above the average, presenting Italy as a promising market for franchising.

Actually, considering Italy as a unique and homogeneous area is not recommended. Recent research (Higgins, 2006) points out that some international groups underline that one of the main barriers to franchising in Europe is that Europe is sometimes considered as one place; in reality, of course, it comprises many, distinct cultural units. Also, Italy presents significant differences among its own regions – not only from a diversity of tourism attractions and natural resources, but also related to significant differences in terms of destination-marketing activities developed by regional and local tourism institutions. As an aside, it is noteworthy that the regions in the South of Italy, which have a strong pull for tourists, receive only one third of the number of arrivals of either of the Centre or the North of the country (Tci, 2006). Furthermore, what was underlined by the hotel managers is the strong incidence of seasonality, which doesn't allow everyone to exploit the economies of scale which are particularly important for international hotel chains. All of these aspects combine to create limitations for the development of franchising in the sector.

5.3.2.3   *Entrepreneurial culture and managerial knowledge*

The variables which seem to be more critical for the development of the franchising culture in Italy can be mostly identified in the entrepreneurial and managerial philosophy existing in the tourism system. When Marriott, in the development of its franchising network in Italy as well as all over Europe says "... we are focused on making sure they work within our standards and brand promise. But at the same time, when we do have a franchise operator we are comfortable with, we work very aggressively to find as many opportunities as we can" (Higgins, 2006).

The contrast with Italy's entrepreneurial culture becomes evident for different reasons. During the interviews, many managers and consultants pointed out that Italian entrepreneurs tend to begin their operations through a generational transition and/or as a makeshift solution. As a result, business sectors that are perceived to be more profitable, such as real estate or construction, attract more potential franchisees. For this reason, they are not likely to evaluate development opportunities from a medium/long-term perspective: with franchising, it is not possible to see an immediate result in term of profitability; thus, franchising is not seen as an opportunity by most Italian entrepreneurs – who seem unable to evaluate the impact of the affiliation cost as regards to the direct and indirect benefits that franchising is able to produce over the long term.

The lack of development of hotel franchising was noted by one of our interviewees, a Manager from PKF Consulting:

> The main obstacles that limit the development of franchising in the Italian industry can be found, in my opinion, in the low efficiency of these formulas in Italy. Italian hotels use franchising lightly with the international brands such as Sofitel, Marriott, and Hilton leading the way. This may be an intermediate strategy suitable for Italian entrepreneurial learning.

This lack of strategic thinking demonstrated by Italian entrepreneurs in the hospitality industry represents an obstacle also for those international chains willing to expand in the country. As Contractor and Kundu (1998a) point out, with franchising the legal form may be a contract, but de facto organizational behavior is an evolving strategic partnership between the franchisor and its franchisees: in the case of an international hotel company, each franchise comprises a piece of an overall global strategy. In almost all of the interviews, managers and consultants pointed out how the adoption of this (more) strategic role can be undertaken only with great difficulty by Italian entrepreneurs, who often decide to affiliate based solely on opportunistic, short-term considerations.

A general perception that emerged several times in the interviews is that managerial capabilities are decreasing significantly in Italy. The overall sense is that the consistent growth of Italian hospitality structures has not led to a corresponding, analogous development of managerial skills, since new hotels are frequently managed by owners whose experience in the hospitality business is sometimes scarce or even nonexistent. "The main obstacle to the development of franchising in Italy is the provincialism and the lack of real hotel managers," said one of our interviewees. Nevertheless, also from a managerial point of view, there seems to be a weak perception of the values inherent in developing managerial capabilities by affiliation with more experienced international brands. For their part, some entrepreneurs feel that binding themselves to a relevant, albeit powerful, brand could undermine their managerial freedom, revealing again a utilitarian and short-term vision.

Finally, another aspect which has to be considered is the perception of training. It has been pointed out in the literature that franchising seems to be positively associated with an importance accorded to training. Again, this represents an obstacle for the diffusion of franchising in a country where professional education in the hospitality industry is still limited.

In conclusion, from both entrepreneurial and managerial points of view, there are a great many obstacles to the diffusion of franchising networks in the country. For all the reasons previously pointed out, franchising is perceived as more of a risk than an opportunity. This negative perception justifies the preference for aggregative contracts based more on soft variables (brand, communications, and image) than on hard features (ownership, technological standards, physical attributes, etc.). From this perspective, Best Western's expansion in Italy represents a signal success: its form of franchising, being very soft, can be defined as atypical (in fact it is often recognized by the official sources more as a consortium than as a franchising network); but it is primarily for this reason that the chain has been accepted by some Italian entrepreneurs. This choice is not without risks: for this reason another hotel chain, Golden Tulip, is trying to shift from a softer to a harder form of franchising, in order to strengthen its control over its affiliates.

5.3.2.4 *Financial and technological issues*

Financial and technological issues are strongly related to the characteristics of the Italian hospitality industry – with its entrepreneurial/managerial culture. From the franchisor's point of view, the research has pointed out the difficulties associated with finding an Italian partner who is not only reliable but who also has conspicuous financial capabilities – necessary for a serious and lasting franchisor-franchisee relationship. Furthermore, one of the main obstacles perceived by potential franchisees is that national and international hospitality chains usually request methods of financial analysis and interpretation that small- or medium-size Italian companies do not find easy to understand or apply. Another aspect which has been pointed out by some managers is the existence, related to the cultural approach of the country, of too many steps of economic/financial valorization in the contractual relation, which can hamper the development of a franchising network. Finally, even an understandable request – financial transparency – is unacceptable to many Italian entrepreneurs. Inevitably, such resistance works against the possibility of creating a trust-based relationship and long-term affiliation.

From a technological point of view, consultancy companies have been quick to recognize the significant competitive advantage an Italian franchisee can acquire with the introduction of new technology and its related services. In fact, they strongly emphasize the lack of technological know-how which usually characterizes Italian entrepreneurs. As regards the technology related to reservations systems, franchisees are often required to adopt – by substitution or updating – a more complex system than the ones with which they are used to dealing. This is also considered a significant obstacle: the technological systems provided by the franchisor are rather complex and a great deal of training is required in order to allow the franchisee to understand and use the system. The link between successful franchising and the business environments was summed up well by one of our interviewees, a Sales Manager for Intercontinental Hotels Group, who said: "In Italy a franchising project is only successful if it is carefully calibrated with the technological environment and the characteristics of the local environment."

Franchising can help not only to improve the reservation system but also all the technology which contributes to differentiating hospitality structures; brand differentiation is a spur to future growth of hotel networks (Higley, 2006): electronic communications systems, wireless connections, etc., are today characteristics that certain branded networks use to conquer the preferences of some consumer targets.

5.3.2.5 *Marketing issues: Demand characteristics and brand perception*

The modern hotel is expected to provide high levels of experience, services, and technology to consumers. The constant growth of customer expectations of hotel amenities, together with the increasing level of provision required to remain competitive in the market, represents what has been called the "amenity creep" (Datamonitor, 2005). Consumers search for guaranteed service quality even as they feed a need for intangibles such as emotional fulfillment and unique travelling experiences. This awkward combination of the physical and the intangible has led some researchers to argue for the extreme importance of "the brand" in the modern hotel industry (Taylor, 2002). In addition, what significantly characterizes foreign tourists is often the search for familiar products, which can be offered by a franchising network: "Consumers in Europe are hungry for brands" (Chopra, 2006), and: "Europe is exciting because there is a huge distribution of unbranded hotels... Only 15–20 percent of European hotels are branded" (Higgins, 2006). Consequently, franchising in Italy, seen from both franchisor and franchisee perspectives, can represent an interesting opportunity in terms of branding. The franchisee can have also an opportunity to generate important relations at an international level, having the possibility to place his advertising inside catalogs and other communications channels with an international scope.

Furthermore, based on an analysis of the Italian market (Isnart, 2005), the tourism industry relies strongly on clients who have to travel for business. This trend could represent a benefit especially to those hotel entrepreneurs and managers of smaller establishments who can bring themselves up to date and can innovate in relation to the growth of the potential demand. Unfortunately, many Italian hoteliers have shown themselves to be resistant to change, unprepared to adapt to changing market demands, and unable to deal with the increasing complexities of social, cultural, and technological variations in their chosen industry. According to one of our interviewees, the Director of Alfa@Hotel, "The entrepreneur believes that binding himself to an important brand, as happens with franchising, can undermine his freedom in running the hotel, indicating a utilitarian and shortsighted vision." Franchising can represent an advantage to the local company because it can provide the knowledge and the procedures necessary to survive in a highly competitive, lucrative industry.

5.4   Conclusion

The present research has tried to expose the main peculiarities in relation to the development of a franchising model in the Italian market. The obstacles are numerous. Some of them are perceived by actual or potential franchisors; others are shown by prospective franchisees who frequently try to curb some affiliation requests.

Nowadays it is important to point out that no hospitality chain pursuing a growth strategy can opt for a singular direction. As pointed out by the Accor managers, the company strategy is to be diversified geographically and in terms of types of deals: "We try to have a good balance between company owned, leased, management contracts, and franchising: each model has pluses and minuses" (Higgins, 2005). Nevertheless, it is quite evident that in Italy the introduction of franchising, which has been resisted by entrepreneurs, represents a concrete risk. In fact the fragmentation of the hotel industry and the lack of long-term strategic orientation have been pointed out as some of the major limits.

At the same time it is undeniable that some opportunities exist and perhaps could be exploited by those international hotel chains willing to expand in the Italian market. The analysis of the cultural indices, like that for other European countries, has depicted Italy as a fertile field for franchising from the entrepreneurial perspective. One of the difficulties pointed out during interviews was how to create a positive perception in those local entrepreneurs who would (potentially) significantly benefit from this formula. In which way can this aim be pursued?

It was immediately apparent from the interviews that the most successful franchising in the country can be defined as atypical – i.e. with fewer bonds between the two parties when compared with a traditional franchising model. Real and tangible advantages to the entrepreneurs can be conveyed, especially with reference to sales and marketing activities – which are in any case frequently externalized from the chosen strategic model. This approach can be the first step of a transitional process toward a stronger, normative, franchising model, one which should lead to a more trusting relationship.

However, it is important to stress the importance, especially in the Italian context, of involving franchisees more directly in the decision-making process (Watkins, 2006). In fact, a strong franchising brand, again, with reference to the Italian market, cannot ignore the powerful pulls of the local context; rather, franchise relationships should be created that derive from a coherent unification of the advantages of the global image with those that are specific to local realities.

After creating the basis for long-term relations, it is possible to start a second process geared to a reinforcement of the business bond. Specifically, franchisors can move from softer to harder contractual models: up-to-date technology, financial improvements, and innovative standards can be introduced to stabilize quality and ensure managerial efficiency.

An important focus has to be on training, which becomes more and more important in an industry where customers are have a constant rise in expectations and where the market arena is becoming highly competitive. Moreover, branding is a relevant issue which can favor the development of franchising. Introducing a brand culture in the Italian system could also be useful as a "demonstration effect" for those Italian chains which could have the opportunity to expand abroad.

In conclusion, what seems to be necessary in the Italian market is a precise strategic design developed by those hotel chains willing to invest in the country. Not only should they be able to the communicate significant perceived benefits to local entrepreneurs, but they should also lay foundations and create competencies among Italian hoteliers in order to help them understand the advantages of international developments in managerial, financial, and marketing activities.

The main limit of this research is to be found in its exploratory method, justified by the fact that the topic analyzed has never been previously studied in the Italian context. In addition, the analysis of the opportunities and risks of franchising in the Italian market is mainly based on the perceptions of investors and consultancy companies which have constant contacts with local hotels. Hence, a possible direction for future research should be the development of a quantitative analysis of the perception of the franchising model by local entrepreneurs who might consider affiliations with international networks in the hospitality industry. Another opportunity for analysis could be the development of cross-cultural research involving other European countries relevant to the hospitality industry, where a more detailed focus on cultural indices could also be provided.

Note

1. The index was built as following: where I_{ij}

stands for the index for the ith cultural dimension and jth country, V_i is the variance of the index of the i_{th} dimension, u indicates the country considered in the analysis (in our case it will be the Italian market), CD_j is the cultural difference of the j_{th} country from the country considered in the analysis. The index takes into consideration only four of the five indices proposed by Hofstede (1980) because the value of long term orientation is not available for all the countries.

References

Alon, I. (1999). *The Internationalization of U.S. Franchising Systems*. New York: Garland Publishing.

Alon, I. (2004). "Global Franchising and Development in Emerging and Transitioning Markets," *Journal of Macromarketing* 24 (2), 156–67.

Alon, I. (2005). *Service Franchising: A Global Perspective*. New York, NW: Springer.

Alon, I., and E. Kellerman (1999). "Internal Antecedents to the 1997 Asian Economic Crisis", *Multinational Business Review* 7 (2), 1–12.

Alon, I., and D.L. McKee (1999). "Towards a Macro-Environmental Model of International Franchising," *Multinational Business Review* 7 (1), 76–82.

Alon, I., R. Perrigot, and G. Cliquet (2004a). "Affiliated Networks: The Case of Best Western Internationalization," *Journal of International Business and Entrepreneurship Development* 2 (1), 78–87.

Alon, I., R. Perrigot, and G. Cliquet (2004b). "The Internationalization of French and American Franchisors in the Hotel Sector," *Sasin Journal of Management* 10 (1), 4–18.

Alon, I., and D. Welsh (2001). *International Franchising in Emerging markets: Central and Eastern Europe.* Chicago: CCH Incorporated.

Altinay, L. (2004). "Implementing international franchising: the role of entrepreneurship", *International Journal of Service Industry Management* 15 (5), 426–43.

Assofranchising (2005). *Il franchising in Italia: proiezioni 2005*; Milan: Quadrante.

Burgess, C., A. Hampton, L. Price, and A. Roper (1995). "International Hotel Groups: What Makes them Successful?" *International Journal of Contemporary Hospitality Management* (7) (2/3), 74–80.

Chopra, C. (2006). "Perspectives for the franchising sector in Europe – 2006," *Franchising World* 38 (3), 15–18.

Connell, J. (1997). "International Hotel Franchise Relationships-UK Franchise Perspectives," *International Journal of Contemporary Hospitality Management,* 9/5/6, 215–20.

Contractor F., and S. Kundu (1998a). "Franchising Versus Company-Run Operations: Modal Choice in the Global Hotel Sector," *Journal of International Marketing* 6 (2), 28_53.

Contractor F., and S. Kundu (1998b). "Modal Choice in a World of Alliances; Analyzing Organizational Forms in the International Hotel Sector," *Journal of International Business Studies* 29 (2) 325–56.

Datamonitor (2005). *Hotels & Motels in Europe: industry profile.* London: Datamonitor plc.

Davé, U. (1984). "Us Multinational Involvement in the International Hotel Sector: an Analysis," *Service Industries Journal* (4), 48–63.

Dev, C.S., K. Erramilli, and S. Agarwal (2002). "Brands across Borders: Determining Factors in Choosing Franchising or Management Contracts for Entering International Markets," *Corner Hotel and Restaurant Administration Quarterly* 43 (6), 91–104.

Falbe, C.M., and D.H.B. Welsh (1998). "NAFTA and Franchising: A Comparison of Franchisor Perceptions of Characteristics Associated with Franchisee Success and Failure in Canada, Mexico and the United States," *Journal of Business Venturing* (13), 151–71.

Gannon, J., and K. Johnson (1997). "Socialization Control and Market Entry Modes in the International Hotel Industry," *International Journal of Contemporary Hospitality Management* 9 (5/6), 193–98.

Hall, E.T. (1990). *Understanding Cultural Differences.* Yarmouth, ME: Intercultural Press.

Higgins, S.M. (2005). "Accor's Growth Plan Targets Franchising," *Hotel and Motel Management* 220 (13), 4, 29.

Higgins, S.M. (2006). "Brand Focus on Worldwide Growth," *Hotel and Motel Management* 221 (4), 30–32.

Higley, J. (2006). "Leaders: Technology to Drive Hotel Growth," *Hotel & Motel Management*, May 15, 4, 44.

Hofstede, G. (1980). *Culture's Consequences: International Differences in Work-Related Values*. Newbury Park, CA: Sage.

Hofstede, G. (1991). *Cultures and Organizations: Software of the Mind*. London, McGraw-Hill.

Hofstede, G. (2001). *Culture Consequences: Comparing Values, Behaviors, Institutions and Organizations Across Nations*. Newbury Park, CA: Sage.

Hollensen, S. (2004). *Global Marketing*. Harlow, UK: Pearson Education Limited.

Hong, J.H., P. Jones, and N. Sirisena (2000). "Hotel Development in Southeast Asia and Indo-China," Fourth International Conference "Tourism in South East Asia & Indo-China: Development, Marketing and Sustainability," June.

Hoover, V.L., D.J. Jr., Ketchen, and J.G. Combs (2003). "Why Restaurant Firms Franchise: an Analysis of Two Possible Explanations," *Cornell Hotel and Restaurant Administrative Quarterly* 44 (1), 9–16.

Hopkins, D.M. (1996). "International Franchising: Standardization Versus Adaptation to Cultural Differences," *Franchising Research: An International Journal* 1 (1), 15–24.

Isnart (Ed.). (2005). "Impresa Turismo, Ia Assise Nazionale Degli Amministratori Camerali Del Turismo," Roma.

Ista (2005). *Rapporto 2005 sul sistema alberghiero in Italia* Rome: Edizioni Ista – Istituto Internazionale di Studi e Documentazione Turistico Alberghiera.

Kaufmann, P.J., and S. Eroglu (1998). "Standardization and adaptation in business format franchising," *Journal of Business Venturing* 14 (1), 69–85.

Kogut, B., and H. Singh. (1988). "The Effect of National Culture on the Choice of Entry Mode," *Journal of International Business Studies* 19 (3), 411–32.

Kotler, P., J. Bowen, and J. Makens (2003). *Marketing for hospitality and tourism*, International Edition. Upper Saddle River, New Jersey: Prentice Hall.

Litteljohn, D. (1997). "Internationalization in Hotels: Current Aspects and Developments," *International Journal of Contemporary Hospitality Management* 9 (5/6), 187–92.

Michael, S.C. (1999). "Do Franchised Chains Advertise Enough?" *Journal of Retailing* 75 (4), 461–78.

Olsen, M.D., and A. Roper A (1998). "Research in Strategic Management in the Hospitality Industry," *International Journal of Hospitality Management* 17, 111–24.

Petersen, B., and L.S. Welch (2000). "International Retailing Operations: Downstream Entry and Expansion Via Franchising," *International Business Review* 9 (4), 479–96.

Pine, R., H.Q. Zhang, and P. Qi (2000). "The Challenges and Opportunities of Franchising in China's Hotel Industry," *International Journal of Contemporary Hospitality Management* 12 (5), 300_10.

Scoviak, M., and S. Wolchuk (2004). "Hotels' 325," *Hotels*, 38 (7), 36–39.

Taylor, S. (2002). "An Alternative to Franchising," *Lodging hospitality*, July 15, 39–40.

Tci (2006). *Annuario del turismo e della cultura*, Milan: Touring Club Italiano.

Toncar, M., I. Alon, and D. McKee (1999). "Cultural Determinants of International Franchising: an Empirical Examination of Hofstede's Cultural Dimensions,"

Seventh Cross-Cultural Consumer and Business Studies Research Conference, Cancun, Mexico December 12–15.

Trompenaars, F. (1993). *Riding the Waves of Culture: Understanding Cultural Diversity in Business*. London: Economic Books.

Vianelli, D. (2003). "Franchising as a Mode of Entry for Italian Companies in International Markets," in I. Alon and D. Welsh (Eds.), *International Franchising in Industrialized Markets: Western and Northern Europe*. Washington DC., CCH Publishing, 331–51.

Watkins, E. (2006). "The New Franchising Dynamic," *Lodging Hospitality* 62 (7), 2.

Welch, L.S. (1990). "Internationalization by Australian franchisors," *Asia Pacific Journal of Management* 7 (2), 101–21.

Williamson, O.E. (1979). "Transaction Cost Economics: the Governance of Contractual Relations," *Journal of Law and Economics* 22(2), 233_62.

Zhao, J.L., and M.D. Olsen (1997). "The Antecedent Factors Influencing Entry Mode Choices of Multinational Lodging Firms," *International Journal of Hospitality Management* 16 (1), 79–98.

6
Franchising in Morocco

Ilan Alon and Rachid Alami

6.1 Introduction: the Moroccan franchising market

6.1.1 An overview

This study tries to isolate critical factors affecting the performance of North American fast-food franchises within the Moroccan business environment, with a primary focus on the roles of culture, business rules, and tradition. Specific cases of companies currently operating in Morocco's the fast-food business sector will be analyzed.

The franchises to be compared and contrasted are McDonald's, a franchise that has succeed in the Moroccan market and has encountered minimal obstacles, and Subway, one that failed and abandoned the market after less than four years of activity.

The main objective of this study is to outline what mistakes have been made and what type of strategies franchisees in the fast-food sector should implement in order to succeed in Morocco. One of the most important aspects that organizations should take into account before going abroad is cultural adaptability. This study will focus on this dimension in order to demonstrate that globalization, a well-known brand, and standard quality of food can sometimes lead organizations to underestimate the role of cultural differences, both in business culture and food traditions.

The next section will give an overview of the franchise sector in Morocco and how this type of collaboration has grown dramatically over the last decade. The global economic and political situation will be presented as the main factor likely to affect a franchisor's decision to go abroad. A significant emphasis will be put on Morocco's potential market and opportunities for foreign investors who want to invest in emerging markets (according to the World Bank definition) with a medium level of risk.

The second part is a review of the existing literature. We will focus on what authors and scholars have stated on franchising. We will also discuss advantages of the franchising format for both franchisor and franchisee. We will then emphasize entry modes into new markets and factors that influence that lead to choice of one entry mode over another. The third section presents the field study, the methodology, and the technical analysis that were used to obtain data and produce results.

Finally, this paper is a study of specific cases. A discussion should be held about any limitations and bias that might be encountered during the research process.

What we propose in this paper is to identify the most important factors for success that any fast-food brand should take into account before going into the Moroccan market. It is clear that we are not trying to create a universal model. There is no "one best way" to succeed as Davel et al (2008) have said. But investing in an Arabic and Muslim market requires some precautions. We are going to give some recommendations for those who want to invest directly or indirectly in Morocco, either through franchise or subsidiary mode, hoping that this study contributes, at least in a small way, to future avoidance of such bad experiences as those of Subway and Dairy Queen.

6.1.2 Growing of franchising sector in Morocco

Franchising in Morocco appeared in the 1960s but has really taken off since the 1990s. Today, Morocco hosts more than 120 franchised brands (Ministry of Economy, 2007). Franchises have opened in cities where the average income is higher, like Casablanca, Rabat, or Tangier. The country offers political and socioeconomic advantages. As the political environment has remained stable and inflation under control, more businesses have been willing to venture into Morocco. McDonald's opened its first Moroccan fast-food restaurant in 1999, and has now more than 20 other restaurants over the country. Subway came to Morocco in 2000 with its first and only branch in Casablanca. It went out of the market in 2004. The number of franchises has grown up from ten in the early 1990s to 350 in 2008, as we can see in Figure 6.1.

The franchising business is growing rapidly in Morocco. According to the Moroccan Ministry of Economy (2008), there are many reasons for this growth. First, international opportunities have expanded

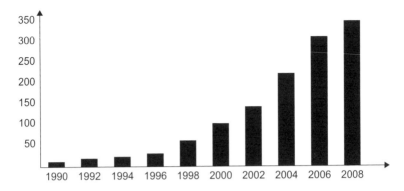

Figure 6.1 Number of franchises in Morocco 1990–2008
Source: French franchising obervatory.

because of increased global media promoting brand names. Moroccan economic integration with European and North American markets and trade agreements between Morocco and other nations have reduced the entry barriers that previously existed. Furthermore, Moroccan demand for foreign goods and products has increased dramatically since the country has opened its borders to foreign investors and capital markets. These include increased demand for goods and services, expanding urbanization, increasing mobility, and increasing average income. Alon et al (2006) have shown that emerging markets represent a "huge pent-up demand for western-style goods and services." Morocco, as an emerging market according to The World Bank, is no exception. The Moroccan consumer is eager for foreign goods and fashionable products from Europe and North America. The latest statistics show that France and U.S. represent the higher number of franchises

6.1.3 Mode of entry for U.S. companies

Almost 90 foreign franchises have successfully implemented operations in the sectors of fast food, clothing, furniture, cosmetics, office cleaning, and auto repair since the first Pizza Hut in Morocco was established in 1992 (Ministry of Economy, 2008). Franchise holders are attracted to the marketing image and financial security of well-known American products and brands such as Pepsi Cola, McDonald's, Domino's Pizza, KFC, Haagen-Daz, Budget, New Balance, FutureKids, Office 1 Superstore, and Midas. The success of franchising stems from an expanding base of young entrepreneurs, many of whom are educated in America or Europe and have the financial means to develop master franchises.

Moroccans are increasingly interested in joint-venture business opportunities with American partners as a way of modernizing their factories or licensing a technology.

Beginning in the 1960s, the manufacturing of U.S. products has typically started through joint ventures or the acquisition of a local Moroccan firm. The best examples are Gillette, Coca-Cola Export Corp., Procter & Gamble, Colgate Palmolive, Clark Gum, Fruit of the Loom, Jacob Delafon (Kohler), Johnson & Johnson, Pfizer Laboratories, Pepsi Cola, Simmons Maroc, Kraft Foods, and Steelcase. Morocco also provides a good geographic location for exporting to the EU and the rest of Africa . If Morocco is a country that has succeeded so well in franchising because of it being an emerging market and a poorly exploited growing economy, as well as a politically stable country with talented young entrepreneurs, more in-depth research should be done to understand why franchises like Subway, Dairy Queen, or La Brioche Dorée have failed. This is the purpose of this article.

6.1.4   The global situation at the macro level in Morocco

At the macro level, the PEST (political, economic, sociological, and technical) analysis shows the main issues and challenges that could influence the decisionmaking process of investors and FDIs (foreign direct investments) in the fast-food industry (Table 6.1).

Although these indicators seem to facilitate the entry of franchises into foreign markets, caution must still be exercised before transferring one's business across national borders. Not every company may be suitable for international expansion without making adjustments to product, operations, or format (Alon et al 2006). Examples of failed franchise operations in the international market demonstrate that regardless of how successful a business may be domestically, attention must be given to the local culture the company is entering in order to achieve success over the long term.

As stated by Shane (1996), the skills and abilities needed to franchise abroad are quite different from those needed to franchise domestically. The availability of information for international expansion is limited, and even more so in the area of cultural aspects. A better understanding of the relationship between culture and business practices in the Morocco case is needed given the size of the market, its population and traditions, and its recent opening and growth.

Table 6.1   Morocco PEST analysis

	Opportunities	Threats
Political factors	Liberal economic system Favorable national trade regulations Flexible employment laws Political stability Court dealing with trade disputes Accommodate FDI policies Free capital transfer No double income tax	Islamic and terrorism
Economic factors	Strong economic growth Stable exchange rates Low inflation rate Strong consumer confidence Low cost labor Unstaturated market Competitive production costs Free trade zone with U.S. and Europe (in progress)	High levels of taxation and income tax Dependency on climate
Sociocultural factors	More balanced income distribution Strong population growth rate Islam as dominant religion Specific diet habits (hot meal – no prok or alcohol)	Poor public health system Strong local competition for low product prices
Technological factors	Credit card network Development infrastructure Good communications and transported networks	Land-buying process Avaliability of stores

As the political environment remains stable and inflation is controlled (World Bank), more businesses are willing to venture into Morocco. Aside from those incentives to enter Morocco, competition is strong, creating a need for more detailed, tailored, and flexible approaches in order to remain profitable. This can only be achieved by knowing the culture of Morocco. Before we can do that, we will give an overview of what authors and scholars have said and shown about franchising.

6.2   Franchising: an overview of existing literature

Franchising is an agreement between organizations whereby the producer of a product or service grants rights to independent entrepreneurs to conduct business in a specified way, in a designated place, and during a certain time frame (Nègre, 2000). The type of franchising that is most common today is called "business format franchising" or "package franchising." With this type of franchising, the franchisee receives more than just the rights to use the product, service, and trademark. They receive the whole business plan including the standardized marketing strategy, operating and training manuals, quality control, support from the franchising company, store layout, etc. The other form of franchising is "product and brand," which was the original version of franchising at the beginning of the twentieth century. In this form, a brand of product or service is resold by another. Typical examples are the beverage industry, gas stations, and auto dealerships.

The concept of franchising dates back to the Middle Ages, but the widespread use of franchise strategies began in the U.S. around 1850 when Singer Sewing Machines, located in New England, decided to market its products throughout the country. At the time, the "franchising" element (product and brand) consisted only of the right to use the brand name at a store and sell the product. Toward the end of the century General Motors and Coca-Cola began to use the franchising concept to expand the markets in which they could sell their products. Throughout the twentieth century, franchising expanded gradually into other industries. In 1917 the first franchised grocery store, the Piggly Wiggly, went into business. Hertz began franchising auto rentals in 1925 and the first fast-food franchise, A & W, opened in the same year (Kalika et al 1999).

The largest expansion of franchising occurred in the late 1940s after the end of World War II, when many veterans returned home desiring

Table 6.2 Advantages of the franchising format

Franchisor	Franchisee
According to Preble (1992):	**According to Preble 1992:**
Cost sharing	Ability to start a business at a low
Rapid market penetration at a relatively	cost with a proven standardized
lower cost than establishing one's own	product or service
distribution system	Support received from the
Economies of scale	franchiser for the brand concept
According to Alon et al (2006):	
Fewer financial resources required	
Raw materials can be produced internally	
Less susceptibility to political, economic	
and cultural risks	
Franchisees are more familiar with local	
laws, culture, business norms and practices	

to open their own businesses. In the 1950s major fast-food chains like Burger King, McDonald's and Dunkin' Donuts began to appear. From the 1960s on, these and other American fast-food chains began their expansion into international markets (Risner, 2001).

6.2.1   Entry modes – macrolevel factors

Justis and Judd (1989) classify forms of entry into foreign markets by fast-food franchisers in the following ways: direct investment setting up subsidiaries, joint-venture agreements with a foreign partner or government, and franchising rights with a master license. The most popular modes for franchise expansion tend to be joint venture and master licensing. Aydin and Kacker (1990) state this is so because these forms of entry create the least amount of financial burden for the franchising company. Joint ventures also allow for investment, control, shared profits, and entrepreneurial initiative, and generally meet government requirements for local equity participation.

Through master franchise licensing, an individual purchases the franchising license which entitles him or her to open up stores within a specific country or territory. The master franchiser receives training from the franchise company and is expected to transfer this acquired know-how to franchisees. In both modes, it is advantageous to have an indigenous entrepreneur who knows the local environment. The selection of a qualified, local master franchiser is especially crucial because of the possible risk of a company losing control of the quality and standards of its brand (Preble, 1992). However, some authors like Alon (2005) and Preble (1992) have raised macrolevel factors that could influence positively or negatively the mode of entry every franchisor is likely to choose. Table 6.3 shows the considerations involved when determining the way companies enter foreign countries.

It can be seen that the Moroccan global situation matches five times with master franchise and joint venture entry modes, whereas it presents only two commons points with subsidiary entry mode.

At first glance, it seems that both master franchising and joint venture are not bad choices for franchisors in a foreign country like Morocco. But, as we are about to see, it is far from being enough to make the right decision to go abroad.

6.2.2   The role of culture in international business

Many definitions have been formulated for culture. This concept seems to be unclear and uncertain. Kroeber and Kluchhon cited in Usunier and Lee (2005) have found more than 160 definitions of culture. Culture is

Table 6.3 Influencing factors that lead to an entry mode

Factors that are likely to influence entry mode	Subsidiary is the best if factor is : (Preble, 1992)	Joint venture is the best if factor is : (Preble, 1992)	Master franchise is the best if factor is : (Alon, 2000)	Morocco's situation (World Bank and official institutions)
Economic potential	HIGH	HIGH	LOW	HIGH
Level of corruption	–	–	LOW	HIGH
Level of Competitive intensity	LOW	HIGH	HIGH	HIGH
Demand variability	LOW	LOW	HIGH	LOW
Franchise knowledge	LOW	LOW	HIGH	HIGH
Masculinity	–	–	HIGH	HIGH
Individualism	–	–	HIGH	LOW
Geographical/ Cultural distance	LOW	HIGH	HIGH	HIGH
Country risk	LOW	HIGH	HIGH	HIGH
Legal protection	HIGH	HIGH	HIGH	LOW

much more than a set of processes or habits. Culture is a set of dimensions as Usunier and Lee (2005) described. He said culture is a complex and interrelated set of elements, such as knowledge, beliefs and values, arts, law, manners, and morals. In the Figure 6.2, we can see the set of dimensions Usunier and Lee (2005) has set out.

For this study, the most relevant factors that could influence whether or not a franchise would be a success – besides the financial, political, economic, and management aspects – are religious traditions. Indeed, with an Islam-based constitution, Morocco has a population of 33 million people of whom 98 percent are Muslims (French Franchise Observatory). Considerations of diet and habits are crucial as we shall see. Furthermore, Malinowski (1944) has posited that the biological needs of people and the way in which they are organized and regulated within the framework of the cultural community are strongly related. He studies the example of eating habits, which must be regarded as both biological and cultural. A study conducted by Hopkins (1996) attempts to shed light on this challenge. His findings reveal that franchisers feel that cultural differences do affect demand for their products or services; however, they prefer keeping the brand standardized to too much cultural adaptation. Hopkins found that most alterations that had to be made for an operation to be successful were in the areas of promotion and advertising, pricing, product/service characteristics, and financial requirements. The results of this

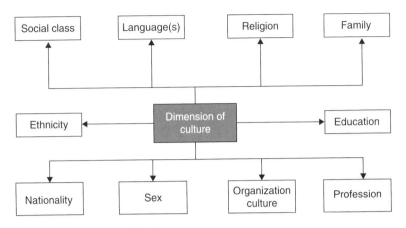

Figure 6.2 Dimensions of culture
Source: Usunier and Lee (2005).

study also showed that there was a slight tendency for franchises to make more changes when entering a market with more extreme cultural differences. At the same time, Hopkins has shown that companies that adapted their products or services too much tended to be less successful.

However, it is difficult to define Moroccan culture because of the cultural "chaos" it seems to reflect with the many contradictory and heterogeneous characteristics it possesses because of its mix of heritages of European, Arabic, Berber, and African descent. There are at least six dialects in Morocco and the country has been tremendously influenced by French and Spanish colonizations. The blend between all these streams of traditions and cultures has left indelible marks on Moroccan society. We will now try to outline why a fast-food brand like McDonald's succeeded while others like Subway failed.

6.3 Methodology and research approach

This study draws on qualitative interviews of franchisees and a few bankers, secondary sources of data from franchisors and official representatives, and a presentation of the two cases: McDonald's and Subway. On the ground observations (when possible) will provide more information, e.g. on the way each franchisee deals with consumers, the physical set-up and menues offered with regard to religious restrictions and dietary habits.

To my knowledge, no research study has been conducted in this field in the Moroccan market to explain why the fast-food industry faces obstacles regarding cultural challenges and business rules.

The approach is based on comparison and contrast McDonald's and Subway. These franchises are similar and successful fast-food chains within the U.S. market and around the world, except in certain countries like Brazil and other Arabic countries where Subway has also failed (Risner, 2001). Both have ample experience in domestic and international markets.

A successful fast-food franchise is defined in this study as a restaurant brand that has entered the Moroccan market and has not suffered major setbacks or had to withdraw or close locations because of financial difficulties. A failed franchise for these cases is defined as a brand that has had negative experiences in the Moroccan market such as closure, bankruptcy, or almost totally withdrawal from the market like Subway.

The methodology used for this research is an interpretation-based one. We have taken an exploratory and descriptive approach to outlining the root causes of the phenomena. By using an inductive approach, we would be able to put into general use these phenomena but only after studying more examples.

6.4 Results of research study

On the one hand, we will compare and contrast major aspects of the strategies Subway and McDonald's used to break into the Moroccan market. These main dimensions are: menus and products, price, operations, store layout and location, and adaptation to local needs.

On the other hand, we will go through interviews and articles to outline major aspects that have arisen as significant factors that might contribute to either success or failure for both fast-food brands: entry strategy, franchisee relationship, and training and local networking. We will thus be able to compare what each of them has done and bring to light key factors for success.

6.4.1 Comparison of main aspects

In this section, we are about to compare what Subway and McDonald's have provided as services and products and contrast the results with Moroccan culture. The question here is: what are the basic factors associated with successful fast-food franchising in Morocco?

First of all, Table 6.4 gives basic information on the beginning of McDonald's and Subway's tale. We can draw important details from

Table 6.4   Summary of company information

General information	McDonald's	Subway
Year founded	1955	1965
Year began franchising	1955	1974
International expansion	1967	1984
Year entered Morocco	1999	2000
How entered Morocco	Joint venture	Master franchise
Presence in other countries	120	72

Source: Company web sites.

this table. The first is that McDonald's began its foreign investment and franchising earlier than Subway. It has more than 15 years' greater experience of expanding abroad than Subway. The second is that McDonald's has set up in more than 120 countries, far more than Subway. These two facts seem to be important and tend to confirm what authors have stated (Alon and Welch, 2001) on the importance of having experience before considering breaking into new markets that are geographically and culturally different.

In Table 6.5 we compare the main characteristics of McDonald's and Subway's services that are visible to consumers. Then, we compare them with Moroccan cultural aspects, indicating the degree of importance for Moroccan customer and see the gap.

This table shows the main visible factors for Moroccan consumers. We draw from it seven critical characteristics (marked as "important" or "very important") that seem to be the most crucial factors likely to influence positively a fast-food outlet's success: ingredients, adaptation to local taste, preparation time, price, meal temperature, store format, and location. It is remarkable that Subway does not fit five out of the seven criteria whereas McDonald's achieves six out of seven, which means McDonald's was always more likely to meet Moroccan consumer needs.

On the other hand, there are other, less visible factors in fast-food franchise. These "behind the scenes" factors are summarized in Table 6.6. We are going to compare these criteria with what authors have given as critical characteristics that are likely to have an impact on international expansion when brands go abroad.

It is clear from this table that Subway has underestimated the most important factors that lead franchisors to succeed abroad. Lack of commitment has put the business on the wrong track from the start. Subway didn't invest enough in training even though authors tell us to consider

Table 6.5 Comparative study between McDonald's and Subway's services and products

VISIBLE CRITERIA From consumer point of view	What McDonald's has done and proposed?	What Subway has done and proposed?	What are Moroccan consumers willing to pay for?	Degree of importance for Moroccan consumer
Ingredient-based products	Halal meat and chicken, fish, bread, cheese, salad, fries	Halal meat and chicken, bread, cheese, salad, chips	Halal meal, fries, spicy	Very important
Product characteristics	Fat-heavy meals and fried ingredients	Healthy menu – fresh meals with low fat and not fried	Healthy menu	Less important
Adaptation to local tastes	McArabia – McFtour (special Ramadan meal)	No adaptation at all	Foreign products but aligned with religion and tastes	Important
Time lining up and preparation	5 min	4 min	Not willing to wait	Important
Meal temperature	Hot temperature	Warm temperature	Hot meal	Very important
Prices (small combo)	$5	$6	$4	Very important
Store format	Standard store, McDrive, space game, huge outdoor space, large number of seats– playground terrace – large parking stand	Standard store to be able to operate from a small base, one hundred square meters, minimal seating, no space game	Large space with playground and games for children, eating at store – parking	Important
Operations	Cooking in the store	No cooking in the store – Sandwich gets prepared in the presence of the customer	No preference	Very important
Localization	Main streets and shopping area centre – Beach, train stations, business area	No parking – far from shopping centre – No playground	Respectable area – cross activities (shopping, cinema, entertainment...)	Less important

Table 6.6   Comparison between McDonald's and Subway's strategies and against theory

INVISIBLE CRITERIA From consumer point of view	McDonald's franchising approach	Subway's franchising approach	Theory: what authors have stated about general approach
Franchisee relationship	Deep relationship and mutual trust	I couldn't get information (franchisee is gone)	The better the relationship, the more the chances to succeed
Training (intensity and duration of training, preparation, manual)	Organizes frequent training for employees	Training was organized only once before opening the store	Crucial factor
Marketing strategy	Television commercials and billboards when they started running business	Waiting until the brand was recognized before launching an AD campaign	Think global, act local
Franchisee's previous experience in franchise	45 years of experience before coming to Morocco	26 years of experience before coming to Morocco	The more experience you have, the more likely you will succeed
Royalties	5%	8%	Nothing is mentioned by authors
Local partner's competences	Big advantage by having a prestigious partner	Franchisee with few years of experience	Your partner must have experience in franchising
Origin of ingredients (yogurt, chips, logistics, ...)	Some ingredients are imported (bread)	couldn't get information	Nothing is mentioned by authors

Source: Based on interviews and articles written by many authors.

this factor as crucial. By waiting until the brand gets recognized before launching advertising campaigns, Subway and its Moroccan franchisee have certainly reduced their chances for success, knowing that McDonald's invested a lot in advertising and publicity at the beginning of its venture. Having more years of franchising experience seems to be a determining factor that made McDonald's well prepared to face cultural differences. We notice that McDonald's invests a lot of money in training but it suffers from a high level of turnover.

6.4.2   Subway's failure

Based on what we have stated so far on Subway's experience in Morocco, we can summarize all the facts in order to get a clear and precise overview of the errors and mistakes that have been committed, on both the cultural and the general sides (Figure 6.3).

Even though we have seen before in this study (Table 6.5) that a master franchisee would be a better choice for franchisors to invest in Morocco, McDonald's have made the choice to go for a joint venture. In fact, the franchisee told us that McDonald's has evaluated Morocco as a strategic place for investment. The reality is that McDonald's, as a very well known and successful brand, had little choice but to have a prestigious Moroccan partner in the country's capital, which was represented by a member of the Royal family. But I have to say that many other franchises are doing well without having a close relationship with what we call in Morocco "the Crown." But the fact is that McDonald's is so prestigious and so profitable that it's not easy to slip through the net.

Subway's mistakes: cultural factors
1. Lack of knowledge of local business rule
2. Keep products as they are without any adaptation to local tastes
3. Assuming that foods brought from U.S. will work in Morocco
4. Lack of knowledge of food tradition
5. Underestimating business processes and bureaucracy
6. Difficulties to find the right location at the right price

Subway's mistakes: general factors
1. Poor selection of master franchiser
2. Inadequate training for operating a chain of restaurants in Morocco
3. High prices and royalties comparing to what they offer
4. Lack of local market expertise from inadequate pre-market research

Figure 6.3   Factors in Subway's mistakes

6.5　Proposition of a business framework

We would like to finish this study by presenting a standard business framework (Figure 6.4) that could help fast-food companies that want to invest in Morocco to avoid mistakes and errors. Based on our results and findings, it appears that for each level of organization, some adjustments should be done regarding to what we call "visible criteria" and "invisible criteria" from the consumers' point of view (Figure 6.5).

Visible criteria　These represent contacts and links with consumers. Quality of food, ingredients, prices, store, and location are among other factors that the consumer tastes and evaluates at the first contact. By adjusting these criteria, the franchisor will adapt its "menu elements" to local expectations. We have seen in the case of Subway that the franchisee was not authorized to adapt its sandwiches to customers' needs. By maintaining its capital brand, a franchisors will keep its main value added at a high level which represents the most important aspect in consumer perception.

Invisible criteria　These are not visible from the consumers' point of view but are no less important for success. Indeed, as many authors have stated before, franchisors and franchisees should maintain a good relationship. Furthermore, the franchisor must adjust its business approach to local rules by amending its processes and negotiations. Royalties

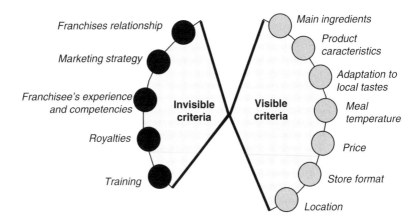

Figure 6.4　Adjustments to visible/invisible criteria

Menu Elements	Visible criteria		Invisible criteria	
	To MAINTAIN	To ADAPT	To MAINTAIN	To ADAPT
	Quality of food	Prices		Training
	Main ingredients	Menus and Flavors		Royalties
	Design and colors	Store and location		Franchisee experience
		Time preparation		

Core Strategy	Visible criteria		Invisible criteria	
	To MAINTAIN	To ADAPT	To MAINTAIN	To ADAPT
	Capital brand	Marketing strategy	Core business model	Business approach
			Organization's values	Franchisee selection
				Term of investment

Figure 6.5 Proposed business framework for fast-food companies to be successful in the Moroccan market

should be set up in order to offset against the market. Franchisee experience represents one of the most important factors to which franchisors should pay. Finally, investing abroad in African markets should be seen as a long-term involvement, according to the expectations of local managers and entrepreneurs (according to banker interview).

6.6 Conclusion

Studying an isolated case in a particular context reduces considerably the scope of this study. According to Wacheux (1996), who has stated that one case study might be a relevant strategy for having an in-depth look at how organizations behave or understand a particular management situation (Eisenhardt, 1989), this paper could be a platform and a springboard for others to confirm or invalidate these results through research. However, authors like Smith (1991) have denied and discredited this approach. In any case, there are more than ten fast-food franchises currently operating in Morocco and more than ten others that have failed. Furthermore, 100 franchise brands from all over the world are doing business in Morocco, so it should be possible to gather a sufficient number of samples to get a statistical correlation and significant findings on key factors that lead franchisors to success in the Moroccan market.

Another limitation that we faced in this paper is that Subway closed its restaurant in 2004 and we could not talk to the franchisee or other managers to get more information. However, many secondary data were available about this famous failure.

This paper has suggested that while one of the advantages of expanding abroad through franchising is the standardization of the brand (which provides economies of scale and mitigates risks), product, and format it also brings about a dilemma when expanding globally. This is the key issue in this study, which examines how to balance adaptation and standardization in order to be successful internationally. Reaching a balance between visible and invisible aspects (from a consumer's point of view) in the franchisor's strategy is particularly challenging in geographically remote and culturally different host countries (Alon, 2005). To what extent should the franchise adapt to its new cultural environment without losing its brand image and its familiar format?

Even though franchising has proved to be one of the best ways to succeed, many franchisors have gone out of business or have overestimated targets by underestimating cultural differences and obstacles. As well as Subway, several other franchisors were not able to break into the Moroccan market where traditions and religious aspects are intense and where customers are both price sensitive and eager for foreign products. Brands like Nectar, Benetton, Megastor, NafNaf, Simon Mahler, Dunkin' Donuts, Wimpy, Glup's, Dairy Queen, and KFC have failed in their attempt to captivate the Moroccan consumer (*La Tribune*, 2007). The general model that we have developed in this paper certainly needs to be confirmed by others through in-depth research studying the root causes of fast-food franchise failures. We hope that this research has opened a gateway to bring more evidence to light in order to help foreign investors mitigate risks when they go abroad.

References

Agrawal, S., and S.N. Ramaswami (1992). "Choice of Foreign Market Entry Mode: Impact of Ownership, Location and Internationalization," *Factors Journal of International business studies* 23 (1, March), 1–27.

Alon, Ilan (2005). *Service Franchising: A Global Perspective*. New York: Springer.

Alon, I. (2006a). *Executive insight: evaluating the market size for service franchising in emerging markets*. Winter Park, FL: Rollins College, Crummer Graduate School of Business.

Alon, I. (2006b). "Market Conditions Favouring Master International Franchising," *Multinational Business Review* 14 (2); AB/INFORM Global, 67.

Alon, I., and D. McKee (1999). "Towards a Macro Environmental Model of International Franchising," *Multinational Business Review* 7 (1), 76–82.

Alon I, M. Tuunamen, and N. Anttonen (2005). "The international business environments of franchising in Russia," *Academy of Marketing Science Review* 2005 5, 1–18.

Alon, I., and D.H.B. Welsh, Eds. (2001). *International Franchising in Emerging Markets: China, India and Other Asian Countries.* Chicago: CCH Inc. Publishing.

Alon, I., D.H.B. Welsh, and M. Fable (2006). "An Examination of International Retail Franchising in Emerging Markets," *Journal of Small Business Management* 44 (1, January); ABI/INFORM Global, 130.

Aydin, N., and M. Kacker (1990). "International Outlook of US-based Franchisers" *International Marketing Review* 7 (2).

Davel, E., J.P. Dupuis, and J.F. Chanlat, Eds. (2008). *Gestion en milieu interculturel: Approches, problématiques, pratiques et plongées.* Quebec: Presses de l'Université Laval.

Eisenhardt, K.M. (1989). "Building Theory from Case Study Research," *Academy of Management Review,* 14, 532–50.

French Franchise Observatory *Guide Pratique de la Franchise et des adhérents de la FFF,* Puteaux: Fédération Française de la Franchise.

Hopkins, D.M. (1996). "International Franchising: Standardisation Versus Adaptation to Cultural.

Justis, R., and R. Judd (1989). *Franchising.* Cincinnati, OH: South-Western Publishing Co.

Kalika, M., N. Dubost, C. Gauzente, and V. Guilloux V (1999). *La décision d'achat d'une franchise: étude empirique du processus d'achat et de la satisfaction du franchisé.* Paris: Université de Paris IX Dauphine, CREPA.

La Tribune (2007). http://www.latribune.fr/accueil/a-la-une.html

Malinowski, B. (1944 [1960]). *A Scientific Theory of Culture, and other Essays.* London: Oxford University Press.

Ministry of Economy of Morocco (2007). www.finances.gov.ma.

Ministrty of Economy of Morocco (2008). http://www.araboo.com/site/morocco-finances-gov-ma-24320.

Nègre, C. (2000). *La franchise : Recherche et Applications.,* Paris: Éditions Vuibert, 14.

Preble, J.F. (1992). "Franchising A Growth Strategy for the 1990s," *Mid-American Journal of Business* 7(1), 35–41.

Risner, E. (2001). *Successful fast-food franchising in Brazil and the role of culture: Four cases* University of Florida thesis.

Shane, S. (1996). "Why Franchise Companies Expand Overseas," *Journal of Business Venturing* 11, 73–88.

Smith, N.C. (1991). "The Case study: A vital yet Misunderstood Research Method for Management," *The Management Research Handbook* New York: Routledge, 145–58.

Usunier, J.C., and J.A. Lee (2005). *Marketing Across Cultures* (4th edition). Englewood Cliffs, NJ/London: Prentice Hall/Financial Times.

Wacheux, F. (1996). *Méthodes quantitatives et recherches en gestion.* Paris: Economica.

Welsh, D.B.H., and Alon, I. (2001). *International Franchising in Emerging Markets: Central and Eastern Europe and Latin America.* Chicago: CCH Inc. Publishing.

7
Franchising in Croatia

Ilan Alon, Mirela Alpeza, and Aleksandar Erceg

7.1   Introduction

Scientific research in the field of franchising as a business model has been conducted for more than 20 years, but it was only during the 1990s that research interest in this area became more intense, particularly research that focused on the global context. During this period franchising became an increasingly interesting business concept to scientists and researchers from different areas, because the variables involved in franchising merit specific study (Combs and Ketchen, 2003) to entrepreneurship experts, because franchising represents a driving force for starting a business venture; to marketing experts, because it represents one of the main distribution channels in new economies; to strategic management experts, because it represents and important organizational form; and to financial experts, because they are interested in capital investment structures in franchise businesses.

This increase in the scientific community's interest in franchising's opportunities and challenges has coincided with increased intensity of franchises being implemented worldwide over the last two decades, especially in the U.S. and Europe (Alon and McKee, 1999). International Franchise Association (IFA) research from 2004 shows that 45 percent of retail business in the U.S. is conducted via franchising with more than 18 million people employed directly or indirectly in over 80 different industries (IFA, 2004). According to European Franchise Federation (EFF) data, there are over 5500 franchisors with over 266,000 franchise locations in Europe.

Although franchising as a business model undoubtedly shows exceptional potential and adaptability to different industries and business environments – even four decades after the first franchise appeared in the Croatian business environment – it still hasn't been fully developed as a business model in the country. This paper explores the current condition of franchising in Croatia, together with its development potential, and identifies the main obstacles to a broader implementation and acceptance of franchising as a desirable business model for entrepreneurs looking to start or grow their companies. We combine primary information from industry participants – bankers, lawyers, consultants, franchisors, and would-be franchisees – with previously published statistics in order to gain a better understanding of Croatian franchising, in particular, and franchising in transitioning and emerging economies more generally.

7.1.1 Defining the concept of franchising

A "franchise" represents a business relationship where "...one firm (the franchisor) sells the right to market goods or services under its brand name and using its business practices to a second firm (the franchisee)" (Combs et al, 2004). Curan and Stansworth (1983) provide a narrower definition:

> ... a business form essentially consisting of an organization (the franchisor) with market-tested business package centered on a product or service, entering into a continuing contractual relationship with franchisees, typically self-financed and independently owner-managed small firms, operating under the franchisor's trade name to produce and/or market goods or services according to a format specified by the franchisor.

Kidwell et al (2007) emphasize that the franchise concept is one of the key strategies for growing a business worldwide; however, the success of this strategy relies heavily on the relationship developed between the franchisor and the franchisee, i.e. on the franchisor's ability to prevent opportunistic behavior on franchisee's side (e.g. lowering production costs which results in negative effect on product/service quality and thus can result in losing the brand identity). Combs et al (2004) present two main distinctive characteristics of franchising in comparison to other organizational forms: first, franchise business models are most often developed in industries where services are an important component and there is a need to bring them closer to the end user; second, franchise agreements commonly determine a unique allocation of responsibilities, decision-making rights and profit-sharing models between a centralized principal (franchisor) and decentralized agents (franchisees).

The majority of scientific research on franchising is based on agency theory and/or resource scarcity theory. Major assumptions and predictions of these theories are summarized in Table 7.1.

7.1.2   Advantages and disadvantages of franchising

A franchise agreement governs the business relationship between two parties – the franchisor and the franchisee. As is the case with any business relationship, this one also implies certain advantages for both parties, while each party agrees to a certain level of compromise when signing the agreement.

Table 7.1   Major assumptions and predictions about franchising according to resource scarcity and agency theories

	Major assumptions	Major predictions
Resource Scarcity Theory	Large chains possess substantial scale advantages Firm ownership is more profitable than franchisee ownership Franchisee labor (i.e. managerial ability and local market knowledge) and capital are easier to obtain than alternatives	Small/young firms are more likely to grow through franchising Franchising is related to growth and survival, but not necessarily profitability Mature firms will grow through firm ownership and by repurchasing existing franchises
Agency Theory	Economic actors are rational and self-interested Economic actors have different goals but are otherwise homogeneous Franchising substitutes powerful ownership incentives for costly direct monitoring Employee-managers in company-owned outlets will be less motivated (vertical agency) Franchisees that do not depend on repeat business will free ride on the brand-building efforts of others (horizontal agency)	Firms will franchise those outlets that would be costly to monitor and where potential for freeriding (horizontal agency) is low Franchise contracts will provide franchisees with a quasi-rent to keep them in the contract and optimally motivated Firms that franchise where it is most efficient to do so will have greater performance

Source: Combs et al (2004), 908.

From a franchisor's viewpoint there are many advantages, i.e. arguments in favor of choosing franchising as a business expansion model: minimizing business risks, lower staffing needs, brand strengthening, and increased competitiveness. Spasić (1996) outlines the following advantages of franchising from the franchisor's standpoint: rapid expansion, the benefit of using the local market expertise of the franchisee, and better managerial skills combined with the greater drive and motivation of the franchisee (when compared to an employed manager, e.g. an outlet manager). The most serious potential disadvantage is the franchisee's infringement of agreement provisions dealing with quality standards. Parivodić (2003) identifies potential loss of control over the franchise network as one of the main disadvantages from a franchisor's viewpoint, with other authors listing additional disadvantages: reduced profit, potential conflicts with franchisees, and the lack of capacity to influence the franchisee's recruitment policy.

Franchisees, on the other hand, find starting their own businesses with a proven business idea and a well-known brand and trademark to be the major benefits of entering a franchisor's network. Other advantages include training, economies-of-scale advantages, fewer potential errors in business processes, product and quality standardization, and access to the franchisor's research programs knowledge base. The main disadvantages connected with franchise purchase are limited decision-making freedom, i.e. dependency on an occasionally inflexible franchising system; the relative inequality of the parties as they negotiate the agreement; and the franchisee's obligation to pay all debts without regard to his or her own financial status.

However, despite all the potential disadvantages, franchising has become a broadly implemented business model; a healthy balance of mutual interests can be established between the franchisor and the franchisee where every franchisee's success contributes significantly to the development of the franchise network as a whole (Alon, 2005).

7.2 The economic and entrepreneurial environments of franchising in Croatia

The possibilities for the development of franchising in Croatia are directly influenced by the general state of the Croatian economy. Economic indicators like GDP growth rate (as shown in Table 7.2) and the unemployment rate (Table 7.3) over the last few years, together with the number of new companies established, show a rather slow rate of

Table 7.2   GDP per capita and growth rates for Croatia over the period 2001–2006

	2001	2002	2003	2004	2005	2006
GDP per capita (EUR)	4997	5507	5905	6461	7038	7706
GDP year-on-year rate of growth	4.4	5.6	5.3	4.3	4.3	4.8

Source: Croatian National Bank (http://www.hnb.hr/statistika/e-ekonomski_indikatori.htm May 20, 2007).

Table 7.3   Unemployment rate in Croatia 2001–2006, by International Labor Organization, persons over 15 years of age

	2001	2002	2003	2004	2005	2006
Unemployment rate	15.8%	14.8%	14.3%	13.8%	12.7%	11.2%

Source: Croatian National Bank (http://www.hnb.hr/statistika/e-ekonomski_indikatori.htm May 20, 2007).

national economic recovery from the consequences of war, privatization, and economic transition processes.

According to the Strategic Development Framework 2006–2013 (2006), the key problems for Croatian economic development are:

- Systems of government and culture generally inconsistent with Western forms of state involvement in private business, such as franchising;
- Lack of an entrepreneurial climate; and
- Unfinished privatization and restructuring processes.

Low levels of entrepreneurial culture, combined with the prolonged privatization and restructuring processes, have slowed investment by both domestic and foreign investors. As a result of the prevailing economic conditions, foreign investors (potential franchisors included) are still cautious when considering business expansion to Croatia, and those who do decide to enter the Croatian market have a hard time finding entrepreneurs interested in establishing business partnerships.

Although figures for Croatia show an increase of entrepreneurial activity measured by the Total Early-stage Entrepreneurial Activity (TEA) index published by the Global Entrepreneurship Monitor (GEM) year on year. GEM is a joint research project between 42 participating countries with the purposes of measuring entrepreneurial activity within them, identifying factors that influence entrepreneurial activity, and drafting proposals for policy actions which can facilitate entrepreneurial activity level within a respective country. Entrepreneurial activity is measured by the TEA index, which represents the percentage of startup entrepreneurs in the total of adult population sample (age 18–64).

Croatian entrepreneurship is characterized by a larger number of entrepreneurs starting their businesses out of sheer necessity (measured by TEA Necessity index) – i.e. the need to solve their unemployment problems – in comparison to the number of entrepreneurs who are trying to seize a perceived market opportunity (measured by the TEA Opportunity index). In 2005, Croatia was the only country within the GEM research project in which the TEA Necessity index outnumbered the TEA Opportunity index. In 2006, however, Croatia managed to turn the numbers in favor of opportunity-seeking entrepreneurs, but was still ranked at the bottom of the 42 participating countries (Singer et al, 2005). These "necessity entrepreneurs" embark on their business ventures with minimal investment and are unlikely to become potential franchisees who, as a rule of thumb, need to be able to invest larger initial capital in their business. See Table 7.4.

The other problem in Croatian entrepreneurship in the context of franchising development lies in the low rate of transition of startup entrepreneurs to entrepreneurs active still active after 42 months: i.e. the low maturation rate of business ventures and the low share of growing companies in the economic structure. Table 7.5 shows the ratio between TEA Necessity and TEA Opportunity indexes in 2006 and the "growing up" index, which is even lower than the one measured in 2005 (0.48 for 2006, 0.60 for 2005). Businesses that successfully survive the transition phase and "grow up" can be observed as potential Croatian franchisors, and the GEM research project indicates an insufficient pool

Table 7.4 TEA indexes for Croatia (2002–2006)

	2002	2003	2004	2005	2006
TEA	3.62	2.56	3.74	6.11	8.58
TEA Opportunity	2.18	1.74	2.04	2.92	4.41
TEA Necessity	0.85	0.59	1.57	3.09	3.81

Source: Singer et al, 2005, 17.

Table 7.5   Entrepreneurial capacity of the Croatian economy, 2006

		2006
Motivation index*	Croatia	1.16
	GEM countries average	6.06
Growing-up index**	Croatia	0.48
	GEM countries average	0.81

*Ratio between TEA Opportunity and TEA Necessity
**Ratio between "entrepreneurs" and "beginners and start-up entrepreneurs"

Source: Singer et al 2005, 29

Table 7.6   Expected competition intensity, 2006, percentage (how many entrepreneurs offer the same product?)

	2006
Startup entrepreneurs	
Many	53%
A few	38%
None	9%
"Grown up" entrepreneurs	
Many	76%
A few	23%
None	1%

Source: Singer et al 2007, 33

of companies with franchisor potential in Croatia. Both startup entrepreneurs and their "grown up" counterparts conduct their respective businesses in an environment of intense competition and low level of innovation (Table 7.6).

According to the "Global Corruption Report," an assessment of the public perception of corruption among public servants and politicians conducted by Transparency International and published in 2007, Croatia ranked 69 out of 163 countries surveyed. Croatian businessmen and analysts taking part in this assessment have given Croatia an overall grade of 3.4 (on a scale where 10 represents total lack of corruption, and 0 represents a highly corrupt environment), which shows a high level of mistrust towards public institutions in Croatia. One of the key characteristics of successful franchising is a mutual trust relationship between the franchisors and the franchisee, because the franchisor enables the franchisee to use its brand name and business expertise. Low levels of trust in Croatia do not represent a healthy basis for franchise partnership development.

7.2.1 The legal environment for franchising in Croatia

Over the last few of years, Croatia has adopted numerous legal documents which gave it access to World Trade Organization (WTO) and Central European Free Trade Agreement (CEFTA) membership and laid the foundation for starting negotiations for accession to the European Union. Nevertheless, there is currently no specific legal framework for franchising in Croatia.

The concept of "franchising" was first introduced to the Croatian legal system by the Trade Act of 2003. However, the activity is insufficiently regulated as no regulation specific to franchising was introduced. Instead, current civil, contractual, and commercial laws govern the franchising relationship. A provision in Article 21 of the Trade Act (Trade Act, *Official Gazette*, 2003) states that the "Franchise Agreement governs the business relationship where the franchisor – a specialized wholesale company and a company who developed a successful form of service business – provides the franchisee – a retail company or a service industry company, with the right to use the franchise for selling certain types of products and/or services."

Since October 1, 2003, in accordance with the provisions of the Competition Protection Act, the Competition Protection Agency is responsible for evaluating every franchise agreement within 30 days of the signing of the agreement. On the other hand, pursuant to Article 11 Section 4 of the Trade Act, the agency can initiate an agreement evaluation procedure if the effects of the respective agreement (individual or cumulative) with other similar agreements in a relevant market do not fulfill the conditions for exclusion. These changes in the Competition Protection Act are the result of the screening process and the necessary adjustments of the Croatian legal system to fit the European Union legal system. The European Union provides exemption for franchising in its competition law.

Since a franchise business model takes advantage of all the economic functions of a trademark – guarantee, advertising, competitive, and promotional – franchising is largely influenced by the provisions of the Trademark Act. The previous Trademark Act provided for the trademark assignment to be connected to the assignment of the technology which guarantees the same product and/or service quality. The new Trademark Act (NN 173/03) no longer has this provision, but a provision of Article 699 of the Civil Obligations Act (NN 35/05), which ensures the quality of the products offered under the same trademark in licensing agreements, can be applied. The trademark owner has a right to perform the necessary quality control actions in order to protect the quality standards of products and/or services sold under its trademark.

7.2.2 The current state of franchising in Croatia

Even though the franchise business model has been present in Croatia for over four decades, the real development of this business model still lies ahead. The first franchise came to Croatia in 1969 with Diner's Club International. A franchise agreement enabled the franchisee based in Zagreb to operate in the whole of the former Yugoslavia and other Balkan countries. The Croatian Diner's Club franchisee received two awards from the franchisor for exceptional business results achieved in the Eastern European market (Viducic et al, 2001).

The first significant discussions on the advantages and disadvantages of the franchise business model in Croatia occurred when McDonald's entered the market in the early 1990s. McDonald's established a company, McDonald's Hrvatska Ltd., and signed business agreements with key suppliers – strategic partners in Croatia some of whom made further investments in their production capacities to meet the needs and quality requirements of this multinational company. McDonald's expanded throughout Croatia by opening its own "company" restaurants or by franchising other outlets. McDonald's presentations in cities where the franchisor sought partners/franchisees generated great interest from potential franchisees with debates on the nature of the franchise agreement offered by McDonald's, i.e. on the rights and obligations of both sides in a franchise relationship.

A couple of years after McDonald's entered the Croatian market, several other franchisors appeared, with the Hungarian bakery franchise Fornetti and the U.S. restaurant franchise Subway among the most recognizable.

In 2006, according to an assessment by the Croatian Franchise Association (Kukec, 2006) there were about 120 franchises operating in Croatia (with 25 Croatian franchisors) (Table 7.7). The same source identifies more than 900 franchise locations with approximately 16,000 employees. Franchising in Croatia encompasses 20 different industries, and more than 20 percent of the total hospitality and trade industries are conducted by companies that use a franchise business model.

7.2.3 Institutional support for franchising in Croatia

The Croatian Franchise Association was established in 2002 to promote and advertise franchise licensing in Croatia, provide a forum for

Table 7.7 Comparison of the number of franchises in Croatia and selected European countries

	Total number of franchises	Number of domestic franchisors
Croatia	125	Approx. 25–30
Czech Republic	90	Approx. 40
Slovenia	100	Approx. 40
Hungary	300	150
Poland	210	117

Source: EFF/IFA, International Symposium, Brussels, October 24–25

franchisors, and establish policies and standards for franchise licensing in Croatia (Croatian Franchise Association, 2007). Even though the mission and objectives of this association are of great significance for franchisors in Croatia, especially taking into consideration the low level of awareness of basic franchising concepts among entrepreneurs, the association (as of the writing of this document in January, 2008) has few members. The main activities of the association have been to promote and advertise franchising opportunities in various media and the coordination of an international forum, The Franchise and Partnership Expo, in Zagreb. Over the past few years (2003–2006), this event offered regular conferences with a number of domestic and international experts who specialized in different aspects of franchising (e.g. bank representatives, lawyers, university professors, and representatives of major franchisors) as guest speakers and participants.

However, the number of exhibitors at The Croatian Franchise Forum has declined over the last few years (in 2003 there were 35 exhibitors; in 2004, 29 exhibitors; in 2005, 15 exhibitors); the main cause for this is the size of the Croatian market (4.2 million people), which is seen as too small for large franchisors.

Another significant institution involved in franchise promotion in Croatia is The Franchise Center, established as an arm of The Center for Entrepreneurship Osijek in 2003. The center is focused on educating interested parties in the process of becoming franchisors and/or franchisees. The Center for Entrepreneurship became a franchisee of The Franchise Center El Paso (established by the University of Texas at El Paso), and brought its seminar, "The Big Picture," to Croatia. Working materials used in this seminar have been adjusted according to legal and economic aspects of Croatian business practice and a new educational program, "Franchise from A to Z," was developed. This seminar is held twice a year (spring and fall) in The Franchise Center of Center for Entrepreneurship Osijek, and in late 2006, the USAID project "Entrepreneurial Croatia" cofinanced the effort to take the seminar to ten other Croatian cities. More than 200 potential franchisees and franchisors participated in educational programs offered by The Franchise Center. In addition to educational programs, The Franchise Center's employees work as consultants and intermediaries in bringing together potential franchisors and franchisees in Croatia.

In addition to these two institutions, there is also a privately owned company, "Promaturo, an entrepreneurial franchise center," which operates from Zagreb and offers agency services for a number of foreign franchisors interested in finding franchising partners in Croatia. Promaturo provides its clients with consultancy services in establishing franchise networks of Croatian companies and advises all clients interested in becoming franchisees of an available franchise business.

7.3   Primary information from franchising stakeholders

Research entitled "Franchising development perspectives in Croatia" was conducted in September 2006 by The Franchise Center of the Center for Entrepreneurship Osijek. During late 2006, "Entrepreneurial Croatia" – a USAID SME support project in Croatia – cofinanced the visit of Professor Ilan Alon, who worked together with The Franchise Center's representatives and held several workshops on franchising for:

1. Lawyers interested in providing consultancy services to potential franchisors and franchisees;
2. Bankers interested in providing financial support for startup entrepreneurs who start their business ventures as franchisees;
3. Consultants interested in providing counseling services for potential franchisees and creating franchise networks to promote franchising as a new business model for Croatian companies, i.e. potential franchisors.

Each of the workshops offered a survey where all the participants were asked to fill out a questionnaire designed to analyze macroenvironmental factors influencing the development of franchising in Croatia. PEST analysis (analysis of political, economic, social, and technological factors) was used for environmental scanning purposes. The questionnaire used in the survey can be found in Appendix 7.1. In all, 45 participants took part in the survey (15 lawyers, 15 bankers, and 15 consultants).

The majority of survey participants agreed on two service-based industries with promising franchise-based growth potential: tourism and hospitality.

Major operational challenges influencing the development of franchising, as identified by the survey participants, are: lack of legal regulation of franchising as a business model; the slow justice system – interconnected with the mistrust of foreign franchisors and their lack of interest in entering into Croatian market; and the general lack of knowledge about the advantages and opportunities of franchising as a new business model among all groups who could benefit from franchising development (bankers, entrepreneurs, support institutions, and consultants).

The main operational challenges influencing the development of franchising in Croatia identified by the survey participants (bankers, lawyers, and consultants) are shown in Figure 7.1.

Lack of awareness of franchising as a business model in the Croatian business environment is highlighted as one of the major opportunities for franchise development by the majority of survey participants, while insufficient legal protection of franchisors' rights stands out as the most frequently mentioned threat. These and other opportunities and threats identified in the survey are shown in Table 7.8.

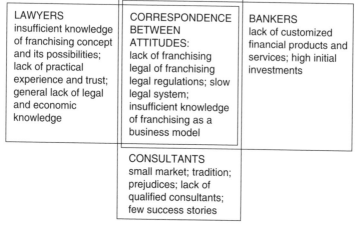

Figure 7.1 Franchising stakeholders' perceptions

Table 7.8 Major opportunities and threats for franchise development in Croatia

	Opportunities	Threats
Lawyers	Development of the service industries sector; Insufficient awareness of franchising as a business model	Lack of governmental and banking sector support; Insufficient protection of franchisors' rights; Frequent regulation changes; Insecurity of conducting business and debt collection due to slow justice system
Bankers	Customers increasingly focus on quality service and quality control; Market still not saturated by this business concept;	Slow legal system; Low TEA index; Mentality
Consultants	Country in transition economy; Incentives for franchise development; Croatia facing EU accession	Low attractiveness of Croatian market to foreign franchisors, Lack of expertise and experts; Croatia facing EU accession; Lack of adequate knowledge

Survey participants were expected to identify major political/legal, economic, social and technological factors influencing the development of franchising as a business model in Croatia. All of the collected answers were systematized and put in the matrix overview, which shows the PEST analysis of the major environmental factors influencing franchise development in Croatia (Table 7.9).

Survey participants have made extremely positive forecasts on the development of franchising in Croatia with the accession to the European Union being identified as the development accelerator. The number of franchisors and franchisees is expected to grow by 30–50 percent over the next five to ten years. Participants anticipate bigger and faster growth of foreign franchisors in comparison to their domestic counterparts, with major franchise networks concentrating in the areas in and surrounding Zagreb, Split, and Istria.

7.4 Conclusion

Franchising represents a business growth model with a broad array of possibilities for implementation in developed and developing economies worldwide. Key advantages of this business model lie in quick growth

Table 7.9 PEST analysis of the major environmental factors influencing franchise development in Croatia

Political factors	Economic factors
No registry of movables which could be used as collateral	Croatia is not recognized as a tax-friendly country
Bureaucracy	Small market
Insufficient protection of franchisors' rights	Lack of public institutional support (e.g. HAMAG)
Lack of legal experience in regulating franchise as a business concept	Unwillingness of banks to participate in financing franchise purchases
Insufficient use of arbitration	Low purchasing power with relatively high franchise product/service prices
Possibility of sudden regulatory interventions by legislators	
No state regulations on franchise agreements	Insufficient economic development
Inadequate intellectual property rights protection	High unemployment rate
Lack of lawyers who are highly specialized and trained in franchise business models	Lack of adequate financial tools
Social factors	Technological factors
Mentality (infringements of business agreements, expectations of quick profits)	Lack of adequate knowledge
	Low R&D investment rates
Low standard of living	Poor infrastructure
Lack of knowledge	Low level of technological education
High indebtedness of the population	Underdevelopment
Atmosphere of mistrust	Technology obsolescence and low rate of adoption of new technology trends' adoption
Intellectual property rights violations	

and expansion possibilities, risk minimization, and reduced investment. Its success derives from establishing and managing a healthy balance of mutual interests between the franchisor and the franchisee.

Franchising has been present in Croatia since the late 1970s, but the first real promotion of this business model brought McDonald's into the country in the 1990s. However, franchising growth in Croatia has stagnated to a degree as a result of the general economic situation, the weak entrepreneurial climate, and the low level of innovation and competitiveness of Croatian companies. At the same time, there are only two franchise support institutions operating in Croatia – The Croatian Franchise Association and The Franchise Center of the Center for Entrepreneurship Osijek, both with the mission of promoting franchises as a business model.

Eye Optics Lens

Dubravka and Damir B. opened Eye Optics Lens – the first privately owned optical store in Osijek in the late 1980s. After several years, they started to grow their business to manufacturing spectacles and soon became the fourth largest spectacles manufacturer in Croatia. Their business soon expanded to opticians' equipment distribution, servicing for a top-quality Japanese manufacturer, and the exclusive dealership agreement for a broad geographical area. This expansion, optical equipment distribution and sales of spectacles in both retail and wholesale markets, helped them to establish business contacts with a number of optical retail businesses in Croatia. They have also received many inquiries from entrepreneurs interested in starting their own optical businesses. Dubravka and Damir have provided these entrepreneurs with optical equipment, free information, and advice on running their businesses, and have assisted them in establishing new business contacts. Now with 15 years of expertise in the optical industry and consultancy, they have decided to systematize their knowledge and try to offer it to potential buyers using franchising as a business growth model.

After the final decision to create their own franchise network was made, they faced numerous challenges in trying to bring their idea to life: the potential buyers' market wasn't sufficiently educated on the possibilities and advantages of franchising; there was a paucity of legal experts with experience in dealing with the franchise business concept; there was no legal framework established for this business model; and there were no financial products and services offered by the banking industry to facilitate the growth of the potential franchise market. After facing these challenges and realizing the current state of franchising in Croatia, Dubravka and Damir have decided not to follow up on their idea of developing a franchise network. They became aware that becoming a franchisor in Croatia today implies entering a brand new industry with their business becoming a product to sell to an insufficiently educated buyers' market with no actual demand. They have decided to return to their core business instead. Franchising as a business growth model will have to wait for better times in their case.

Companies which today decide to expand their businesses by becoming franchisors in Croatia are facing a legally unregulated area, insufficiently educated potential franchisees, and a dearth of adequate financing products and services for franchise purchase. Many potential franchisees, faced with these challenges, decide to give up their idea of growing their businesses via franchising (see, for example, the Eye Optics Lens case study), which leaves a total of between 25 and 30 Croatian franchisors operating currently in Croatia (based upon unofficial information provided by Croatian Franchise Association), a significantly smaller number when compared to some other transitional countries. The results of a research project, "Franchising development perspectives in Croatia," conducted in September 2006 with lawyers, bankers, and consultants as target groups, indicate that Croatia will witness a major development of franchising as a business model over the next five to ten years, with tourism and hospitality being touted as drivers of franchising development.

The environment for franchising in Croatia is less than hospitable, with low levels of entrepreneurship (particularly opportunity-driven entrepreneurship), lack of franchising know-how, mistrust in society, corruption in public spheres, lack of a legal framework for franchising, and a small population, to mention a few reasons. Offsetting such pessimism are two salient factors: (1) EU integration will lead to harmonization of rules and possible convergence in consumption patterns promoting franchising; and (2) the tourism and hospitality industries, which need the international standards offered by franchising, are both organized and growing, providing an opportunity for franchising development. We believe that gradual implementation of franchising, through the development of local chains, conversion of existing businesses, and entry of foreigners, will ultimately give stimulate these sector's' development and prosperity.

Appendix 7.1   Questionnaire used for the survey purposes in "Franchising development perspectives in Croatia" research

---

Which industries in your opinion show the biggest potential for growth by using franchise as a business model?

Identify the major operational challenges that, in your opinion, have the biggest influence on the development of franchising in Croatia.

Identify the major opportunities and threats for franchisors in Croatia.

Identify the major political and legal factors influencing franchise development in Croatia.

Identify the major economic factors influencing franchise development in Croatia.

Identify the major social factors influencing franchise development in Croatia.

Identify the major technological factors influencing franchise development in Croatia.

How do you see franchising as a business model in Croatia in the next five to ten years?

References

Alon, I. (2005). *Service Franchising: A Global Perspective.* New York: Springer.
Alon, I., and D.L. McKee (1999). "Towards a Macro-environmental Model of International Franchising," *Multinational Business Review* 7 (1), 76–82.

Alon, I., and D. Welsh (2001). *International franchising in emerging markets: China, India and other Asian Countries*. Chicago: CCH Inc.

Combs, J.G., and D.J. Ketchen, Jr. (2003). "Why do firms use franchising as an entrepreneurial strategy? A meta-analysis," *Journal of Management* 29 (3), 443–65.

Combs, J.G, S.C. Michael, and G.J. Castrogiovanni (2004). "Franchising: A review and avenues to greater theoretical diversity," *Journal of Management* 30 (6), 907–31.

Competition Protection Act (2003). *Official Gazette*, 122/03, Article 11, www.nn.hr, [Accessed May 20, 2007].

Croatian Franchise Association (2007). http://www.fip.com.hr/fipHr/index.asp?lang=hr,]Accessed May 20, 2007].

Curan, J., and J. Stanworth, (1983). "Franchising in the modern economy/towards a theoretical understanding," *International Small Business Journal* 2 (1), 8–26.

IFA, (2004). Economic Impact of Franchised Business, National Economic Consulting Practice of PriceWaterhouseCoopers, IFA Educational Foundation

Kidwell, R.E., Nygaard, A., and Silkoset, R. (2007). "Antecedents and Effects of Free Riding in the Franchisor-Franchisee Relationship," *Journal of Business Venturing*, Elsevier 22(4), 522–544.

Kukec, L.J. (2006). "Franchising in Croatia" – round table. Address by the President of the Croatian Franchise Association, EFF/IFA International Symposium, Brussels, October 24–25.

Parivodić M. (2003). *Pravo međunarodnog franšizinga*, Službeni glasnik, Beograd.

Singer et al. (2005). *Strategija razvoja Osječko-baranjske županije*, Osijek.

Spasić, I. (1996). *Franchising posao*, Institut za uporedno pravo, Beograd.

Vidučić, Lj., G. Brčić, I. Alon, and D.Welsh (2001). "*International Franchising in Emerging Markets – Central and Eastern Europe and Latin America*, CCH Inc., Chicago, USA.

8
Microfranchising in Less Developed Countries

Ilan Alon, Matthew C. Mitchell, and J. Mark Munoz

8.1 Introduction

Microfranchising has matured from its beginnings in nonprofit development communities to capture the attention of the wider business community. Its successful proliferation in diverse emerging economies such as Kenya, El Salvador, and India has led to the establishment of profitable organizations, the creation of jobs, the alleviation of poverty, and sustainable economic development. We are aware of the great potential of this emerging business model, but are concerned about the paucity of academic literature on the subject. This article is an attempt to remedy this situation by synthesizing existing perspectives and stimulating new avenues of research. Specifically, we explore viable models in the practice of microfranchising by revisiting literature pertaining to its precursor – franchising. Contemporary cases are also highlighted in order to identify effective and successful strategies.

To achieve these objectives the article is organized into three sections: first, the main franchising concepts are reviewed, including research findings on challenges, opportunities, and existing models. The following section on microfranchising reviews current cases to describe the salient characteristics of an emerging business model and the main drivers for microfranchising success. Finally, an analysis and discussion is presented which includes a model for effective implementation of microfranchising, directions for future research, and implications for practitioners.

8.2 Review of franchising literature

Franchising is not a new business concept. The terminology originated in France, and translates as the provision of a right (Williamson, 1992).

While franchising as a business model has been in use for a long time, its application has evolved into diverse forms. At its core, franchising is an organizational form that enables a transfer of systems via contractual arrangements involving payments of fees and royalties (Alon, 2004). At their core, franchised business models provide key services which include 1) business concept and management systems, 2) provision of equipment, 3) access to start-up funds, 4) ongoing support, and 5) lobbying to local and national entities (Henriques and Nelson, 1997).

Over the past decade, viewpoints on franchising have gravitated from an organizational focus to a focus on processes. For example, Elango and Fried (1997) defined franchising as an organizational model where one enterprise grants another the right to conduct business using a prescribed methodology in a specific place over a period of time, in exchange for specified fees or royalties. However, in recent years franchising has been viewed as a strategic business model that empowers its associates and significantly impacts the surrounding economic environment (Spinelli, 2007). Even with a diversity of perspectives, common agreement exists on the fact that franchising has a favorable impact on company profitability, local job creation, and the wider economy. Franchises account for 10–20 percent of GDP in the majority of developed economies (Magelby, 2006).

Franchise operations offer benefits to both the giver (franchisor) and the recipient (franchisee). Ascribed benefits for the franchisor include 1) the ability to expand with only limited resources, 2) the transference of risk to franchisees, 3) the benefits from economies of scale, 4) the profit potential derived from motivated, self-employed franchise partners, and 5) operational independence (Andaleeb, 1996; Kaufmann and Eroglu, 1999). For the franchisee, benefits include 1) access to an implementation-ready business model with a proven methodology, 2) a recognized trademark and brand, and 3) the backing of experienced training and operational support (Hutchinson, 1999). Furthermore, major attractions of the franchise system are its growth potential, operational enhancement, and profitability. Johns et al (1989) pointed out that combined advertising, volume discounts, mentoring, and support added a unique appeal to the franchise system. A final advantage of franchising lies in its ability to mitigate risk. With numerous ascribed benefits of a franchising approach, risk associated with business start-ups is minimized (Henriques and Nelson, 1997). This is because the franchisee can rely on some of the experience of the franchisor and the proven business concept.

Franchising, however, is not an appropriate mode for all business situations. Certain conditions need to exist in order that a franchise strategy may be optimized. Dyl (1991) demonstrated that franchising is most suitable when 1) a quality trademark is present, 2) the opportunity to decentralize a product/service exists, and 3) the product/service is close to the site of consumption. In essence, brand appeal, scalability, and product-to-market factors, among others, need to be considered.

A wider review of the literature indicates several defining characteristics of franchising. These include:

Ability to operate in diverse forms and structures There are many ways in which franchising is practiced. Franchise operations vary according to types, size, operational mode, and contractual arrangements (Kaufmann and Kim, 1995).

Need for value perception For franchise operations to be successful, the value added component needs to be fully understood by both the franchisor and franchisee. Rawlins (1992) pointed out that perceived benefits to the franchise protagonists should exceed costs.

Driven by leveraging of skills With evolving and competitive business environments, the ability of franchise operations to optimize skill sets is essential. Spinelli (2007) shows that contemporary franchising has resulted in a shift away from traditional managerial roles and toward a more creative leveraging of diverse skill sets.

Franchisor-franchisee relationship is important Price and Arnould (1999) demonstrate that franchise operations are often defined by their level of reciprocity. Mutually beneficial, win-win scenarios need to be cultivated for long-term sustainable success. The synergistic and mutually beneficial relationship between a franchisor and franchisee is sometimes viewed as a partnership or strategic alliance (Stanworth and Kauffman, 1996). The ability to manage this alliance efficiently is critical (Spinelli, 2007).

Anchored on innovation In response to changing business conditions, franchising is largely an innovation that is implemented in response to local environmental characteristics, or as a result of specific management choices in the execution of overall strategy (Hoffman and Preble, 2001).

Strengthened by business connectivity The ability to streamline linkages between production and consumption, which is common in service industries such as retail and food, enhances the franchise model (Erramilli, 1990).

Suitable for specific industries   The business methodology associated with franchising is common in the service industry where the franchisor provides certain assets, franchise structure, information, and intellectual property among other items. The service industry is suitable for franchising because of the heightened consumer confidence it provides as a result of brand recognition, standards, and quality perceptions (Cross and Walker, 1987; Hoffman and Preble, 2001). Therefore, franchising has been common in service industries such as the retail and food sectors (Erramilli, 1990).

Branding is a key consideration   Strategic leveraging of the brand can lead to franchise success. A strong brand name can be a powerful tool in franchising, as in any business (Day and Wensley, 1988).

Defined by internal and external forces   Franchising operations are affected by both external forces (i.e. competition or the economy) as well as internal (i.e. organizational framework or procedures) (Alon, 2006). Additionally, factors such as capital access and growth opportunities in the area of operation shapes franchise management approaches and strategies.

Assessment of operational environment is necessary   Market environments are diverse and some conditions are more suitable for franchise operations than others. Studies suggest that in cases where high capital investment is required or the growth rate is high, franchising can be an attractive option for expansion (Thompson, 1992).

   While there are several characteristics that define the franchising practice, the description above provides a preview of some of the essential attributes that shape its functionality. In the next section, we revisit franchise theories and models to further explore viable operational forms.

8.2.1   Franchise theories and structures

There are several theories and models that attempt to describe and define franchising. In particular, two theories stand out: first, resource scarcity theory stresses the need for value added mechanisms where capital access and managerial know-how paves the way for enterprise growth and success (Carney and Gedajlovic, 1991). Second, agency theory makes use of the necessity for efficient control in order to manage differences between the agent and principal (Brickley and Dark, 1987). Other perspectives frame the franchise concept in the context of 1) transaction cost economics where parties provide an added value to gain market advantage or operational efficiencies and 2) relational exchange theory in which a need for commonality of perceptions across parties is stressed because governing norms vary between relational exchanges (Spinelli, 2007).

In addition to the diverse theoretical perspectives that describe franchising, a variety of views also exists describing franchise implementation modes. The classification of franchising structures most evident in the literature is listed below.

Classification based on relationship type Franchising may be classified according to the type of relationship between the franchisor and the franchisee. Franchising comes in diverse forms and may be an agency, cooperative, distributor, or representative model (Magelby, 2006).

Classification based on work function The type of activity can also define how a franchise operation can be classified. Magelby (2006) cites potential franchising models as product, business format, informal business format, buyer's cooperative, producer's cooperative, owner operator, delivery route, manufacturer's representative, journeyman, piecework jobber, independent operator, local agent, local distributor, local purveyor, local promoter, finance franchise, and agricultural producer.

Classification based on organizational arrangement Henriques and Herr (2007) alluded to two types of franchising model based on organizational arrangement. First, top-down franchising exists when a business owner (franchisor) provides the right to a business person (franchisee) to implement a similar business model subject to paid fees, adherence to standards, and provision of business support. This model 1) offers a complete and detailed operating system, 2) is market-driven, 3) is dependent on good franchisor management skills, 4) requires proper intellectual property rights protection, 5) requires healthy and safe work environments, 6) employs active advocacy approaches, and 7) is constrained by challenges such as quality, capital, franchisor selection, contractual rigidity, transferability, product line limitations, overdependence on franchise name, and lack of flexibility, among other things. The second organizational arrangement is a bottom-up franchising model where a group of small enterprises operates under a combined system to optimize performance, heighten productivity, and improve competitiveness. This model 1) evolves over time, 2) is driven by members goals and initiatives, 3) provides market access, 4) has less emphasis on the protection of trademark and property rights, 5) incorporates group based initiatives, 6) exhibits strong advocacy functions, 7) offers benefits to business formalization, and 8) is constrained by challenges such as diversity of membership goals and ambitions, potentially slow decisionmaking processes, and difficulty of brand protection.

Classification based on operational approach   Some organizations identify their franchise strategy based on the business approach taken. Franchising may also be classified into product/brand name franchising where suppliers engage in a contract with individuals to sell their products (Falbe and Dandridge, 1992) or business format franchising where a business model, including standards and control, is passed by the franchisor to the franchisee (Kostecka, 1988).

Classification based on strategic choice   The type of strategic action selected by organizations also defines their classification. In recent years, there has been growth in conversion franchising, where franchisors pick new franchisees who operate independent businesses or the franchises of competitors (Hoffman and Preble, 2003).

8.2.2   Franchising in international venues

The diverse implementation of franchising has been evident not just in how the businesses operate, but also where they operate. Franchising has grown in popularity in recent years especially as a business model for a globalizing environment (Preble and Hoffman, 1995; Swartz, 1994). According to the literature, there are several key considerations when franchising in emerging, new, or foreign markets which include:

Need for a clear vision and specific goals   Firms need to fully understand their competencies, where they want to go, and what they are looking to achieve. For example, franchisors tend to stay domestic when the local market is large and there are limitations in management and financial resources (Aydin and Kacher, 1989).

Understand market conditions and plan accordingly   When franchising internationally, economic factors such as market size, competitive intensity, and extent of demand shape entry decisions (Alon, 2006). A clear understanding of the prevailing conditions aids in developing viable strategies. When looking to expand overseas, franchising is an attractive entry mode in locations where population size or per capita income does not warrant a large-scale investment (Whitehead, 1991).

Anticipate risks   New markets or new locations pose a level of risk. While numerous franchising opportunities in foreign venues have opened up, threats and challenges do exist (Amies, 1999). Knowledge of foreign markets reduces those associated risks (Eroglu, 1992).

Plan for market shifts and evolution   Business environments evolve, so it is therefore important to understand the demographic changes that are taking place and respond accordingly. For instance, urbanization and participation of women in the workforce have significantly contributed to franchise growth (Alon and McKee, 1999; Yavas and Vardiabasis, 1987).

Keep a close eye on government policies and legal frameworks   There is a need to be vigilant about government policies and procedures. Policies enforced by governments on matters pertaining to fiscal and regulatory measures tend to impact business functions such as importation and repatriation, and subsequently affect profitability (Alon and McKee, 1999). Additionally, there are political and legal considerations as well resulting from issues such as political risk, corruption, and the extent of regard for rule of law (Alon, 2006; Falbe and Dandridge, 1992; Justis and Judd, 1986).

Prepare and train managers for new markets   Managers expanding into new territories can benefit from past experience, mentors, and training. Studies suggest that the likelihood of franchise internationalization is heightened when company managers are open to foreign markets and overseas opportunities (Kedia et al 1995). Furthermore, greater franchise experience contributes to confidence in overseas expansion (Shane, 1996).

While there are challenges relating to franchise expansion overseas, there are also benefits to be realized for both the organization and the country of operation. For instance, the process of business adaptation can lead to new ideas and innovation that can be employed to further the venture's growth and evolution (Elango, 2007). Alon (2004) identified several ascribed socioeconomic benefits including output creation, job creation, tax base increases, tariff gains, economic modernization and infrastructure development, economic clustering, reduction in capital flight, long-term economic growth, stimulation of entrepreneurship, supply chain efficiencies, expertise expansion, and the broadening of consumer choice, among others.

8.2.3   Franchise challenges

While there are numerous benefits associated with franchising, challenges do exist. Hutchinson (1999) pointed out that potential disadvantages for franchisees include 1) costs and fees, 2) restriction of freedom, 3) moral challenges, and 4) expansion limitations, while for franchisors, a major disadvantage lies in the reliance on the franchisees to maintain franchise image and corporate reputation. Typical franchise challenges are listed here.

Unprepared management team   The type, qualifications, and inclinations of the management team can shape the franchise's future. Management limitations can hinder franchise growth (Combs and Castrogiovanni, 1994).

Lack of preparation for conflict   Numerous potential areas of conflict exist between franchisors and franchisees. Reflecting business in general, there have been documented cases of conflict between franchisors and franchisees (Frazer 2001; Kaufmann and Dant, 1996). Often conflict occurs when one party acts in a way that deviates from the norm (Parsa, 1996). Common issues of conflict involve advertising fees, territorial rights, pricing, and product mix, among others (Grunhagen and Dorsch, 2003; Shivell and Banning, 1996).

Lack of safeguards against opportunism   Opportunism can be viewed as a challenge in the franchise system (Doherty and Alexander, 2004). Proper safeguards and protection need to be in place.

Inability to homogenize   It is a challenge to homogenize or standardize franchise operations as a result of the diversity of cultural and business platforms (Aydin and Kacker, 1990). Efforts need to be made in developing system commonality and compatibility.

Existence of moral hazards   In franchising, there are moral hazards that exist for both the franchisor and franchisee (Lafontaine, 1992). Because of the cultural, business, and political diversity in franchise operations moral mindsets vary, and there are therefore countless opportunities for transgressions and misunderstandings. Setting ground rules and codes of conduct early may help address this challenge.

The challenges highlighted above are but a few of the numerous ones encountered in franchise operations. As business models vary, the types of challenges encountered by franchise firms may also differ.

8.2.4   Drivers for franchising success

In this article we have explored franchising definitions, structures, modes of implementation, and challenges in order better to identify viable methodologies for microfranchising. In this section, we evaluate the literature on strategies that contribute to franchise success. From our review of the literature, we will proposed a model for microfranchising success. Specifically, in this section, the main drivers of successful franchisees are classified into external and internal approaches. Internal approaches refer to courses of action undertaken within the boundaries of the firm. External approaches refer to initiatives undertaken by the franchise in response to the changing characteristics of the external business environment.

8.2.4.1 Internal approaches

Goal compatibility among protagonists   Goal congruence is a significant factor in franchise operations along with commitment level (Baucus et al 1996; Spinelli and Birley, 1996).

Effective resource utilization   Effective utilization and leveraging of resources is essential. Barney (1991) classified key firm resources as 1) physical capital, 2) human capital, and 3) organizational capital. Strategic combination of resources possessed by the franchisor and franchisee adds value and strength to the franchise system and lead to success (Elango and Fried, 1997).

Strategic leveraging of scale   Operational size factors into franchising operations since economies of scale contribute to lowering monitoring costs for franchisees (Huszagh et al 1992).

Mutuality of goals and values   Mutual values, cooperation, trust, and ethical commonality contribute to a successful franchise relationship between principal and agent (Inma 2005; Juste and Redondo, 2004; Shaw et al 2000).

Attention to the brand   Maintaining brand equity facilitates expansion through cost benefits accrued to promotional economies of scale and operational cost reductions (Carney and Gedajlovic, 1991).

Effective communication channel   An effective platform for efficient communication is vital to franchising success (Hoffman and Preble, 2001).

Proper compensation   The amount of royalty also factors into franchise performance, success, and sustainability (Agrawal and Lal, 1995; Alon, 2001).

Viable foundation for support and assistance   Franchise operations tend to perform well when appropriate assistance and support are provided and when franchisees are involved in the decisionmaking process (Guiltinan et al 1980; Hunt and Nevin, 1974).

Commitment to training and development   Often, the lack of business experience on the part of the franchisees requires a significant investment in training from the franchisor (Swerdlow and Roehl, 1998).

Suitability of leadership and management style   The franchisor's leadership style, as well as the extent to which the franchisor relies financially on the franchisor factors into the long-term success of the relationship (Lewis and Lambert, 1991; Schul et al 1983).

Leveraging of competencies   Franchise systems need to optimize the use of competencies and reduce inclinations towards opportunism (Marks, 2004).

Viable control mechanisms   Control mechanisms are essential in the franchise system (Malhotra and Murnighan, 2002). In instituting control, franchisors have the option to utilize coercive or noncoercive measures in order to ensure cooperation and support and to heighten motivation (Rahatullah and Raeside, 2008). Coercive approaches typically refer to contract enforcement and financial leveraging, while noncoercive measures refer to support activities that help develop the business and strengthen franchise relationships (i.e. training, promotional support, etc.).

Appropriate legal frameworks   Sound legal contracts may also be used to ensure cooperation (Sobel, 2006).

Engagement of the franchisee   It is important to view the franchisees as contributors to the system, as they are directly in contact with customers (Elango and Fried, 1997). Franchise operations tend to perform well when franchisees are a part of the decisionmaking process (Guiltiran et al 1980).

Sharing of knowledge and information   Sharing of accumulated information and innovative pursuits can offer significant benefits to all parties involved in the franchise relationship (Gassenheimer et al 1996). There are many opportunities for learning under the franchise system (Fiol and Lyles, 1985).

8.2.4.2   *External approaches*

Proximity to market demand   A factor in franchise success is mobility or the ability to deliver specific products or services in close proximity to where an existing demand exists (Preble and Hoffman, 1998).

Dynamic networking   The ability to cooperate and involve a network of people is important in the franchise system (Baucus et al 1996; Shane and Hoy, 1996)

Awareness of changing market conditions   Sensitivity to changing market conditions is important. Markets tend to be volatile as a result of the interplay of factors such as technological changes, macroeconomic evolution, and demographic and sociocultural shifts, etc. (Hill et al 1990).

Need for adaptability   Franchise systems need to be adaptable to local conditions because numerous operational and market variations exist (Feltenstein, 1997; Hadjimarcous and Barnes, 1998).

The path toward franchising success requires a combination of approaches. In addition to the drivers outlined above, Spinelli (2007) summarized the key lessons associated with successful franchise implementation, which include 1) the greatest efficiencies are gained when parties deliver numerous skills and competencies; 2) a clear understanding of value propositions offered by participating parties leads to better performance; 3) developing a well conceived organizational structure enhances output; and 4) shared inputs on the business form, structure, and responsibilities can lead to business improvement. Kartarik (2009) also identifies behaviors that are key to franchising success which include 1) Sharing the global view, 2) encouraging franchises to share, 3) building expectations, 4) communicating effectively, 5) supporting needs, 6) partnering for testing, 7) considering multiconcept forms, and 8) ensuring adequate financing.

8.3   Microfranchising: an emerging phenomenon

The exploration of the franchise literature in this paper has been intended to help identify viable approaches in the practice of microfranchising. From the terminology, it can be inferred that microfranchising is essentially franchising on a far smaller scale. The reviewed literature suggests that the practice has a strong socially directed focus where creative organizational forms are used to unite a profit generation opportunity with a social agenda. Microfranchising may be defined as a socially oriented business systemization or replication with the objective of helping the poor to improve their economic state (Fairbourne, 2006).

Evidence suggests that there has been interest in the replication of socially directed enterprises via a franchising mode. Emerson (1999) alluded to the growth in social enterprises' business activities, while Tracey and Jarvis (2007) suggest that franchising can be a viable expansion strategy for social enterprises. Additionally, there has been a notable evolution of the more traditional philanthropic or government-subsidized organizations to successful profit-generating enterprises (Amin et al 2002).

While the field is growing, there is a paucity of academic literature that clearly defines microfranchising. Foremost on our agenda are two key questions. First, what aspects of the wealth of franchise literature are applicable to microfranchising? Second, based on the relevant franchise literature, can a business model be developed that would enhance the practice of microfranchising?

Existing microfranchising literature has started to define the practice. Salient characteristics of the business model are as follows.

Facilitates connectivity   Through microfranchising, even individuals and organizations with limited capital can participate in a diverse set of opportunities brought about by globalization. Microfranchising is a business approach that enables the poor to connect to the global economy by owning a business and progressing towards self-reliance and prosperity (Fairbourne, 2006).

Anchored on business efficiencies   Microfranchising provides a framework for improving business modes. It strengthens the value chain, cultivates mentoring, and leads to creative methodologies (Ivins, 2008).

Relationship-based   Similar to the case of franchising, the ability to manage the franchisor-franchisee relationship is a key factor for success. Microfranchising requires a mentoring relationship between franchisor and franchisee so that standards and systems are upheld (Fairbourne, 2006).

Offers personal and organizational merits   There are several ascribed benefits of microfranchising, among them the ability for poverty alleviation and the provision of financial independence and security to the participants (Fairbourne, 2006).

Positively impact the society   There are several ascribed benefits of microfranchising in broader society. It has the ability to contribute to the economic development of the individual and society by favorably impacting issues such as inadequate jobs, skill set limitations, and insufficiency of goods and services (Fairbourne, 2006).

Implementable and proven methodology   Microfranchising is a viable model to help emerging entrepreneurs implement a tested model and avoid common pitfalls of neophyte business people (Ivins, 2008).

Offers raised skills and developmental opportunities   Microfranchising facilitates developmental opportunities through training that opens the door to more efficient business delivery (Ivins, 2008).

Requires close financial partnerships   Microfranchising and microfinance go hand in hand and have a symbiotic relationship (Fairbourne, 2006).

Operate in a diversity of models   There are many models for microfranchising (Fairbourne, 2006). As with franchising, numerous creative forms of microfranchising are in existence.

Driven by economies of scale   Through microfranchising, efficiencies can be gained by economies of scale, and the model can lead to venture sustainability (Fairbourne, 2006).

Impacted by several external factors   Microenterprises are confronted by several limiting factors such as 1) poor credit access, 2) inefficient networks, 3) unproductive approaches, 4) unsuitable working conditions, 5) availability of marketing and supply support, 6) educational and training barriers, 7) infrastructure, 8) legal factors, and 9) other barriers such as bureaucracy and harassment (Becker, 2004; Henriques and Herr, 2007; ILC, 2002).

Opportunities in diverse sectors   Magelby (2006) offers a list of potential microfranchises that could spur economic development in developing nations: 1) accounting services, agricultural inputs, and apparel; 2) bakeries, barber shops, beauty parlors, bicycles, building materials, and butcher shops; 3) construction, cooking oil, cosmetics, and courier services; 4) electrical contracting, and equipment rental (wheelbarrows, bicycles, etc.); 5) financial services, food, fuel, and furniture; 6) hardware, housewares, and other specialty retail; 7) movie theaters; 8) plumbing contracting; 9) renewable energy and repair shops; and 10) transportation for commodities and for people.

Need support to thrive   Research suggests that microfranchises require effective internal and external support systems in order to thrive. For instance, training support (internal) as well as financial access (external) are needed (Fairbourne, 2006; Ivins, 2008). Other supporting factors that can add value include infrastructure, technology, networking opportunities, and business support services.

By exploring the characteristics of microfranchising, an understanding of the practice is achieved. We will now further examine field cases to shed light on the critical business methodologies.

8.3.1　Microfranchising landscape

There has been a diversity of microfranchising approaches in many parts of the world including Africa, Latin America, India, and Southeast Asia. For example, in Ghana, a company called Fan Milk sells milk products through a network of bicycle riding sales people (Ivins, 2008). In Kenya, a microfranchise endeavor successfully facilitated the distribution of inexpensive generic drugs to help address infectious diseases in the country. The HealthStore Foundation provides microfinancing services to healthcare workers to allow them to operate Child and Family Wellness Shops (CFW Shops) that distribute medicines and healthcare services to remote communities in the country (Flannery, 2007). In many African nations a project called KickStart lifted many farmers out of poverty by utilizing the principles of scalability. This business model was anchored on the principles of social impact, cost efficiency, sustainability, and replicability (Starr, 2008).

In El Salvador, a microfranchise sells and distributes eyewear through microfranchisees known as vision advisors. The Scojo Foundation trains entrepreneurs to perform vision screening and operate a business, and provides them with tools for successful marketing. Franchisees invest in a kit worth about U.S.$130 and can eventually earn around U.S.$80 a month. The foundation uses a consignment system to attract a larger base of franchisees (Fairbourne, 2006).

In India, a telecommunications provider implemented a microfranchising approach using a base station. The company typically appoints a 25–35 year old male who is the son of a village storeowner. The franchisee is then trained in sales and marketing and develops a network of resellers within a 5–7 km radius. The enterprise has gained business momentum by tapping into the strengths of local networks and utilizing microfinance to facilitate consumer purchases (Anderson, 2007).

In the Philippines, a company called Cellular City has a model where franchisees sell second-hand cell phones, prepaid call cards, and accessories to consumers (Fairbourne, 2006; Ivins, 2008). The startup cost is about U.S.$8000 and outlets are located in high foot-traffic areas. Several other microfranchise models have succeeded in the Philippines. For example, the Reyes family expanded to more than 200 barber shops, and a local bakery called Julie's has grown to over 300 outlets (Magelby, 2006).

8.3.2　Drivers for microfranchising success

Working with the diversity of operational styles, products, and geographic locations we will now examine the cases and related literature in order to determine commonalities and identify principles for success. From our case studies and the available literature, we have compiled a list of principles for success in the practice of microfranchising:

Keen market understanding and identification of opportunities Market diversity exists and the ability to understand the market and plan accordingly is critical. In the case of CFW Shops in Kenya, the market environment was characterized by 1) a lack of government regulations, 2) limited suppliers and resources, 3) a fragmented market with unfulfilled need (for instance, 80 percent of doctors live in urban locations while 70 percent of the population live in rural areas), 4) proliferation of unscrupulous business practices, and 5) lack of high quality and reliable supply (Flannery, 2007). This landscape provided the backdrop for the implementation of a microfranchise operation that was in demand at the right time. A significant amount of research and preparation can be helpful (Starr, 2008).

Scalability is a key consideration Microfranchises need the ability to gain a broad reach in order to capture advantages from economies of scale. In the KickStart project in Africa, scalability of the franchise model was given utmost attention and subsequently paid off (Starr, 2008). Other key considerations are simplicity and adaptability.

Standardization of procedures In the CFW case, implementation of standardized procedures was emphasized (Flannery, 2007). Microfranchising allows a specific format to be followed (Fairbourne, 2006).

Strategic planning Thinking through the appropriate strategy is essential. It starts with a comprehensive understanding of the organization's mission (Starr, 2008). In the case of the CFW shops in Kenya, the strategy was built around improving the quality and availability of healthcare. The company pursued a compartmentalized approach by establishing two divisions: drug stores and clinics. The centers were subsequently selected based on market demand and franchisee competencies (Flannery, 2007).

New models and innovation In their study on socially directed enterprises, Anderson and Kupp (2008) observed a common pattern in approaches relating to 1) value chain reconfiguration, 2) collaboration with nontraditional partners, and 3) building local capacity. The authors cited the case of India Reliance Infocomm which saw its sales escalate when it offered a mobile phone worth $120 to consumers for a U.S.$10 upfront fee and a 36-month fee of U.S.$4.

Resource utilization   The ability to optimize the use of resources can lead to optimal results. In the case of CFW Shops in Kenya, an abundant supply of nurses and healthcare workers means that they can screen then select the very best franchise applicants and have a large pool of potentially qualified franchisees (Flannery, 2007). In the case of Cellular City in the Philippines, after the owners noticed an abundant supply of potential franchisees they leveraged this resource to expand to other franchise lines such as bakeries and pharmacies (Fairbourne, 2006).

Well-positioned franchise fee   The size of the franchisee fee required needs to be high enough to allow careful screening and selection of franchise candidates, but it should be low enough to attract good candidates who might not have all the required capital. The CFW Shops in Kenya have a U.S.$300 franchise fee. This amount is significant in a country where per capita income is U.S.$360 a year. Because the franchise's operations can favorably impact a community, some franchisees get support from the local community (Flannery, 2007).

Financial support   HealthStore Foundation lends $800 to franchisees to cover startup costs and initial inventory (Flannery, 2007). Scojo, a company that provides eyewear through microfranchising in El Salvador, uses a consignment system to lower financial barriers to business entry (Fairbourne, 2006).

Franchisee training   Franchisees are generally required to participate in an intense month of training in order to learn business operations such as standards and procedures, merchandising, store layout, etc. (Fairbourne, 2006; Flannery, 2007). Training has also been used to seal gaps in operational or infrastructure deficiencies (Anderson and Kupp, 2008). In South Africa, Vodacom provides extensive training to thousands of franchisees who operate telecom kiosks (Magelby, 2006).

Emphasis on quality   The HealthStore Foundation often conducts unannounced inspections and quality checks to ensure standards and procedures are consistently followed. Franchisees who violate the rules can be subject to revocation of the right to operate (Flannery, 2007).

Market adaptation   Business adaptation can come in many forms. In the telecoms industry, creative alliances with nontraditional institutions helped franchises expand into new markets (Anderson and Kupp, 2008). HealthStore Foundation opted to use the franchise approach to allow community members to operate a business in an environment with which they are familiar (Flannery, 2007).

Location is critical   The selected location for the microfranchise factors into its future success (Flannery, 2007). In the case of Cellular City in the Philippines, the retail shops are situated in high foot-traffic areas where they are accessible to many potential customers. New sites are selected based on population density and size of the city (Fairbourne, 2006). In the telecoms sector, the small firms devised value-chain enhancements to allow them to reach out to target consumers (Anderson and Kupp, 2008).

With successful microfranchise operations, real value can be added to stakeholders such as multinational corporations, large domestic corporations, humanitarian NGOs, microfinance institutions, and domestic franchisors among others (Magelby, 2006). A sustainable presence of microfranchising operations in countries requires a concerted effort from various stakeholders. As several sectors stand to benefit, interorganizational cooperation involving the private and government institutions would be beneficial. In order to promote microfranchising success in countries, Henderson and Herr (2007) recommend 1) broadening awareness among policymakers; 2) the provision of knowledge and support to relevant private and public institutions; and 3) the establishment of strategic linkages with NGOs, franchise associations, and development agencies.

8.4 A framework for microfranchising

We have made several insights by reviewing the key concepts of the franchise literature and analyzing them alongside microfranchising cases and research. First, we see many similarities between the core characteristics of franchising and microfranchising. Second, there are also similarities between the principles for success associated with franchising and microfranchising. And third, through the assessment of these similarities a model for successful microfranchise implementation can be developed.

Based on the reviewed literature, we will now compare the characteristics of franchising and microfranchising to identify the similarities. As shown in Table 8.1, commonalities between franchising and microfranchising exist in the following areas: 1) they have the ability to operate in diverse forms and structures, 2) they need to add value and business efficiencies, 3) they are driven by effective skills utilization, 4) the relationship between franchisor and franchisee is important, 5) they are strengthened by networks and connectivity, 6) they are defined by internal and external forces, and 7) they require careful assessment of operational environment. It is possible that there are

Table 8.1 Commonalities between franchising and microfranchising characteristics

Franchising	Microfranchising	Commonality
Operate in diverse forms and structures	Operate in diversity of models	Yes
Need for value perception	Anchored on business efficiencies	Yes
Driven by leveraging of skills	Offers raised skills and developmental opportunities	Yes
Franchisor-franchisee relationship is important	Relationship based	Yes
Strengthened by business connectivity	Facilitates connectivity	Yes
Defined by internal and external forces	Positively impact society Offers personal and organizational merits	Yes
Assessment of operational environment is necessary	Impacted by external factors	Yes
Anchored on innovation	–	No comparison
Branding is key	–	No comparison
Suitable for specific industries	Opportunities in diverse sectors	No comparison
–	Implementable and proven methodology	No comparison
–	Requires close financial partnership	No comparison
–	Driven by economies of scale	No comparison
–	Need support to thrive	No comparison

additional compatibilities, but we have chosen to highlight only the clear and obvious parallelism. A description of "No Comparison" is used to suggest that while commonality may exist it is not evident from the reviewed literature.

Data shown in Table 8.2 suggest that the microfranchising success factors identified in the literature have also been identified as success factors for franchise operations. This includes factors such as 1) goal compatibility, 2) resource utilization, 3) leveraging of scale, 4) goal commonality and strategic planning, 5) attention to quality and brand, 6) proper compensation, 7) support and assistance, 8) commitment to

Table 8.2 Commonalities between franchising and microfranchising success factors

Franchising	Microfranchising	Commonality
Internal approaches		
Goal compatibility among protagonists	Standardization of procedures	Yes
Effective resource utilization	Resource utilization	Yes
Strategic leveraging of scale	Scalability is key consideration	Yes
Mutuality of goals and values	Strategic planning	Yes
Attention to brand	Emphasis on quality	Yes
Effective communication channel		
Proper compensation	Well-positioned franchise fee	Yes
Viable foundation for support and assistance	Financial support	Yes
Commitment to training and development	Franchise training	Yes
Sustainability of leadership and management style	–	No comparison
Leveraging of competencies	–	No comparison
Viable control mechanisms	–	No comparison
Appropriate legal framework	–	No comparison
Sharing of knowledge and information	New models and innovation	Yes
External approaches		
Proximity to market demand	Location is critical	Yes
Dynamic networking	–	No comparison
Awareness of changing market conditions	Keen market understanding and opportunity identification	Yes
Need for adaptability	Market adaptation	Yes

training, 9) use of knowledge and innovation, 10) location efficiencies, 11) market understanding, and 12) market adaptation. A few success factors associated with franchising were incomparable to microfranchising and were noted as having "No Comparison."

With this high level of similarity, it is likely that identified franchising challenges such as 1) unpreparedness of the management team, 2) lack of preparation, 3) lack of safeguard against opportunism, 4) inability to homogenize, and 5) the existence of moral hazards would likely be also applicable to microfranchises. In the same manner, some of the factors relating to franchise internationalization may also be applicable to micro-franchises.

From Tables 8.1 and 8.2, it can be inferred that the practice of franchising is in fact very similar to microfranchising and that the abundant research on franchising can likely be utilized to develop viable models relevant to the practice of microfranchising.

Based on the list of success factors for microfranchises, we now offer a viable model for successful implementation. In the process of implementation, prioritization needs to be considered. Therefore, we further classify the microfranchise success factors based on priority (Table 8.3).

Priority 1 refers to measures that relate to activities pertaining to organizational and market understanding (i.e. goal compatibility assessment, market research and understanding, and strategic planning). Priority 2 refers to activities relating to business planning and management (i.e. location efficiencies, resource utilization, leveraging of scale, attention to quality and brand, and proper compensation). Priority 3 refers to activities relating to maintenance and control (i.e. provision of support and assistance and commitment to training). Priority 4 refers to activities pertaining to growth, development, and enhancement (i.e. market adaptation, use of knowledge, and innovation. To illustrate, Figure 8.1 shows the proposed model for microfranchise implementation (MMI).

The MMI takes into account the success factors relating to microfranchises and frames them according to priority and action timeline. We have added a final factor titled "review and reinvention" to highlight the

Table 8.3   Microfranchise success factors (based on priority)

Priority 1 organizational and market understanding	Priority 2 business planning and management	Priority 3 maintenance and control	Priority 4 growth and development
Goal compatibility assessment	Location efficiencies	Provision of support and assistance	Market adaptation
Market research and understanding	Resource utilization	Commitment to training	Use of knowledge and innovation
Identification of goal commonality and strategic planning	Leveraging of scale		
	Attention to quality and brand		
	Proper compensation		

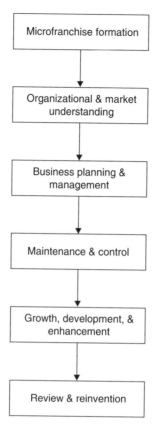

Figure 8.1   Model for microfranchise implementation (MMI)

fact that microfranchise models need to undergo changes in response to shifts in market conditions.

We believe the compiled literature and the presented MMI model further our understanding of microenterprises and their effective management. We are aware of the need for caution about generalization of the findings when based solely on academic literature and case studies. In the future, specific surveys in diverse industries and settings can test the theories and expand on our understanding of the subject. Additionally, further exploration on the similarities and differences between the franchising and microfranchising models would be of great value given the rapid proliferation of franchising concepts in both public and private spheres.

8.4.1 Implications for microfranchise practitioners

This study suggests that there are several commonalities between the practices of franchising and microfranchising. It would therefore be worthwhile for microfranchise owners and practitioners to review franchising literature in order to identify potentially viable strategies and approaches.

In the study, some of the characteristics and success factors of franchising vs. microfranchising were described as having "No Comparison." These areas of noncomparability potentially indicate knowledge gaps in the existing literature. It would be interesting to see additional research on the subject in both the academic and field settings. Microfranchise practitioners need to share their findings and experiences so that a broader body of literature on the topic may be available. Much can be learned when microfranchising experiences and lessons are shared globally.

While the term "micro" tends to suggest something small, the successful implementation and replication of a microenterprise highlights the need to understand the "macro" forces with which the enterprise interacts. We believe that although the microfranchise phenomenon has just started, it will likely expand through more creative organizational forms across many more countries in the years to come.

References

Agrawal, Deepak, and Rajiv Lai (1995). "Contractual Arrangements in Franchising: An Empirical Investigation," *Journal of Marketing Research* 32 (2), 213–19.

Alon, Ilan (2001). "The Use of Franchising by Us Based Retailers," *Journal of Small Business Management* 39 (2, April), 111–22

Alon, Ilan (2004). "Global Franchising and Development in Emerging and Transitioning Markets," Journal of Macromarketing 24 (2), 156–167.

Alon, Ilan (2006). "Market Conditions Favoring Master International Franchising," *Multinational Business Review* 14 (2, Fall), 67–82.

Alon, I., and D. McKee (1999). "Towards a Macroenvironmental Model of International Franchising," *Multinational Business Review* 7 (1), 76–82.

Amies, M. (1999). "The Wilder Shores of Franchising," *Franchising World* 31 (1), 27–28.

Amin, A., R. Hudson, and A. Cameron (2002). *Placing the Social Economy.* London: Routledge.

Andaleeb, Syed, S. (1996). "An Experimental Investigation of Satisfaction and Commitment in Marketing Channels: The Role of Trust and Dependence," *Journal of Retailing* 72, 77–93.

Anderson, Jamie (2007). "Developing a Route to Market Strategy for Mobile Communications in Rural India," *International Journal of Emerging Markets* 3 (2).

Anderson, Jamie, and Martin Kupp (2008). "Serving the Poor: Drivers of Business Model Innovation in Mobile," *Info* 10 (1), 5–12.

Aydin, N., and M. Kacker (1989). "International Outlook of U.S.-Based Franchisors," *International Marketing Review* 7 (2), 43–53. http://www.emeraldinsight.com/Insight/viewContentItem.do?contentType=Article&contentId=855182

Aydin, N., and M. Kacker (1990). "International Outlook of Us-Based Franchisers," *International Marketing Review* 7 (2), 43–53.

Baucus, David A, Melissa S. Baucus, and Sherrie E. Human (1996). "Consensus in Franchise Organizations: A Cooperative Arrangement Among Entrepreneurs," *Journal of Business Venturing* 11, 359–78.

Barney, J. (1991). "Firms' Resources and Sustained Competitive Advantage," *Journal of Management* 17 (1), 99–120.

Becker, Kristina Flodman (2004). *The Informal Economy – Fact Finding Study.* Stockholm: Swedish International Development Cooperation Agency (SIDA).

Bordonaba-Juste, Maria Victoria, and Yolanda Polo-Redondo (2004). "Relationships in franchised distribution systems: the case of the Spanish market," *International Review of Retail, Distribution, and Consumer Research* 14 (1, January), 101–27.

Brickley, James A and Frederick H. Dark (1987). "The Choice of Organisational Form: The Case of Franchising," *Journal of Financial Economics* 18, 401–20.

Carney, Mick, and Eric Gedajlovic (1991). "Vertical Integration in Franchise Systems: Agency Theory and Resource Explanations," *Strategic Management Journal* 12, 607–29.

Combs J.G., and G. Castrogiovanni (1994). "Franchisor strategy: A proposed model and empirical test of franchise versus company ownership," *Journal of Small Business Management* 32 (2), 37–48

Cross, J.C., and B.J. Walker (1987). "Service Marketing and Franchising: a Practical Business Marriage," *Business Horizons* 30 (6), 50–58.

Day, G.S., and R. Wensley (1988). "Assessing Advantage: a Framework for Diagnosing Competitive Superiority," *Journal of Marketing* 52 (2), 1–20.

Doherty. A.M., and N. Alexander (2004). "Relationship Development in International Retail Franchising – Case Study Evidence from the U.K. Fashion Sector," *European Journal of Marketing* 38 (9/10), 1215–35.

Dyl, E. (1991). "Financial Issues in Franchising," in R. Yazidipour, Ed., *Advances in Small Business Finance.* Dordrecht: Kluwer Academic Publishers, 93–108.

Elango, B. (2007). "Are Franchisors with International Operations Different from Those Who Are Domestic Market Oriented?" *Journal of Small Business Management* 45 (2, April), 179–93.

Elango, B., and V. Fried (1997). "Franchising Research: a Literature Review and Synthesis," *Journal of Small Business Management* 35 (3), 68–81.

Emerson, J. (1999). "Five Challenges in Social Purpose Enterprise Development" working paper. San Francisco: Roberts Enterprise Development Fund. Available at http://www.redf.org/download/boxset/REDF_vol2_11.pdf

Eroglu, S. (1992). "The Internationalization Process of Franchise Systems: a Conceptual Model," *International Marketing Review* 9 (5), 19–30.

Erramilli, K.M. (1990). "Entry Mode Choice in Service Industries," *International Marketing Review* 7, 50–62.

Falbe, C.M., and T.C. Dandridge (1992). "Franchising as a Strategic Partnership: Issues of Cooperation and Conflict in a Global Market," *International Small Business Journal* 10, 40–52.

Fairbourne, Jason S. (2006). "Microfranchising: a new tool for creating economic self-reliance," *ESR Review* 8 (1, Summer), 18–23.

Feltenstein, T. (1997). "Think Global, and Act Local," *Franchising World* 29 (5), 30–31.

Fiol, C.L., and M.A. Lyles (1985). "Organizational Learning," *Academy of Management Review* 10 (4), 803–13.

Flannery, Jessica (2007). "Microfranchise against Malaria," *Stanford Social Innovation Review* 5 (4, Fall), 69–70.

Frazer, L. (2001). "Causes of Disruption to Franchise Operations," *Journal of Business Research* 54 (3), 227–34.

Gassenheimer, J., D. Baucus, and M. Baucus (1996). "Cooperative Arrangements among Entrepreneurs: an Analysis of Opportunism and Communication in Franchise Structures," *Journal of Business Research* 36 (1), 67–79.

Grunhagen, Marko, and Michael Dorsch (2003). "Does the Franchisor Provide Value to Franchisees? past, Current, and Future Value Assessments of Two Franchise Types," *Journal of Small Business Management* 41 (4, October), 366–84.

Guiltinan, J.R, I.B. Rejab, and W.C. Rodgers (1980). "Factors Influencing Coordination in a Franchise Channel," *Journal of Retailing* 56 (3), 41–58.

Hadjimarcou, J., and J.W. Barnes (1998). "Case Study: Strategic Alliances in International Franchising – the Entry of Silver Streak Restaurant Corporation into Mexico," *Journal of Consumer Marketing* 15 (6), 598–607.

Henriques, Michael, and Robert E Nelson (1997). "Using Franchises to Promote Small Enterprise Development," in Malcolm Harper (Pub.), *Small Enterprise Development* (March edition). Bhubaneswar (India).

Henriques, Michael, and Mathias Herr (2007). "The Informal Economy and Microfranchising,"in J. Fairbourne, ed. *Microfranchising theory*. http://www.amazon.com/MicroFranchisingCreating-Wealth-Bottom-Pyramid/dp/1847201083/ref=sr_1_1?ie=UTF8&s=books&qid=1260648792&sr=8-1

Hill, C.W.G., H. Peter, and W.C. Kim (1990). "An eclectic theory of the – choice of international entry mode" *CD Strategic Management Journal* 11, 117–28.

Hoffman, Richard, and John Preble (2001). "Global Diffusion of Franchising: a Country Level Examination," *Multinational Business Review* 9 (1, Spring), 66–76.

Hoffman, Richard, and John Preble (2003). "Convert to Compete: Competitive Advantage through Conversion Franchising," *Journal of Small Business Management* 41 (2, April), 187–204.

Hunt, S.D., and J.R. Nevin (1974). "Power in a Channel of Distribution: Sources and Consequences," *Journal of Marketing Research* (11), 186–93.

Hutchinson, Patrick (1999). "Small Enterprise: Finance, Ownership, and Control" *International Journal of Management Reviews* 1 (3, September), 343–65.

Huszagh, S.M., F.W. Huszagh, and F.S. Mcintire (1992). "International Franchising in the Context of Competitive Strategy and the Theory of the Firm," *International Marketing Review* 9 (5), 5–18.

ILC (2002). "Decent Work and the Informal Economy," *Report VI*. Geneva: International Labor Conference, 90th Session.

ILO (2002). *Women and Men in the Informal Economy – a Statistical Picture*. Geneva: International Labor Office, Employment Sector.

Inma, Chutarat (2005). "Purposeful Franchising: Rethinking of the Franchising Rationale," *Singapore Management Review* 27 (1), 27–48.

Ivins, Tiffany Z. (2008). "Microfranchising Microlearning Centers: a Sustainable Model for Expanding the Right to Education in Developing Countries?" *Journal of Asynchronous Learning Networks* 12 (1), 1–8.

John, B.L., W.C. Dunlop, and W.J. Sheehan (1989). *Small Business in Australia*, 3rd ed. Sydney: George Allen and Unwin.

Justis, R., and R. Judd (1986). "Master Franchising: a New Look," *Journal of Small Business Management* 24, 16–21.

Kartarik, Mark (2009). "Nurturing Multi-Unit Operators to Success," *Franchising World* (April), 13–14.

Kaufmann, P.J., and R.P. Dant, (1996). "Multi-Unit Franchising: Growth and Management Issues," *Journal of Business Venturing* 11 (5), 343–58.

Kaufmann, P.J. and S. Eroglu (1999). "Standardization and Adaptation in Business Format Franchising," *Journal of Business Venturing* 14 (1), 69–85.

Kaufmann, P.J., and S.H. Kim (1995). "Master Franchising and System Growth Rates," *Journal of Marketing Channels* 4 (1/2), 49–64.

Kedia, B.L., D.J. Ackerman, and R.T. Justis (1995). "Changing Barriers to the Internationalization of Franchising Operations: Perceptions of Domestic and International Franchisors'" *International Executive* 37 (4), 329–48.

Kostecka, Andrew (1988). *Franchising in the Economy*. Washington, D.C: U.S. Department of Commerce.

Lafontaine, F. (1992). "Agency Theory and Franchising: Some Empirical Results," *Rand Journal of Economics* 23 (2), 263–83.

Lewis, M.C., and D.M. Lambert (1991). "A Model of Channel Member Performance, Dependence, and Satisfaction," *Journal of Retailing* 67 (2), 205–25.

Magleby, Kirk (2006). *Microfranchises as a Solution to Global Poverty*. Viewable at: http://ascendalliance.org/file.php?id=338. [Accessed May 21, 2009].

Malhotra. D., and J.K. Mumighan (2002). "The Effects of Contracts on Interpersonal Trust," *Administrative Science Quarterly* 47.

Marks. R. (2004). "How to Identify Foreign Markets for Export," *Franchising World* 36 (9), 64–65.

Parsa, H.G. (1996). "Franchisor-Franchisee Relationships in Quick-Service-Restaurant Systems," *Cornell Hotel and Restaurant Administration Quarterly* 37 (3), 42–49.

Preble, J.F., and R.C. Hoffman (1995). "Franchising Systems around the Globe: a Status Report," *Journal of Small Business Management* 33 (2), 80–88.

Preble, J.F., and R.C. Hoffman (1998). "Competitive Advantage through Specialty Franchising," *Journal of Consumer Marketing* 15 (1), 64–77.

Price, L.L., and E.J. Arnould (1999). "Commercial Friendships: Service Provider–Client Relationships in Context," *Journal of Marketing* 63 (October), 38–56.

Rahatullah, M.K., and Robert Raeside (2008). "Toward Operational Excellence in Franchising: Achieving Synergy, Adding Value, and Security Competitive Advantage by Exploiting Entrepreneurial Traits and Core Competencies," *Sam Advanced Management Journal* 73 (3), 25–38.

Rawlins, W.K. (1992). *Friendship Matters*. Hawthorne, NY: Aldine de Gruyter.

Schul, R.L., T.E. Little, and W.M. Pride (1983). "The Impact of Consumer Leadership Behavior on Interchannel Conflict," *Journal of Marketing* 47 (3), 21–34.

Shane, S. (1996). "Why Franchise Companies Expand Overseas," *Journal of Business Venturing* 11 (2), 73–88.

Shane, S.A., and F. Hoy (1996). "Franchising: a gateway to cooperative entrepreneurship," *Journal of Business Venturing* 11 (5), 325–27.

Shaw, Jason D., Nina Gupta, and John E. Delery (2000). "Empirical Organisational-level Examinations of Agency and Collaborative Predictions of Performance-contingent Compensation," *Strategic Management Journal* 21 (5), 611.

Shivell, K., and K. Banning (1996). "What Every Prospective Franchisee Should Know," *Small Business Forum* 14, 33–42.

Sobel. J. (2006). "For Better or Forever: Formal Versus Informal Enforcement," *Journal of Labour Economics* 24, 21197.

Spinelli, Stephen (2007). "Franchises without Borders," *Business Strategy Review* 18 (1, Spring), 50–52.

Spinelli, S., and S. Birley (1996). "Toward a theory of conflict in the franchise system," *Journal of Business Venturing* 11 (5), 329–42.

Stanworth, John, and Patrick Kaufmann "1996). "Similarities and Differences in UK and US Franchise Research Data: Towards a Dynamic Model of Franchisee Motivation," *International Small Business Journal* 14, 57–70.

Starr, Kevin (2008). "Go Big or Go Home," *Stanford Social Innovation Review* 6 (4, Fall), 29–30.

Swartz, L.N. (1994). "International Franchising: an Alternative for Cross-Border Expansion," *International Insights: An Arthur Andersen Report* (September), 31–32.

Swerdlow, S., and W. Roehl (1998). "Direct and Indirect Effects of Training and Organizational Commitment among Hospitality Employees: Implications for Lodging Franchisors," in F. Lafontaine, Ed., *Proceedings of the Society of Franchising.* Las Vegas: NV: Institute of Franchise Management.

Tracey, Paul, and Owen Jarvis (2007). "Toward a Theory of Social Venture Franchising," *Entrepreneurship: Theory and Practice* 31 (5), 667–85.

Thompson, R.S. (1992). "Company Ownership versus Franchising: Issues and Evidence." *Journal of Economic Studies* 19 (4), 31–42.

Welsh, Dianne, Ilan Alon, and Cecilia Falbe (2006). "An Examination of International Retail Franchising in Emerging Markets," *Journal of Small Business Management* 44 (1, January), 130–49.

Whitehead, M. (1991). "International Franchising – Marks and Spencer: A Case Study," *International Journal of Retail and Distribution Management* 19 (2), 10–12.

Williamson, G. (1992). *Franchising in Australia: The Practical Guide to All the Promises and Pitfalls.* Australia: Allen & Unwin Pty Ltd.

Yavas, B.F., and D. Vardiabasis (1987). "The Determinants of U.S. International Fast Food Franchising: an Application to the Pacific Basis," in J.M. Hawes and G.B. Glisan, Eds., *Developments in Marketing Science* 10: 161–64.

Part III
International Franchising Cases

9
Ruth's Chris Franchises Expand Internationally

Ilan Alon and Allen Kupetz

> Well, I was so lucky that I fell into something that I really, really love.
> And I think that if you ever go into business, you better find something
> you really love, because you spend so many hours with it...
> it almost becomes your life.

Ruth Fertel, 1927–2002
Founder of Ruth's Chris Steak House

9.1 Introduction

In 2006, Ruth's Chris Steak House was fresh off a sizzling initial public offering (IPO). Dan Hannah, Vice President for Business Development since June 2004, was responsible for development of a new business strategy focused on continued growth of franchise- and company-operated restaurants. He also oversaw franchisee relations. Now a public company, Ruth's Chris had to meet Wall Street's expectations for revenue growth. Current restaurants were seeing consistent incremental revenue growth, but new ones were critical and Dan knew that the international opportunities offered a tremendous upside.

With restaurants in just five countries including the U.S., the challenge for Dan was to decide where to go to next. Ruth's Chris regularly received inquiries from would-be franchisees all over the world, but strict criteria – liquid net worth of at least US$1 million, verifiable experience within the hospitality industry, and an ability and desire to develop multiple locations – eliminated many of the prospects. And the cost of a franchise – a US$100,000 per restaurant franchise fee, a 5 percent of gross sales royalty fee, and a 2 percent of gross sales advertising fee – further eliminated some qualifiying prospects. All this was coupled with some debate within Ruth's Chris senior management team about the need and desire to grow its international business. So where was Dan to look for new international franchisees and what countries would be best suited for the fine dining that made Ruth's Chris famous?

9.2   The house that Ruth built

Ruth Fertel, the founder of Ruth's Chris, was born in New Orleans in 1927. She skipped several grades in grammar school, and later entered Louisiana State University in Baton Rouge at the age of 15 to pursue degrees in chemistry and physics. After graduation, Ruth landed a job teaching at McNeese State University. The majority of her students were football players who not only towered over her, but were actually older than she was. Ruth taught for two semesters. In 1948, Ruth married Rodney Fertel, who lived in Baton Rouge and shared her love of horses. They had two sons, Jerry and Randy and opened a racing stable in Baton Rouge. Ruth earned a Thoroughbred trainer's license, making her the first female horse trainer in Louisiana. Ruth and Rodney divorced in 1958.[1]

In 1965, Ruth spotted an ad in the *New Orleans Times-Picayune* for a steak house for sale. She mortgaged her home for US$22,000 to purchase Chris Steak House, a 60-seat restaurant on the corner of Broad and Ursuline in New Orleans, near the Fairgrounds racetrack. That September, just a few months later, the city of New Orleans was ravaged by Hurricane Betsy. The restaurant was left without electricity, so she cooked everything that was in the cooler and brought it to her brother in devastated Plaquemines Parish to aid in the relief effort.[2]

In 1976, the thriving restaurant was destroyed in a kitchen fire. Fertel bought a new property a few blocks away on Broad Street and soon opened under a new name, "Ruth's Chris Steak House," since her original contract with former owner Chris Matulich precluded her from using the name Chris Steak House in a different location. That same year, after years of failed attempts, Tom Moran, a regular customer and business owner from Baton Rouge, convinced a hesitant Fertel to let him open the first Ruth's Chris franchise. It opened on Airline Highway in Baton Rouge. Fertel reluctantly began awarding more and more franchises. In the 1980s, the little corner steak house grew into a global phenomenon with restaurants opening every year in cities around the nation and the world. Fertel became something of an icon herself and was dubbed by her peers *The First Lady of American Restaurants*.[3]

Ruth's Chris grew to the largest fine dining steak house in the U.S. (see Figure 9.1) with an unwavering focus on commitment to customer satisfaction and a broad selection of USDA Prime grade steaks. (USDA Prime is a meat grade label, which refers to evenly distributed marbling that enhances the flavor of the steak – see Figure 9.2). The menu also included premium quality lamb chops, veal chops, fish, chicken, and lobster. Steak and seafood combinations and a vegetable platter were also available at selected restaurants. Dinner entrées were generally priced between US$18 and US$38. Three company-owned restaurants were open for lunch and offered entrées generally ranging in price from US$11 to US$24. Ruth's Chris's core menu was similar at all of its restaurants. The company occasionally introduced new items such as specials that allowed it to give its guests additional choices, such as items inspired by Ruth's Chris New Orleans heritage.[4]

In 2005, Ruth's Chris enjoyed a significant milestone, completing a successful IPO that raised more than US$154 million in new equity capital. In its 2005 Annual Report, the company said it had plans "to embark on an accelerated development plan and expand our footprint through both company-owned and franchised locations." Its 2005 restaurant sales grew to a record US$415.8 million from 82 locations in the U.S. and ten internationally: Canada (1995, 2003), Hong Kong (1997, 2001), Mexico (1993, 1996, 2001), and Taiwan (1993, 1996, 2001). As of December 2005, 41 of the 92 Ruth's Chris restaurants were company-owned and 51 were franchisee-owned, including all ten of the international restaurants (see Figure 9.3 and Table 9.1).[5]

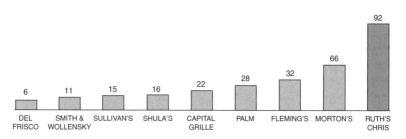

Figure 9.1   Fine dining steak houses by brand in the United States (2005)

Filet

T-bone

New York Strip

Ribeye

Porterhouse

Figure 9.2   USDA Prime Cuts of Beef

Ruth's Chris 51 franchisee-owned restaurants are owned by just 17 franchisees, with five new franchisees having the rights to develop new restaurants, and with the three largest franchisees owning eight, six, and five restaurants respectively. Prior to 2004, each franchisee entered into a ten-year franchise agreement with three ten-year renewal options for each restaurant. Each agreement grants the franchisee territorial protection, with the option to develop a certain number of restaurants in their territory. Ruth's Chris franchisee agreements generally include termination clauses in the event of nonperformance by the franchisee.[6]

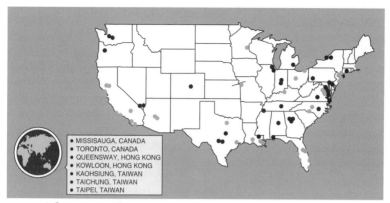

● MISSISAUGA, CANADA
● TORONTO, CANADA
● QUEENSWAY, HONG KONG
● KOWLOON, HONG KONG
● KAOHSIUNG, TAIWAN
● TAICHUNG, TAIWAN
● TAIPEI, TAIWAN

○ Company-owned
● Franchisee-owned

Figure 9.3   Ruth's Chris locations in the United States (2005)

Table 9.1   Ruth's Chris restaurant growth by decade

Decade	New restaurants (total)	New restaurants (company-owned)	New restaurants (franchises)
1965–69	1	1	0
1970–79	4	2	2
1980–89	19	8	11
1990–99	44	19	25
2000–2005	25	12	13
	93*	42	51

Note: *Due to damage caused by Hurricane Katrina, Ruth's Chris was forced to temporarily close its restaurant in New Orleans, Louisiana.

9.3   A world of opportunities

As part of the international market selection process, Dan considered four standard models (see Figure 9.4):

- Product development – new kinds of restaurants in existing markets.
- Diversification – new kinds of restaurants in new markets.
- Penetration – more of the same restaurants in the same market.
- Market development – more of the same restaurants in new markets.

The product development model (new kinds of restaurants in existing markets) was never seriously considered by Ruth's Chris. It had built a

Restaurant brands

		Existing	New
Market	Existing	**Penetration** (more restaurants) *Same market, same product*	**Product development** (new brands) *Same market, new product*
	New	**Market development** (new markets) *New market, same product*	**Diversification** (new brands for new market) *New product, new market*

Figure 9.4   Restaurant Growth Paths[7]

brand based on fine dining steak houses and with only 92 stores, the company saw little need and no value in diversifying with new kinds of restaurants.

The diversification model (new kinds of restaurants in new markets) was also never considered by Ruth's Chris. Although in only four international markets, Dan knew that the current fine dining steak house model would work in new markets without the risk of brand dilution or brand confusion.

The penetration model (more of the same restaurants in the same market) was already underway in a small way with new restaurants opening up in Canada. The limiting factor was simply that fine dining establishments would never be as ubiquitous as quick service restaurants (i.e. "fast food") like McDonald's. Even the largest cities in the world would be unlikely to host more than five or six Ruth's Chris steak houses.

The market development model (more of the same restaurants in new markets) appeared the most obvious path to increased revenue. Franchisees in the four international markets – Canada, Hong Kong, Mexico, and Taiwan – were profitable and could offer testimony to would-be franchisees of the value of a Ruth's Chris franchise.

With the management team agreed on a model, the challenge shifted to market selection criteria. The key success factors were well-defined:[8]

Beefeaters   Ruth's Chris is a steak house (although there are several fish items on the menu) and thus its primary customers are people who enjoy beef. According to the World Resources Institute, in 2002 there were 17 countries above the per capita mean of annual beef consumption for high-income countries (93.5 kg – see Table 9.2).[9]

Legal to import US beef The current Ruth's Chris model is to use only USDA Prime beef, thus it must be exportable to the target country. In some cases, Australian beef might be able to meet the same high U.S. standard.

Population/high urbanization rates With the target customer being a well-to-do beefeater, restaurants need to be in densely populated areas to have a large enough pool. Most large metropolises probably meet this requirement.

High disposable income Ruth's Chris is a fine dining experience and the average meal check for a customer ordering an entrée is over US$70 at a Ruth's Chris in the U.S. While this might seem to eliminate many countries quickly, there are countries (e.g. China) that have such large populations that even a very small percentage of the population with a high disposable income could create an appropriate pool of potential customers.

Do people go out to eat? This is a critical factor. If well-to-do beefeaters do not go out to eat, these countries must be removed from the target list.

Affinity for U.S. brands The name "Ruth's Chris" is uniquely American, as is the Ruth Fertel story. Countries that are overtly anti-U.S.

Table 9.2 Meat consumption per capita (in kilograms)[10]

Region/classification	2002	2001	2000	1999	1998	Growth rate (%) 1998–2002
World	39.7	38.8	38.6	38.0	37.7	5.31
Asia (excluding Middle East)	27.8	26.9	26.6	25.7	25.4	9.45
Central America/Caribbean	46.9	45.7	44.8	42.9	41.3	13.56
Europe	74.3	72.5	70.5	70.6	73.1	1.64
Middle East/North Africa	25.7	25.7	26.0	25.1	24.7	4.05
North America	123.2	119.1	120.5	122.2	118.3	4.14
South America	69.7	68.4	69.1	67.6	64.2	8.57
Sub-Saharan Africa	13.0	12.9	13.1	12.8	12.6	3.17
Developed countries	80.0	78.0	77.2	77.3	77.6	3.09
Developing countries	28.9	28.1	28.0	27.1	26.6	8.65
High-income countries	93.5	91.9	92.0	92.2	90.9	2.86
Low-income countries	8.8	8.6	8.4	8.3	8.2	7.32
Middle-income countries	46.1	44.6	43.9	42.7	42.3	8.98

should be eliminated from – or at least pushed down – the target list. One measure of affinity could be the presence of existing U.S. restaurants and successful franchises.

9.4   What should Ruth's Chris do next?

Dan had many years of experience in the restaurant franchising business and thus had both personal preferences and good instincts about where Ruth's Chris should be looking for new markets. "Which markets should we enter first," he thought to himself? Market entry was critical, but there were other issues too. Should franchising continue to be Ruth's Chris exclusive international mode of entry? Were there opportunities for joint ventures or company-owned stores in certain markets? How could he identify and evaluate new potential franchisees? Was there an opportunity to find a global partner/brand with which to partner?

Dan gathered information from several reliable U.S. government and related websites and set them out as in Table 9.3. He noted that many of

Table 9.3   Country data

Country	Per capita beef consumption (kg)	Population (1000s)	Urbanization rate (%)	Per capita GDP (PPP in US$)
Argentina	97.6	39,921	90	13,100
Bahamas	123.6	303	89	20,200
Belgium	86.1	10,379	97	31,400
Brazil	82.4	188,078	83	8400
Chile	66.4	16,134	87	11,300
China	52.4	1,313,973	0	6800
Costa Rica	40.4	4075	61	11,100
Czech Rep	77.3	10,235	74	19,500
France	101.1	60,876	76	29,900
Germany	82.1	82,422	88	30,400
Greece	78.7	10,688	61	22,200
Hungary	100.7	9981	65	16,300
Ireland	106.3	4062	60	41,000
Israel	97.1	6352	92	24,600
Italy	90.4	58,133	67	29,200
Japan	43.9	127,463	65	31,500
Kuwait	60.2	2418	96	19,200
Malaysia	50.9	24,385	64	12,100
Netherlands	89.3	16,491	66	30,500
Panama	54.5	3191	57	7200
Poland	78.1	38,536	62	13,300

Continued

Table 9.3 Continued

Country	Per capita beef consumption (kg)	Population (1000s)	Urbanization rate (%)	Per capita GDP (PPP in US$)
Portugal	91.1	10,605	55	19,300
Russia	51	142,893	73	11,100
Singapore	71.1	4492	100	28,100
South Africa	39	44,187	57	12,000
South Korea	48	48,846	80	20,400
Spain	118.6	40,397	77	25,500
Switzerland	72.9	7523	68	32,300
Turkey	19.3	70,413	66	8200
UAE/Dubai	74.4	2602	85	43,400
UK	79.6	60,609	89	30,300
U.S.	124.8	298,444	80	41,800
Vietnam	28.6	84,402	26	2800

his top prospects currently did not allow the importation of U.S. beef, but felt that was a political (rather than a cultural) variable and thus could change quickly under the right circumstances and with what he felt was the trend toward ever more free trade. He couldn't find any data on how often people went out to eat or a measure of their affinity toward a U.S. brands. Maybe the success of U.S. casual dining restaurants there might be good indicator for how people in a country felt toward U.S. restaurants? With his spreadsheet open, he went to work on the numbers and began contemplating the future global expansion of the company.

"If you've ever had a filet this good, welcome back."

Ruth Fertel, 1927–2002
Founder of Ruth's Chris Steak House

Notes

1. Answers.com, "Ruth Fertel." Retrieved on June 8, 2006 from http://www.answers.com/topic/ruth-fertel
2. Ibid and Ruth's Chris Steak House 2005 Annual Report, 4.
3. Answers.com, "Ruth Fertel." Retrieved on June 8, 2006 from http://www.answers.com/topic/ruth-fertel
4. Ruth's Chris Steak House 2005 Annual Report, 7.
5. The focus of this case is on market entry rather than franchising, but there are several excellent sources for additional information on franchising as a mode of entry including Ilan Alon (2005), *Service Franchising: A Global Perspective*. New York: Springer.
6. Ruth's Chris Steak House 2005 Annual Report, 10.

7. This diagram is based on Ansoff's Product/Market Matrix, first published in "Strategies for Diversification" (*Harvard Business Review*, 1957).

8. A useful related article is: Ilan Alon (2006), "Evaluating the Market Size for Service Franchising in Emerging Markets," *International Journal of Emerging Markets*, 9–20.

9. World Resources Institute, "Meat Consumption: Per Capita (1984–2002)." Retrieved on June 7, 2006 from http://earthtrends.wri.org/text/agriculture-food/variable-193.html

10. World Resources Institute, "Meat Consumption: Per Capita (1984–2002)." Retrieved on June 7, 2006 from http://earthtrends.wri.org/text/agriculture-food/variable-193.html

10
International Franchising at Best Western

Ilan Alon, Gérard Cliquet, Matthew C. Mitchell, and Rozenn Perrigot

10.1 Introduction

Internationalization remains an important task for network operators in the hotel sector. They must try to adapt their chain to the country they want to penetrate, but this is not always easy. To internationalize their operations the majority of firms choose a franchising system. However, Best Western (BW) has successfully developed and implemented the use of a wholly unique system of internationalization by using affiliated networks. This organizational structure allows for rapid international expansion while retaining the ability to tailor what they are offering to local environments. The purpose of this paper is twofold. In the first section, we review the international tourism and hotel sectors. Then, in the following section, we analyze the internationalization strategy and processes of Best Western. Its organization is neither franchised nor company owned, but rather an affiliation network, which is worth studying in the context of internationalization. Finally, the limitations of this paper and tracks for future research are summarized in the Conclusion.

10.2 International tourism and the hotel sector

In this section, the international tourism and the hotel sector are reviewed to reveal the organizing principals of this US$ 1.1 trillion industry (World Travel and Tourism Council, 2009).

10.2.1 International tourism

The economic concept of tourism includes personal travel (for leisure and other purposes) and business trips both domestically and internationally. Even in the face of the recent global financial crisis the tourism industry is projected grow by 3.0 percent in 2009 and 4.4 percent over the next ten years (Baumgarten and Kent, 2008). In fact, over the last five years, from 2004–2009 the industry has steadily grown worldwide by about 4.0–7.0 percent annually and contributed U.S.$5890 billion to global GDP in 2008. The projected growth rates for the next ten years vary region by region. The European Union's tourism industry projects the slowest growth at 2.7 percent while the highest annual growth rates are expected for South Asia (7.2), Central and Eastern Europe (5.7), and North East Asia (5.3). Moreover, the travel and tourism industry's share in world GDP remains fairly constant at around 10 percent. This is because the largest tourism volumes are in regions where industry growth is in line with general economic growth (Baumgarten and Kent, 2009).

Despite recent declines resulting from the uncertainties surrounding the global financial crisis and the H1N1 outbreak, international tourism has grown faster than domestic tourism in general. According to the UN and the World Travel and Tourism Council (WTTC) international tourist arrivals have grown at an average annual rate of 7.5 percent since 1950 and are projected to grow at an average annual rate of 4.5 percent over the next 20 years. However, in recent years, the development of international tourism has been no quicker than the growth of the world economy as a whole, which averages about 3.0 percent (World Travel and Tourism Council, 2001). During 2008, almost 922 million tourists went abroad and they spent a total of more than U.S.$944 billion while there. International tourism adds nearly 25 percent to domestic tourism's GDP worldwide, with certain regions depending more markedly on international tourism than others. For example, in the Caribbean nearly 15 percent of the workforce is employed either directly or indirectly by the tourism industry which accounts for nearly one-fifth of the region's countries' GDP (World Travel and Tourism Council, 2009).

The demand for tourism services is shifting qualitatively. Travel is seen as a necessary activity for a substantial proportion of the population, especially in wealthier developing countries. Trips have become shorter but more frequent. New market niches are being exploited, such as health/spa and ecotourism accommodation (IBISWorld, 2009). For example, tourists are becoming more knowledgeable and proactive about the ecological impacts of their behavior and therefore purchase their travel packages accordingly. The spread of information technology enables travel providers to customize their products and services more efficiently to these informed and diversified consumers.

Global tourism has been strongly supported by the deregulation of air transport. In developing countries, no fewer than 80 percent of international tourists arrive by air. Air fares have fallen drastically as a result of increased competition and the abolition of national monopolies. The General Agreement on Trade in Services (GATS) has had an impact on the liberalization of the international tourism economy. Most countries have made tourism-related commitments under GATS concerning issues such as commercial presence or access to technology. Tables 10.1a and 10.1b shows the estimated share of global tourism in terms of generated revenue and transactional activity.

Table 10.1a Estimated share of global tourism revenue and travel activity by region (2009)

Region	$US (Billions)	% Revenue	% Activity
Europe	2,579.0	39.1	37.8
North America	2,033.5	30.9	29.4
Northeast Asia	1,078.3	16.4	18.5
South America	163.4	2.5	4.4
South East Asia	235.6	3.6	3.2
Oceania	149.5	2.3	2.7
Middle East/Africa	276.1	4.2	2.1
South Asia	72.3	1	1.9
Total	6587.7	100	100

Source: World Travel and Tourism Council (2009).

Table 10.1b Share of international travelers by global subregion

Region/Sub-region Europe	% Share (2008)
Northern Europe	6.5
Western Europe	17.7
Central/Eastern Europe	10.8
Southern/Medite rranean	19.5
Asia	
North-East Asia	11.1
South-East Asia	6.4
Oceania	1.2
South Asia	1.1
America	
North America	10.7
Caribbean	2.3
Central America	0.8
South America	2.2
Africa	
North Africa	1.8
Subsaharan Africa	3
Middle East	4.8

Source: World Travel and Tourism Council (2009).

Economic blocs also promote the increase of tourism activities among their member countries and support their development as global tourism destinations. In particular, the European Union (EU) and the Association of South-East Asian Nations (ASEAN) are known for having specific tourism promotion policies. In 2007, under the Portuguese presidency, the EU initiated a series of efforts focusing on sustainable tourism, which was deemed critical for Europe's continued prosperity (European Commission, 2007). Furthermore, the Caribbean Tourism Organization coordinates and manages regional tourism promotion on behalf of its 32 member countries (*Caribbean Tourism Organization, 2009*).

As broadband connectivity has spread, the Internet is increasingly being used to market worldwide destinations to developed and developing countries' populations. Tourism has become one of the most important application domains on the World Wide Web. According to one survey conducted by the Association of British Travel Agents, nearly 60 percent of all travelers book their travel online (Le Fevre, 2008). This number is increasing rapidly as Internet sales of travel products reduce costs and present low entrance barriers in terms of financial investment and know-how. E-commerce therefore clearly increases the opportunities for developing countries to reap the benefits of their competitive advantage as tourism destinations (Mills and Law, 2004).

10.2.2   The hotel industry

Large hotel chains are constantly increasing their business through mergers, as well as franchising and management contracts. The largest hotel chain, Intercontinental HG, operates 3741 hotels with a total of 556,000 rooms. Over the last ten years the industry has witnessed an increasingly active period of mergers and acquisitions. The key competitors emerging from this activity are found in Tables 10.2 and 10.3, which shows the top ten hotel groups by number of rooms and the top ten hotel brands worldwide respectively.

Among these ten, many are multibrand groups, which means that they own several hotel chains with different brand names. For instance, the Wyndham Worldwide group has nine brand names which include Amerihost Inn, Days Inn, Knights inn, Ramada, RCI, Fairfield Communities, Super 8 Motels, Travelodge, Villager, Howard Johnson, and Wingate Inns – of these Super 8 Motels and Days Inns are by far the largest brands with more than 2000 locations each (IBISWorld, 2009).

Table 10.2 Top ten hotel groups worldwide (in rooms)

Rank		Group	Country	Hotels		Rooms		Change	
2007	2006			2007	2006	2007	2006	Rooms	%
1	1	Intercontinental HG	GB	3,741	3,606	556,246	537,533	18,713	3.5
2	2	Wyndham Worldwide	USA	6,473	6,348	543,237	532,669	10,568	2.0
3	3	Marriott Int.	USA	2,775	2,672	502,089	485,979	16,440	3.4
4	5	Hilton Corp.	USA	2,901	2,744	497,738	472,510	25,228	5.3
5	4	Accor	FRA	4,121	4,065	486,512	475,433	11,079	2.3
6	6	Choice	USA	5,316	5,145	429,401	418,488	10,913	2.6
7	7	Best Western	USA	4,164	4,195	315,401	315,875	−474	−0.2
8	8	Starwood Hot. & Res.	USA	871	845	265,598	257,889	7,709	3.0
9	9	Carlson Hospitality	USA	945	932	145,933	146,785	−852	−0.6
10	10	Global Hyatt	USA	733	738	141,011	144,671	−3,660	−2.5
		Total		32,042	31,302	3,883,369	3,787,832	95,537	2.5

Source: MKG Consulting (2008; Travel Industry Wire (2007).

Table 10.3   Top ten hotel brands worldwide (in rooms)

Rank				Hotels 2007	Rooms 2007	Change	
2007	2006	Chain	Group			Rooms	%
1	1	Best Western	Best Western	4,164	315,401	–474	–0.2
2	2	Holiday Inn	Intercontinental H.G.	1,395	260,470	–7,346	–2.7
3	3	Marriott	Marriott Int.	537	190,434	6,976	3.8
4	4	Comfort	Choice	2,439	184,714	2,243	1.2
5	5	Hilton	Hilton Corp.	498	172,605	7,439	4.5
6	6	Days Inn of America	Wyndham World.	1,859	151,438	1,136	0.8
7	7	Express by HI	Intercontinental H.G.	1,686	143,582	10,028	7.5
8	8	Hampton Inn	Hilton Corp.	1,392	138,487	4,366	3.3
9	9	Sheraton	Starwood	396	135,859	1,852	1.4
10	10	Super 8 Motels	Wyndham World.	2,054	126,475	2,144	1.7
		Total		16,420	1,819,467	28,364	21.3

Source: MKG Consulting (2008); Travel Industry Wire (2007).

10.3   The internationalization of Best Western

This section is divided into two parts and examines the unique and successful internationalization processes of Best Western. The first part describes the company, its organizational structure by affiliation, and the services it offers to the affiliated hotels. The second part presents its internationalization process and strategy.

10.3.1   Best Western company presentation

By all estimates BW has risen from humble roots in the American West to become the largest branded hotel chain in the world. According to its own historical account:

> Best Western was founded in 1946 by M.K. Guertin, a California-based hotelier with 23 years of experience in the lodging industry. Best Western International began as an informal referral system among member hotels. By 1963, Best Western was the largest chain in the industry, with 699 member hotels and 35,201 rooms. In 1964, when Canadian hotel owners joined the system, Best Western took the first step toward global expansion. Best Western entered Mexico, Australia and New Zealand in 1976, further establishing its international presence. (Best Western Website, 2009)

BW is the largest hotel chain in the world according to MKG Hospitality, which is the industry standard for measuring capacity (MKG Consulting,

2008). BW International Inc. is the largest hotel brand with more than 4000 independently owned and operated hotels in over 80 countries, about 2200 of which are in the U.S., Canada, and the Caribbean (Hoovers, 2009).

In 2001, BW underwent a significant period of internationalization and welcomed 111 new hotels in North America and 141 new hotels in the other countries. Its resulting global presence is significant and is shown in Table 10.4.

The primary international market is Europe with 1312 hotels (Best Western website, 2009). The percentage of sales coming from overseas

Table 10.4   Best Western Hotels Worldwide

Country	Hotels	Country	Hotels	Country	Hotels	Country	Hotels
Argentina	4	Egypt	1	La Reunion	1	Republic of Korea	3
Aruba	1	England	273	Latvia	1	Romania	4
Australia	243	Estonia	1	Lebanon	1	Russia	3
Austria	46	Finland	21	Lithuania	2	Scotland	48
Bahrain	1	France	200	Luxembourg	1	Slovakia	2
Bangladesh	1	French Guiana	1	Malta	1	Slovenia	2
Belgium	34	Germany	135	Mexico	48	South Africa	1
Belize	1	Grand Bahamas	1	Morocco	1	Spain	30
Bolivia	1	Greece	29	Netherlands	41	Sweden	55
Brazil	22	Guatemala	1	New Caledonia	1	Switzerland	73
Canada	165	Honduras	1	New Zealand	67	Tunisia	1
Channel Islands	1	Hong Kong	1	Nicaragua	1	Turkey	19
Chile	12	Hungary	6	Norway	25	United Arab Emirates	1
Columbia	1	India	16	Oman	2	United States	2117
Costa Rica	8	Indonesia	1	Pakistan	1	Uruguay	4
Cyprus	1	Ireland	27	Peru	7	Venezuela	5
Czech Republic	9	Israel	3	Philippines	1	Vietnam	1
Denmark	31	Italy	127	Poland	4	Virgin Islands	3
Dominican Republic	1	Japan	1	Portugal	20	Wales	19
Ecuador	1	Jordan	4	Puerto Rico	1	Yugoslavia	1

Source: Best Western Inc. (2002).

was 44 percent in 2001 and the revenue from basic member services at that date was US$129,281,970. Detailed data regarding the percentage of sales are found in Table 10.5 (note: 2002 is the last year for which these data were made available).

10.3.2   Best Western's organization: affiliation

In its annual report BW describes its business and its organization this way:

> Best Western International, Inc., and subsidiaries is a membership organization incorporated as a non-profit organization... The company is an association of member hotels established solely to provide revenue generating opportunities and the leverage of purchasing power to benefit its members. (Best Western Inc., 2009)

In pursuit of these goals over the last eight years the company has increased its investment in advertising and has added upscale accommodation in non-U.S. markets to increase its competitiveness (Hoovers, 2002; Hoovers, 2009). With its strong global presence and consumer brand recognition, its generates added exposure for a property that

Table 10.5   The percentage of sales coming from overseas (1999–2001)

	2001	2000	1999
Revenues (USS)			
Basic Member Services	129,281,970	127,978,202	111,835,776
Membership and			
Affiliations:			
North America	2,289	2,272	2,308
International	1,764	1,822	1,704
Total:	4,053	4,094	4,012
Proportion of Revenue			
Based on Number			
of Properties			
North America	56%	55%	58%
International	44%	45%	42%
Revenues from			
Basic Member Services			
(USS)			
North America	73,014,170	71,022,588	64,336,234
International	56,267,800	56,955,614	47,499,542

Source: Hoovers (2002)

wants to become a member. In addition, members look to one another for referral business.

BW strives to provide the lowest fees among any major hotel chain in their industry segment. Affiliates must renew their membership annually, so there are no long-term obligations. This feature protects BW from having to honor a long-lasting contract with a hotel that may hurt its brand image. Members, as well, may become unaffiliated with BW at any time or even transfer their membership for a minimal fee if the property is in good standing. Offering many benefits to its members, BW maintained an impressive base renewal rate of 99 percent for 11 consecutive years (Best Western Press Release, 2007).

10.3.3 Best Western services

BW provides a wide range of comprehensive member services which include domestic and international reservation systems; worldwide marketing, sales, and advertising; brand identity; facilities design; quality assurance; customer service; education; and training services. All of these services, funded primarily through fees and dues paid by the members, are designed to increase the profitability of the individual member properties. The company does make other services available to its members on a separate fee basis (Best Western Inc., 2002). These include central purchasing, special marketing opportunities, and telecommunications networking programs. These services are described in detail below (Best Western website, 2009).

BW's travelers' guides and road atlases contain color photos, maps, and information on all BW hotels. More than 1.5 million guides are distributed annually in the following countries and regions: the U.S., Canada, Mexico, the Caribbean, Central America, and South America. Other guides published worldwide include the annual editions of the BW International Atlas & Hotel Guide: Europe, Mediterranean, Africa & Asia; and Asia-Pacific. These complimentary guides feature in-depth property listings and detailed road maps. They also illustrate facilities and amenities available at each location.

www.bestwestern.com BW has been a leader in using the technology to attract, satisfy, and retain customers. In 1995 BW launched the hotel industry's most extensive and complete listing of properties on the Internet, making it the earliest and largest hotel brand on the web. The company's website currently showcases all 4000-plus hotels with their own property pages featuring promotions, amenities, and local attraction information with color photos, maps, and online booking. By the turn of the millennium the website was logging more than 182 million unique hits annually which resulted in $97 million in gross room night revenue. BW was also a first mover in the mobile-commerce arena by launching a new application for wireless users in early 2001.

The worldwide reservations system services more than 50 million guests every year with offices in the U.S., Italy, Ireland, and Australia. In 2000, the reservations centers generated $563 million in sales and 6.6 million room nights. BW International Inc. was one of the first lodging brands to provide booking capabilities to Internet users around the world when the hospitality giant added this service on December 19, 1995. Continuing with this success in 2006 the company redesigned several regional booking sites to make them twice as efficient and con-sistent with the company's uniformly branded global website (Best Western Press Release, 2007).

Representation and listings in all major global distribution systems, including Amadeus, Sabre, Galileo, and Worldspan.

The Best Requests program assures guests that they will receive the same key amenities and services at any BW in the world.

Gold Crown Club International is the highly popular global frequent traveler's program currently boasting more than 3 million members worldwide and growing.

> But, what are the differences between a franchised hotel chain and an affiliated one? In fact, a franchised chain operator can offer his franchisee the same services and programs as BW including, direc-tory, sales offices abroad, presence at specialised shows, reservation centers, advertisement and marketing operations, central purchas-ing, staff training, quality control, etc. ... (Robinet and Adam, 2005)

The differences between a franchised system and an affiliated one, such as BW, are not to be found in the services offered by the operator: the differences, however are twofold. First, the contract of affiliation is more flexible in the sense that it must be renewed each year, and not every ten years like in most franchised hotel networks. Furthermore, the fees paid by the affiliated hotels are significantly less than comparable franchisor fees. Second, and perhaps more importantly for the internationalization process, is there is no requirement for concept homogeneity. In the case of franchising, this respect of homogeneity can sometimes curb inter-nationalization progress. Indeed, it is clear that some concepts cannot be reproduced without change in foreign countries and therefore must be adapted to foreign cultures. A particularly striking example of this prerequisite adaptation to local conditions is Disney's forays into France and Japan (Brannen, 2004). The particular case of BW's internationalization is consequently and interesting one to study. Although BW has been criticized for focusing on internal issues and conflicts to the detriment of its position in the marketplace, the company has continued to enjoy international expansion over the last five years (Hoovers, 2009; MKG Hospitality, 2008; Travel Industry Wire, 2007). Since tourism and business travel are uniformly global, BW enjoys the competitive strength of providing primarily a non-culture-specific product that is relatively easy to internationalize. The company's business model of leasing naming rights to members allows local owners to make cultural adjustments in décor, food, and beverage offerings, further simplifying the internationalization process.

10.3.4 The sequence of Best Western's international expansion

After its beginning in the Western U.S., BW took its first step toward global expansion in 1962 when Canadian hotel owners joined the system. This was a natural progression because of the common language, similar economic backgrounds, and relatively open borders.

The company's expansion into Europe occurred mostly during the mid- to late 1960s, a period during which relations between the U.S. and most European countries were very strong. By that time Europe had become a major destination for American tourists, the U.S. dollar was extremely strong, U.S. companies were actively seeking involvement in Europe, and Europeans in general welcomed interaction with Americans. During the same period, BW also entered the Caribbean countries benefitting from the same underlying conditions.

The early to mid-1970s were, for most companies and individuals, a much more difficult period. The energy/oil crisis of 1972 and the subsequent economic recession had a staggering effect on the rate of business and economic growth worldwide. This perhaps explains why no significant international expansion occurred for BW until 1976, when it entered Mexico, Australia, and New Zealand. During the late 1970s, the company further expanded its member structure in Europe, with a particular emphasis on England, Scotland, and Wales.

In the 1980s, BW focused its expansion on Northern Europe and Scandinavia, opening properties in France, Denmark, Finland, and Sweden. Between 1980 and 1986, the company focused mainly on improving its existing operations and expanding its presence within

North America. In 1987, the company entered the only remaining Scandinavian country (Norway) as well as adding member properties in Israel and Portugal.

The fall of the Berlin Wall in 1989 and the collapse of the U.S.S.R. in 1991 resulted in new opportunity for BW to expand into the countries of Eastern Europe and the newly independent ex-Soviet states. Russia and Lithuania were targeted in 1993.

In the closing years of the millennium, following the Asian economic crisis, the company realized that tremendous potential for growth could be found in the areas of Asia and the Pacific rim. The focus of international growth consequently shifted to the Far East, where BW added member properties in China and Vietnam. After 2000, the company continued its expansion in these growing regions, adding properties in Hong Kong, New Caledonia, and South Korea.

Most recently BW has recognized the growth potential of Asia and India. The company plans to open 200 hotels in Asia by 2010, and has successfully negotiated a licensing agreement in India which promises to yield 100 new hotels per year for the next ten years. Finally, in 2008 BW opened its first hotels in Dubai, Colombia, Suriname, and Haiti (Hoovers, 2009). Table 10.6 presents a detailed and dated summary of BW's international expansion.

10.3.5   Best Western's international strategy

Before the global financial crisis and the threat posed by the H1N1 outbreak forced the industry into a defensive posture, the company's international business strategy included aggressive expansion initiatives. These targeted "key international gateways" and 35 North American cities that were previously underserved by BW. Despite the downturn, BW still plans for expansion claiming that it is in a unique position of stability and growth. The company sees opportunities when individuals and firms look to "cut costs by moving their hotel business to the mid-market sector" (Hoovers, 2009). Essentially, their expansion strategy can be described as being threefold.

10.3.5.1   *International (outside North America)*

Moving forward on their international expansion plans will mainly focus on Asia, India, South America, the South Pacific, and Western Europe. Specifically, BW is targeting Asia and India. The company plans to be the largest hotel chain in Asia and it is on pace to have more than 200 hotels in the continent by 2010. By focusing on understanding the local history and culture, the company has been able to develop strong local

Table 10.6 Historical summary of the international expansion of BW hotels

1962	BW had the only hospitality reservation service covering the entire U.S.A and Canada.
1962	There were 670 BW hotels in 25 western states and Canada. All the properties offered free reservation service for their customers.
1966	A major expansion of BW services was announced. Changes included: 1) Establishing a new reservation center offering one-step, toll-free service for business commuters, travel agents and vacationers through arrangements with American Express, 2) Expanding into Europe, the Caribbean and the Pacific, 3) Increasing membership standards, 4) Opening sales offices in Washington, Montreal, Phoenix and Seattle, 5) Establishing tie-ins with airlines and representatives from other transportation industry members, 6) Investigating stronger infiltration of tour and business meeting markets.
1976	An agreement was signed with a group of properties in Mexico further expanding BW's international representation.
1976	BW began its push for foreign expansion. Affiliation agreements were signed with 411 properties in Australia and New Zealand.
1978	BW experienced further international expansion into the European market with the addition of BW Interchange Hotels, a network of 108 hotels and country inns in England, Scotland and Wales. Shortly after this move, BW signed an affiliation agreement with Ireland's Irish Welcome Hotels.
1980	Agreements were signed bringing 19 properties in Denmark, 120 properties in France, 19 properties in Finland, 23 properties in Spain, 19 properties in Sweden and 93 properties in Switzerland into the chain. By this time, BW's 903 international affiliates comprised 34% of the chain's total membership.
1987	BW's worldwide expansion continued with the addition of Israel, Norway and Portugal to its affiliate membership.
1992	BW announced plans to develop consolidated reservations offices (CROs) in Europe. The first, in Frankfurt, opened in Jan. 1992. A month later, a similar center opened in Milan. Another, located in Dublin, was scheduled to begin operation in 1994.
1993	Worldwide growth continued with new affiliate members in Russia, Lithuania and Japan.
1996	BW opens door to new hotels in China and Vietnam. BW named official hotel of Six Flags theme parks. BW Launches call for vintage postcard memorabilia.
2002	Opened first hotels in New Caledonia, Hong Kong, South Korea and Yugoslavia.
2008	Opened first hotels in Dubai, Colombia, Suriname and Haiti.
2009 & Beyond	The Company plans to open 200 hotels in Asia by 2010, and has successfully negotiated a licensing agreement in India which promises to yield 100 new hotels per year for the next 10 years.

Source: Best Western Website (2009).

partnerships with developers. In fact, David Kong, the CEO, confidently claims that "Best Western is quickly becoming one of the most respected hotel brands on the continent" (Best Western Press Release, 2007).

In India, BW has teamed up with Cabana Hotels to realize an aggressive growth strategy that seeks to add 100 hotels and 10,000 rooms in the country over the next ten years. Cabana Hotel Management Pvt. Ltd. will be the master licensee of these properties and intends to invest more than US$1.2 billion in Best Western branded hotels. In addition to providing management services for the hotels, Cabana has established an "advanced hotel management institute" that will provide world class training for employees of the BW hotels (Best Western Press Release, 2007).

Beyond Asia and India, the company completed a round of expansion which opened hotels in Australia (11), Italy (nine), Sweden (10), France (16) and the UK (16) (Best Western Press Release, 2002). To continue with this round of expansion BW Hotels Norway recently announced plans to grow their presence from 12 to 26 hotels in that country by the end of 2009 (Best Western Press Release, 2009).

In South America, BW successfully executed a plan to open 22 new hotels. BW is established its presence in the region by opening offices in Sao Paulo and Buenos Aires, as well as sales offices in Argentina, Brazil, Chile, Peru, and Venezuela. In preparation for this aggressive expansion, BW hired a team of Spanish- and Portuguese-speaking agents to handle reservations and customer service calls (Best Western Press Release, 2002).

10.3.5.2   North America

In North America, BW opened 133 new BW hotels in 2007 through both conversions and new hotel construction (Best Western Press Release, 2007). In addition to the opening of new locations the company has recently formed strategic partnerships with iconic American brand names to cement its own status as "THE WORLD'S LARGEST HOTEL CHAIN®." First, in 2004 it partnered with NASCAR to become the "Official Hotel of NASCAR®" in order to offer special discounted rates and services to race fans (Best Western Press Release, 2007). Second, it partnered with Harley-Davidson to offer the Gold Crown Club International Ride Rewards program which offers members a variety of customized products and services (Best Western Press Release, 2007). The company has formed alliances with these and other key marketing partners in order to continue strengthening the Best Western brand in North America.

10.3.5.3   *The "Premier Hotel" designations*

Additionally, BW has implemented a strategy that gives distinction to their higher end hotels in Europe and Asia, called "BW Premier Hotels." These hotels offer 33 more amenities and services above and beyond the required standard BW offering. There have been many applications for distinction as a Premier Hotel in Austria, Belgium, China, the Czech Republic, France, Germany, Greece, Hungary, Italy, Slovenia, Spain, Sweden, and Switzerland. This designation helps with the company's expansion of four-star designated hotels that provide a greater level of style and amenities (Best Western Press Release, 2002; Best Western website, 2009).

10.3.6   International evolution perspectives

BW has always placed a heavy emphasis on its international business practices. BW's International Board organized a meeting in San Diego where they adopted the association's first-ever global business plan. This plan emphasizes key initiatives in quality assurance, e-commerce, and loyalty marketing. The heart of the new plan contains BW's vision for the future: "to be the preferred mid-scale hotel chain."

BW will leverage its dominance with affiliates in 82 countries all around the world. The new plan highlights the strong brand recognition achieved over many years and will leverage their position in the marketplace. New programs have been created to build momentum and to solidify BW's position as "THE WORLD'S LARGEST HOTEL CHAIN®." "Our global organization has taken some very important steps together recently like establishing our BestRequests™ global product standard," stated Jim Evan, chairman of the International Board and president and CEO of BW International (Business Wire Inc., 2001). The Best Requests™ program was rolled out to all BW hotels worldwide in January 2002. Much of the program's success centers on providing the best services available in a consistent manner across the globe. BW also entered into a joint marketing agreement with the American Automobile Association (AAA). BW will be marketed as the preferred hotel to AAA's 44 million membership. This agreement will enhance the BW reputation in the U.S., Canada, and the Caribbean. "More than 80 percent of BW hotels are AAA inspected and approved which makes our association with AAA a very strategic marketing partnership," said Bob Gilbert, vice president of Worldwide Sales and Marketing for BW (Business Wire Inc., 2001).

BW made extensive investments in software applications and solutions to enhance its offerings to its customers, including the purchase of a number of products from the KANA iCare™ suite. These eCRM solutions enable guests to make reservations in real-time on the Web and every department within BW can access reservation information using KANA software to provide superior customer service at reduced costs. "Standardizing on the KANA iCARE™ suite makes perfect sense for a company like BW that needs to engage international customers across multiple touch points," said Bud Michael, executive vice president of products and marketing of KANA (Business Wire Inc., 2002).

As shown above, BW continues to grow its global presence in the hotel industry. "BW continues to be a very attractive brand for hotel developers because we maintain lower affiliation costs and offer equivalent, if not superior services to that of our franchised competition," said Mark Williams, vice president of North American development. During fiscal year 2006, 133 North American hotels and more than 100 international hotels were brought into the BW association: France opened 16, the UK opened 16, Australia opened 11, Sweden opened 10, and Italy and Germany both opened nine.

BW's current international expansion initiatives seem to be very well planned and coordinated while still allowing the ability for the individual operators to customize their offerings to local tastes and trends. Streamlining their processes and standards will likely have a favorable impact upon their brand image and awareness. Since their brand is the main product leased by affiliation, membership should continue to increase. In conclusion, we anticipate a successful effort in further international expansion by BW International.

10.4   Conclusion

This informative paper illustrates the case of affiliation which is understudied in the literature. In the internationalization context, we often talk about franchised, company-owned, or plural form networks. A common question is how to choose the best managerial form for penetrating a new market. This paper, while generally descriptive, is intended to be both informative and provocative. Indeed, the case of BW presents a successful – yet understudied – expansion mode: affiliation. Each hotel owner is associated with the decisions of the BW (*Franchise Magazine*, 2003). BW's internationalization is already promising. And the fact that each hotel keeps its uniqueness, and above all its architectural uniqueness, is an added value (*Franchise Magazine*, 2003). Various research tracks can be envisaged. Some might deal with the internationalization process, others could employ quantitative analyses to compare the revenues of franchised hotel chains vs. affiliated ones. The facts operators use to make the franchisee vs. affiliate decision could also be examined. What are the advantages and drawbacks of these two perspectives? The similarities and disparities between franchise networks/affiliated networks could be an interesting topic. Finally, the affiliation as the network management choice could be also studied in other industries.

References

Baumgarten, Jean-Claude, and Geoffrey J.W. Kent (2008). *Progress and Priorities 2008/2009*. London: World Travel and Tourism Council.

Baumgarten, Jean-Claude, and Geoffrey J.W. Kent (2009). *Travel and Tourism Economic Impact: Regional Reports*. London: World Travel and Tourism Council.

Best Western Inc. (2002). *Annual Report 2001*. Phoenix, AZ: Best Western Inc

Best Western Press Release (2002). "Best Western Expands in South America," http://www.bestwestern.com/newsroom/pressreleases.asp.

Best Western Press Release (2002). "Best Western to Sign 300 New Hotels in 2002," http://www.bestwestern.com/newsroom/pressreleases.asp.

Best Western Press Release (2002). "BW Premier Designation Launches in Europe," http://www.bestwestern.com/newsroom/pressreleases.asp.

Best Western Press Release (2007). "Best Western and Harley-Davidson Team Up," http://www.bestwestern.com/newsroom/pressreleases.asp.

Best Western Press Release (2007). "BW Plans to be Largest Hotel Chain in Asia by 2010," http://www.bestwestern.com/newsroom/pressreleases.asp.

Best Western Press Release (2007). "BWI & Cabana Hotels Announce India Expansion Plan," http://www.bestwestern.com/newsroom/pressreleases.asp.

Best Western Press Release (2007). "BWI Announces Year-End Results" http://www.bestwestern.com/newsroom/pressreleases.asp.

Best Western Press Release (2007). "BWI to Celebrate April Fools' Day for Race Fans," http://www.bestwestern.com/newsroom/pressreleases.asp.

Best Western Press Release (2007). "New BW Australia Website Halves Booking Time" http://www.bestwestern.com/newsroom/pressreleases.asp; July 13, 2009.

Best Western Inc. (2009). *Annual Report 2008*. Phoenix, AZ: Best Western Inc.

Best Western Press Release (2009). "BW Hotels Norway Continues Strategic Expansion," http://www.bestwestern.com/newsroom/pressreleases.asp.

Best Western website (2009). "Best Western Corporate Fact Sheets" http://www.bestwestern.com/newsroom/factsheet.asp.

Brannen, M.Y. (2004). "When Mickey loses face: Recontextualization, semantic fit, and the semiotics of foreignness," *Academy of Management Review* 29 (4), 593–616.

Business Wire Inc. (2001). "AAA Names Best Western as a Show Your Card & Save Partner."

Business Wire Inc. (2001). "Best Western's International Board Approves Inaugural Global Business Plan."

Business Wire Inc. (2002). "Best Western Standardizes on the KANA iCARE Suite to Provide Superior Customer Service and Reduce Costs."

Caribbean Tourism Organization (2009). "OneCaribbean," http://www.onecaribbean.org/aboutus/.

European Commission (2007). *Initiatives of the Portuguese presidency of the EU in the tourism sector*; http://ec.europa.eu/enterprise/newsroom/cf/.

Franchise Magazine (2003). "Best Western fonce dans les étoiles," 52 (April-May).

Hoovers (2002). *Best Western International, Inc. Profile*. Austin, TX: Hoovers, A D&B Company.

Hoovers (2009). *Best Western International, Inc. Profile*. Austin, TX: Hoovers, A D&B Company.

IBISWorld (2009). *IBISWorld Industry Report: Global Hotels and Resorts: G4611-GL*: Santa Monica, CA: IBISWorld Inc.

Le Fevre, John (2008). "Online Travel Bookings Soar but Internet Video Advertising Flops: Travel Agencies Facing Pressure While Online Advertising Myth Busted;" http://photojourn.wordpress.com/2008/10/08/online-travel-bookings-soar-but-internet-video-advertising-flops/.

Mills, Juline E., and Rob Law, Eds. (2004). *Handbook of Consumer Behavior, Tourism, and the Internet*. Binghamton, NY: Haworth Hospitality Press Inc.

MKG Consulting (2008). MKG Hospitality Database. Paris: MKG Consulting.

MKG Hospitality (2008). HotelCompset Database. Paris: MKG Hospitality.

Robinet, Jean-Claude, and Claude Adam (2005). *Management hôtelier: Théorie et pratique*. Paris: De Boeck Université.

Travel Industry Wire (2007). "MKG Consulting – The Official 2007 Ranking Of Groups And Hotel Brands Worldwide," http://www.travelindustrywire.com/article27273.

World Travel and Tourism Council (2001). *UNWTO World Tourism Barometer*.

World Travel and Tourism Council (2009). *UNWTO World Tourism Barometer* 7 (1–3).

11
San Francisco Coffee House Opens in Croatia

Ilan Alon, Mirela Alpeza, and Aleksandar Erceg

11.1 Introduction

Denis Tensek (MBA) and his wife Jasmina Pacek (MFA) spent a considerable amount of time in the U.S.; both went to graduate schools in California and have worked for well known American companies. Armed with the know-how they obtained from their experiences in the U.S. they left their management positions and returned to their homeland of Croatia in order to spend time with their family and to help their country develop.

On their return, they decided to start their own business. While considering many business possibilities and researching the local market for opportunities, they got an idea based on the experience they had gained in the U.S. and opened an American-style coffee house, with an atmosphere reminiscent of San Francisco's. While Croatia had many coffee houses, few had the combination of service, quality, products, and atmosphere that they remembered from their time living in the U.S.

Denis and Jasmina recalled their days in the U.S., and the economic success stories of the major coffee franchise chains such as Starbucks. They even considered taking a master franchise license for Croatia, but the process was long, complicated, and extremely expensive in comparison to the expected return. The fact is that Starbucks has very low local brand recognition in Croatia. The other problem with importing brands is that they often do not allow the adjustments needed for success in local markets, the major one in this case being the pricing of their products simply being too high for the local purchasing power of a developing country such as Croatia.

Therefore, Denis and Jasmina decided to open their own coffee house, one unique to the Croatian environment – a California-style coffee house offering the quality of service , product assortment, ambiance, and efficiency found only in sophisticated coffee shops in the

U.S., and all of it at locally affordable prices. The pricing was an even more important parameter because the plan was to be put into action in the city of Osijek, situated in the region that was most heavily impacted by the war with the Serbs, and still among the least economically developed regions in the country.

Denis and Jasmina started with one single coffee house that from the start had a potential to grow into a franchise. Instead of purchasing a franchise, they went down the other route and created one of their own, that had all the elements of the modern franchise chains that were available on the international market but with the adjustments needed to suit the local market. They decided to use all of their U.S. lifestyle and professional experiences, as well as understanding of habits and behaviors of the local market, to create this new concept in Croatia.

Right from the start, the coffee house was a success. Business was up week by week, month by month. And, operating profits reached a satisfactory level. Motivated with the success of the first coffee shop in one of Croatia's poorest regions, the couple realized that the potential for this concept was national, if not regional or international. But, how would they grow? Should they develop their own outlets or open more company owned outlets?

Growing organically by opening self-owned stores was costly, slow, and hard to control. They had neither the means nor the manpower. They knew they did not want to put more capital at risk, and did not have the time to travel to various locations around the country. Furthermore, their concept had started to get local publicity and inquiries from would-be franchisees began to show. But, how could they franchise in Croatia?

Croatia has a small economy, changing legal system, and little experience in franchising. Growing through franchising was appealing, but they only had one store, the business was young, and franchising was unfamiliar to the emerging market of Croatia. The conditions for franchising were not ideal. They analyzed the coffee house business in Croatia and the infant and risky franchise sector.

Aside from whether to franchise or not, how could they protect their intellectual property, business format know-how? How could they fight off imitators? What would happen if Starbucks or other major coffee chains entered the market? What should be the next steps? How could they become the biggest and most successful coffee house nationally or regionally?

11.2   The entrepreneurs: Jasmina and Denis

In winter 2003, after spending six years in the U.S., spouses Jasmina and Denis returned to Croatia. San Francisco Coffee House (SFCH) is an example of entrepreneurship where two people not only used their life experiences in other societies where a particular product or service was available, but also their specific professional experience to contribute toward creating this unique visual identity and business opportunity. The managerial experience Denis gained by working in large American companies and the educational experience from an MBA from California State University gave him an advantage in creating a world-class business in Croatia that towered above local offerings in service, quality, and customer perceptions. See Figure 11.1.

On the other hand, Jasmina's international design experience, experience working as Art Director in American corporations, and a Masters in Fine Arts and Design from the University of California, gave SFCH a

Figure 11.1   The interior and exterior of the SFCH, Osijek

recognizable visual identity and an interior in which visitors could feel the San-Francisco-style coffee shop atmosphere. Thanks to their successful careers and profitable real estate investments in the U.S., they felt comfortable and confident in returning to Croatia with enough capital to help them in their new venture, and help their country at the same time.

11.3   The environment for franchising in Croatia

The environment for franchising in Croatia is not ideal because there is insufficient regulation, little market know-how about franchising, and low economic development. On the other hand, the emerging market and the new openness to European integration have created opportunities to start bring in new businesses from the outside.

11.3.1   The economic environment

In 1991, after the Republic of Croatia gained its independence, the Croatian market increasingly opened to a great variety of international products and services. As a result of the economic growth which began in the late 1990s, salaries have grown appreciably, especially in the larger cities and in certain other parts of Croatia.[1] Salary growth resulted in increased consumer demand for higher quality global brand names, which were not widely available in Croatia at that time. After independence, the Croatian market became flooded with imported goods of variable quality. The habits of younger Croatian consumers have changed as a result of this increased supply: international brands became must-haves for younger consumers, while older people tended to continue to seek out domestic brands. Inevitably, perhaps, purchasing habits also varied geographically.[2]

Financial institutions in Croatia are mostly owned by foreign banks – around 90 percent according to one source[3] – and many of these acquisitions have occurred in the last few years. Although there is a predictable variety of capitalization options for would-be entrepreneurs, a chief characteristic of the Croatian domestic market is the bankruptcy of small entrepreneurs as they struggle to collect debts. Although barter is a common fixture of the domestic market (i.e. between local companies), the international ownership of local banks makes such traditional arrangements problematic.

Basic statistics on the economy are shown in the Table 11.1.

Table 11.1   Basic socioeconomic data on Croatia

Annual data	2007(a)	Historical averages (%)	2003–2007
Population (m)	4.0	Population growth	0.0
GDP (U.S.$ billion; market exchange rate)	51,452.4(b)	Real GDP growth	4.9
GDP (U.S.$ billion; purchasing power parity)	69,211	Real domestic demand growth	5.0
GDP per capita (U.S.$; market exchange rate)	12,863	Inflation	2.6
GDP per capita (U.S.$; PPP)	17,303	Current account balance (% of GDP)	–7.1
Exchange rate (av) HRK:U.S.$	5.35(b)	FDI inflows (% of GDP)	6.4

Source: *The Economist* (2008) http://www.economist.com/countries/Croatia/profile.cfm? folder=Profile-FactSheet (retrieved June 11, 2008).

11.3.2   Political environment

Creating a vibrant business environment in accordance with the standards of the European Union and with countries embedded in the local market economy is one of the major goals of the Croatian government's policies. The government's dedication to the reform of the national economy can be seen in its desire to attract foreign investment for the development of Croatia's domestic and international markets.

Foreign investments in Croatia are regulated by the Company Act and other legal norms. A foreign investor in Croatia has a number of organizational options available to him or her according to this act: a foreign investor can invest alone or as a joint-venture partner with a Croatian company or private citizen; there are no constraints as to the percentage of foreign ownership that is possible. In addition, in keeping with the government's desire for foreign investment, investors can gain access to a number of newly opened markets; entrants can take advantage of a number of incentives, tax benefits, and customs privileges that are available only to foreign investors.

11.3.2.1   The institutions of franchising

During the last few years, The Republic of Croatia has approved a number of laws which resulted in Croatia's acceptance into the World Trade Organization (TWO) and the Central European Free Trade Agreement (CEFTA); these legal changes have also allowed Croatia to begin negotiations for acceptance into the European Union. Nevertheless, there is no specific legal basis for franchising in Croatia. Franchising is mentioned in the Croatian Trade Act (*Narodne Novine*, 2003), where the generalities of potential franchising agreements are stated, but mention is made in only one article and that mention is very condensed. Therefore, there is no legal standard for the development of franchising and no legal parameters (yet) for franchising agreements: at the present time, business practices on the ground determine the appropriateness of such agreements.

Since the concept of franchising is relatively new to Croatia and its inhabitants, little knowledge exists about it. There are two Centers for Franchising, one in Osijek and one in Zagreb, Croatia's most vibrant city. Each of these centers works with the Croatian Franchising Association to stimulate franchising development in several ways:

Educating about franchising – The Franchise Center in Osijek, for example, has organized seminars called "Franchise from A to Z," in order to educate entrepreneurs about franchising and its benefits;

Franchising promotion – both centers and the association are trying to promote franchising as a way of doing business through local media – interviews, articles in the newspapers and magazines, etc.;

Creating websites with information about franchising on the Internet – with information on the portal with current news;

Connecting franchisors with potential franchisees – one section of the franchise portal contains offers from franchisors interested in the Croatian market; there are several inquiries each week from potential franchisees;

Helping domestic companies to become franchisors – The Franchise Center in Osijek, with the help of Poduzetna Hrvatska, organized training for potential franchise consultants who can help domestic companies if they decide to use franchising as a growth strategy;

Establishing franchise fairs and round tables.

Foreign franchises tend to choose one of two potential pathways into the Croatian market: distribution-product franchising and/or business-format franchising. Larger, better-known franchisors like McDonald's open offices in Croatia and offer franchises to interested entrepreneurs in order to ensure quality control, while smaller and less well-known franchisors sell master franchises to local entrepreneurs in order to ensure the benefits of local knowledge and cost savings.

11.3.3 Barriers to franchising development

In September 2006, the Franchise Center of the Center for Entrepreneurship in Osijek conducted a survey of 50 people, asking what they (representatives of banks, entrepreneurs, and lawyers) thought about the barriers facing franchising in the Croatian. Responses included:

Laws – there is no legal regulation of franchising in Croatia. The word "franchising" is only mentioned in trade law. The absence of clear legal precedent makes it difficult for Croatian lawyers to help their clients, especially during the contracting phase – whether franchisor or franchisee, foreign or domestic investor.

Franchise professionals – there is a dearth of professionals related to franchising: too few educational efforts and few franchise consultants who could help potential franchisors in developing their own networks or advise franchisee about selecting one.

Problems with banks (lack of familiarity with franchising) – banks do not recognize franchising as a relatively safe way of entering into a new business and do not have any specialized loans for the franchising industry. According to a survey conducted by the Franchise Center (2006), some banks' representatives said that they would also ask for a guarantee for a loan from the franchisor. Banks are unwilling to educate their employees about this way of doing business. Banks seem unable to distinguish between start-up entrepreneurs creating footholds in new franchise sectors and franchisees who are entering preexisting, proven franchise systems.

Small market – because there are only about 4 million inhabitants in Croatia, there is pessimism about whether the largest franchisors will come to Croatia because of logistical problems: the perception is that it is much easier to open a site in London than in Croatia. Large and famous franchisors are looking for bigger areas to capture the population, and they often resist adapting to local standards and prices. Smaller franchisors that would like to enter Croatia are not as well known to Croatian entrepreneurs and are, therefore, seldom selected.

Franchising is not a well-known way of doing business – people seldom recognize what franchising is; many think it is connected with insurance. This is the biggest barrier according to the survey because people are not willing to enter into something with which they are unfamiliar. Further seminars and round tables need to be organized in order to educate entrepreneurs about franchising and its costs/benefits.

According to the above-mentioned survey, there are some identifiable reasons for the relatively slow development of franchising in the Republic of Croatia: entrepreneurial thinking, lack of franchising education, and a weak national franchising association. First, many entrepreneurs would rather own their own companies and have complete "business freedom" than submit to the restrictions they see as being related to becoming part of a system – from production and distribution to sales and to the "forced" cleaning of the premises. Second, Croatian entrepreneurs are not completely familiar with the benefits which can be gained by being a member of a successful franchising system.

While the tone above sounds pessimistic, industry experts also reported that there is an excellent chance for franchising in Croatia, that there is the possibility of high growth in this sector (up to 30 percent), and that Croatia's future membership of the EU will provide the necessary boost to franchising development. This survey showed that although franchising is not a familiar way of doing business, experts see a bright future for it in Croatia.

11.3.4   Competition

Franchises have become better known in Croatia since the early 1990s, after the first McDonald's was opened in Zagreb. "McDonald's expansion into the Croatian market has tended to use two franchising methods: direct franchising and business-facility lease arrangements...Such lease arrangements allow for franchisees to become entry-level franchisees using less capital at the outset."[4]

Other franchisors followed McDonald's lead. For example, one of the relatively new restaurant franchising concepts in the Croatian market is the Hungarian company Fornetti, which managed to spread its mini-bakeries business rapidly throughout Croatia by using franchising. It was founded in 1997, and today has more than 3000 sites in Central and Eastern Europe.[5] Other international franchises represented in Croatia include Benetton, Subway, Dama Service, and Remax.

According to the Croatian Franchise Association, there are approximately 125 franchise systems (25 of them domestic) present in the Croatian market. These systems operate approximately 900 outlets and employ almost 16,000 people.[6] Companies in more than 20 industries have chosen franchising as a growth option, with the retail and fast-food sectors accounting for more than 20 percent of the market. Other sectors with important shares include the tourist industry, auto rental companies, courier services, and the fashion industry.

Tables 11.2 and 11.3 show the best known foreign and domestic franchisors in Croatia by industry and number of outlets as of 2007.

While a few restaurant franchisors have already entered the market, no well-known international coffee house has made its mark in Croatia. Competition for coffee houses was mostly local, dating back to Croatia's early days of independence. Local competitors offered a roughly homogeneous product – coffee – and most did not bother to create a visual identity, a brand, or a new concept. Price, location, and ambiance distinguished one coffee bar from another. Competitive rivalry from abroad, however, is imminent. The question is not if international coffee houses will come, but when?

Coffee consumption in Croatia is quite popular; many Croatians spend time between meals, in the morning, or at night at coffee bars, which often also serve beers and other alcoholic products. While regular bars

Table 11.2   Foreign franchisors in Croatia

Franchisor	Industry	Number of outlets
McDonald's	Fast food	16 restaurants
Subway	Fast food	6 restaurants
Fornetti	Bakeries	More than 150 locations
Dama Service	Refilling toner cartridges	3 locations
Berlitz	Foreign language school	1 location
Firurella	Weight loss center for women	2 locations
Berghoff	Kitchen equipment	3 locations

Source: Round table – Franchising in Croatia EFF/IFA International Symposium, October 24–25, 2006, Brussels.

Table 11.3   Domestic franchisors in Croatia

Franchisor	Industry	Number of outlets
Elektromaterijal	Household appliances' distribution	More than 50 stores
X-nation	Fashion	40 stores/units
Rubelj Grill	Grill	17 restaurants
Skandal	Fashion	15 stores
Body Creator	Weight loss center for women	4 centers
Bio & Bio	Health food	3 shops
Bike Express	Courier service	1 location
San Francisco Coffee House	Coffee bar	1 location

Source: Round table – Franchising in Croatia EFF/IFA International Symposium, October 24–25, 2006, Brussels.

and other restaurants compete with coffee shops for customers, coffee shops are relatively cheap, providing a comfortable environment for socializing. Suppliers of coffee are many and include both international and local brands. Coffee, itself, is basically a commodity.

11.4   The opening of the San Francisco coffee house

Osijek is a town with many coffee houses and bars, and visiting them is part of the lifestyle of the local population. But, they all suffer from one competitive problem: they all offer roughly the same limited product line without any differentiating concept. Denis and Jasmina noticed that what was missing in the market was an American-style coffee bar in which most of the offerings would consist of different types of coffee and include the novel (in Croatia) possibility of getting "coffee to go." They decided to adapt this ubiquitous American concept to the local Croatian market. They were under the impression that the "Made in U.S.A." brand would be positively received in their "new" market, so they named the coffee bar "The San Francisco Coffee House." During the development of the business plan, Denis traveled to the U.S. several times, researching ideas, studying the technology of coffeemaking, and bringing back with him some of the supplies and crucial ingredients.

Denis had chosen the location for the San Francisco Coffee House very carefully: he was looking for a location with a minimum of 80 square meters near an area with heavy foot traffic, since their main target market was business people. He found an excellent location in the town's center – across from the green market, near three university departments, several lawyers, and public notaries' offices – for which he signed a five-year lease with provisions for extending the lease and a right to first refusal if the owner wanted to sell the premises. After the first few months, they found that their major client markets were students and business professionals of all ages.

Since SFCH was the first American coffee house in Croatia, this unique place where one can enjoy authentic ambiance of this American city got excellent reviews and unusually large media attention in the first six months of its existence. *Elle Décor* categorized it among the six best decorated service industry interiors in the country, complimenting the brave mixture of styles and materials Jasmina used to create this urban, bright, and sophisticated environment. The result was even more amazing taking into account that the entrepreneurs had worked within a limited budget of €40,000 as start-up capital.

The SFCH product range is also unique for this market. It offers its customers coffee in 17 different latte (with milk) and mocha variants and several varieties of American-style muffins. Coffee can be drunk in the relaxing but urban atmosphere of the bar or it can be taken out in "to-go" packaging. In order to adapt to their target market, its guests are provided with Croatian and international newspapers and magazines, and there is free wireless access to the Internet (which is extremely rare in Croatia). The ambience is also enhanced by smooth jazz and chart music from the 1970s, 1980s, and 1990s.

SFCH has eight employees and is managed by Tanja Ivelj. The employees are all young people, some of them without any previous employment experience, and most of whom have worked in SFCH since its inception. When searching for employees, Denis looked for trustworthy, loyal, and honest people. For each workstation, employees have a detailed job description and detailed checklists for each shift and for weekly and monthly routine duties.

Once employed, all employees take a course in working in a coffee bar. Their salaries are almost 20 percent higher than those of comparable employees at other local coffee shops. Every six months all employees have scheduled performance review. If this is satisfactory there is a further 5 percent salary increase. Human resource management is one of the areas where Denis has brought his American corporate experience into Croatia. In Croatia, employee rights, salaries, and general terms of employment are in most cases ambiguous. In addition, contrary to common practice in Croatia, SFCH provides full paid vacation and benefits for its employees. As a result, in an industry where the turnover rate is extremely high, SFCH was able to achieve less than 20 percent staff turnover over the first three years of operation. As Denis said: "satisfied and motivated employees offer high standard of service to the end customer."

SFCH has made an extra effort to maintain excellent relationships with its suppliers, settling bills promptly in a market that is known for its slackness. Wise and responsible financial management is the company's priority.

The market has also rewarded SFCH. The summary of the financial performance of the company's operations is shown in Table 11.4.

11.5 What should be done next?

Jasmina and Denis looked at the facts: franchising is one of several possible models for business growth and is widely used in economically

Table 11.4   SFCH financial performance

Income data	2006	2007
Net revenue	20,000.00	25,000.00
Total expenses	130,000.00	140,000.00
Direct costs	760,00.00	81,000.00
Depreciation	4000.00	11,000.00
Gross profit	120,000.00	158,000.00
Operating expenses	54,000.00	59,000.00
Earnings before I&T	66,000.00	99,000.00
Taxes	14,520.00	21,780.00
Earnings after I&T	51,480.00	77,220.00

developed countries throughout the world. Some of the reasons why companies prefer to develop franchise networks rather than to grow organically include lower financial investment, lower risk, faster growth, local market knowledge by franchisee, and the latters motivation to succeed. They wanted these benefits too.

The barriers which SFCH faced in franchising in the local market are challenging:

There is just not enough information about franchising. As a result, entrepreneurial and institutional awareness of franchising is quite low;

There are no well-established support organizations for the development of franchise networks in Croatia. There are only two Entrepreneurship Centers in Croatia which offer services regarding franchise network development;

There is no significant support from financial institutions. Banks fail to recognize the relatively low risk of investment in start-up entrepreneurs/franchisees compared to independent start-up entrepreneurs, among other factors mentioned earlier.

Moreover, the company was still young and as yet unproven in other locations. The couple could simply enjoy their local success, they could open additional stores by themselves, or they could try to sell franchises of their concept. All three options had significant upside and downside risks. Their intuition told them they should use franchising, but serious limitations existed. Could they develop franchising in a market where local conditions are less than conducive? Could they gain national prominence? The couple had never run a franchising business and did not have the necessary experience and knowledge. How could they overcome these weaknesses and the environmental threats? How could they seize the opportunities in the marketplace using their unique experiences, capabilities, and strengths?

Notes

1. Državni zavod za statistiku (2006) **Statistical information 2006**, http://www.dzs.hr/Hrv_Eng/StatInfo/pdf/StatInfo2006.pdf, [Accessed on October 26, 2006].
2. GfK (2005), **Građani o markama**, Survey conducted by GfK, March 2005, http://www.gfk.hr/press/marke.htm, http://www.gfk.hr/press/marke2.htm, [Accessed on January 3, 2007].
3. Hrvatska narodna banka (2006) **Standardni prezentacijski format**, http://www.hnb.hr/publikac/prezent/hbanking-sector.pdf, [Accessed on October 20, 2006].
4. Viducic, Lj., G. Brcic, Ilin Alon, and D. Welsh (2001). *International Franchising in Emerging Markets: China, India and Other Asian Countries*, CCH Inc., Chicago, p. 217.
5. Mandel, K. (2004). "Franchising in Hungary," address given at The Franchise Center Osijek seminar "Franšiza od A do Ž," Osijek, November 2004.
6. Kukec, Lj. (2006). Round table – "Franchising in Croatia," address given at EFF/IFA International Symposium, Brussels, October 24–25.

12
An Athlete's Foot Master Franchisee in China

Ilan Alon

12.1   Introduction

One day in late 2001, Rick Wang, the managing director of RetailCo Inc., the master franchisee for The Athlete's Foot in China, was reviewing the most recent sales report of his company. He found that the sales volume had declined precipitously over the past six months, down almost one-third from what it had been only one year ago. Inevitably, Rick was concerned.

RetailCo Inc. had had a banner year in 2000; however, the company had experienced a cascade of problems beginning in 2001. At the start of that year, the company was forced to deal with pressure caused by a shortage in the supply of its major products, which could deal a death-blow to any small retailer. In quick succession, financial crises and sales problems related to the lack of product created a systemic disaster. Unless he acted quickly and decisively, RetailCo might not survive this confluence of major problems.

12.2   Rick Wang and RetailCo Inc.

Rick Wang was a typical American-born Chinese, able to speak both American English and Chinese. His parents had immigrated to Taiwan and then America when they were fairly young; regardless of their geographic location, however, the family maintained strong cultural ties to its homeland. Rick was raised in a traditional Chinese family in the U.S. After graduating from the University of Southern California with a degree in Communications, he began his career as an account director at Lintas, a well-regarded international advertising agency. After that, he transferred to work for Foremost Dairies Ltd., a leading manufacturer of milk and ice cream in Taiwan, as a marketing director, and thus gained experience in short-shelf-life consumer goods.

In 1992, he moved to his parents' hometown, Shanghai, and worked for Shanghai Fuller Foods Ltd. as vice president of marketing. He assisted in the building of the company's factory in Jinqiao district and developed new brands of Fuller milk and ice cream. Under Rick's leadership, the brands "Qian Shi Nai" (milk) and "San Marlo" (ice cream) quickly achieved market leadership in the area, known by almost all the residents in Shanghai. In late 1997, Shanghai Fuller Foods Ltd. was sold to Nestlé and Rick decided to strike out on his own.

As a result of a chance encounter, Rick Wang became acquainted with the athletics footwear industry and became a retailer. Rick retains a vivid memory of the day he was introduced to the possibilities of this retailing niche:

> One day, when I was playing softball with a bunch of my American friends who then worked at Nike, one of them said to me, "Rick, since your ice-cream business has been sold, what do you want to do now?" I said, "I don't know yet. Maybe I'll go back to San Francisco, or back to Taiwan." He said, "Why don't you consider overseeing our Nike stores in Shanghai?" I asked, "Nike stores? Can I make money?" And he replied immediately, "Sure, they can make a lot of money!" I asked for the financial statement, which he showed me the next day. After looking carefully I said, "Ok. Let's do it."

Rick Wang, at that time, had no experience in either the sports footwear industry or any direct knowledge of in-store retailing, but he was very excited about his new business venture. RetailCo Inc. was established with the intention of managing the retailing of athletics footwear.

His optimism notwithstanding, Rick's hasty involvement and lack of experience in the footwear retailing industry led to the poor performance of his stores. In the six months after the company was established, no profit was made. As the situation worsened, Rick anxiously sought expert advice. He began by educating himself on the Internet, searching terms such as "athletic footwear retail," "sport retail," and "sports shoes retail"; surprisingly, he found that almost every page of his searches revealed one American company, The Athlete's Foot Inc. Like many entrepreneurs, Rick recognized the value inherent in modeling his own activities on those of an industry leader.

12.3   The Athlete's Foot Inc.

The Athlete's Foot Inc, based in Kennesaw, Georgia in the United States, is the world's foremost franchisor of athletics-footwear operations. It grew from a small, family-run store to an international retailer in three decades. Today, The Athlete's Foot owns about 800 corporate and franchise stores in more than 40 countries (see Figure 12.1).

The history of the growth of The Athlete's Foot is a model of aggressive business behavior. In 1971, Robert and David Lando opened the world's first athletics-footwear specialty store – named The Athlete's Foot – on Wood Street in Pittsburgh, Pennsylvania. The very next year, The Athlete's Foot began franchising its business model domestically. The first franchise agreement was signed by Killian Spanbauer, who opened a store at the Sawyer Street Shopping Center in Oshkosh, Wisconsin. After that, The Athlete's Foot began a period of focused expansion: by 1976 there were more than 100 stores; only two years later, there were more than 200 Athlete's Foot outlets in the U.S.

That same year, the company began to internationalize its franchising efforts; in 1978, the first of what was to become many international franchises opened, at 16 Stevens Place, in Adelaide, Australia. This milestone event encouraged The Athlete's Foot to franchise an additional 150 stores in international markets by 1979.

After a decade of successful market penetration, the Athlete's Foot, in its second decade, began a period of adjustment. In the early 1980s, Group Rallye purchased The Athlete's Foot from the Lando family. This buyout provided crucial financial support to the company at a time when it needed to pay more attention to product design and customer

Antigua	Venezuela	Greece	Nicaragua	St. Kitts
Argentina	Cyprus	Honduras	Martinique	St. Lucia
Aruba	Denmark	Indonesia	Panama	St. Maarten
Australia	Dominican Republic	Italy	C.I. Jersey	Taiwan
Bahamas	Ecuador	Japan	Poland	Thailand
Barbados	El Salvador	Jamaica	Philippines	Turkey
Canada	France	Kuwait	Portugal	Uruguay
Chile.	Guadeloupe	Malaysia	Republic of Palau	United States
China	Guatemala	New Zealand	Reunion Island	Trinidad
Costa Rica	Guam	Malta	Spain	South Korea

Figure 12.1   Countries where the Athlete's Foot stores are located
Source: www.theathletesfoot.com.

service – rather than focusing exclusively on expansion. For example, the company inaugurated a systemwide commitment to customer service. In order to help customers to find the "right" footwear, or at least to help to determine the proper fit, sales associates underwent training at "Fit University," introduced by The Athlete's Foot Wear Test Center in order to provide education on the physiology and anatomy of the feet and to enable sales associates to fit athletics footwear properly. This focus on educating its sales force – who, in turn, educated customers about the value of relying on The Athlete's Foot as a consumer-oriented facility – paid almost immediate dividends.

In the 1990s, The Athlete's Foot consolidated its market standing even as it continued its enviable international growth. The Athlete's Foot changed its name to the Athlete's Foot Inc. and moved its headquarters to Kennesaw, Georgia, after Euris purchased Group Rallye in 1991. The company's structure was reorganized into two divisions as a result of this change in ownership: a marketing team serviced franchises and a "store team" operated company-owned stores. The marketing team did an impressive job in the years following the reorganization. The Athlete's Foot Inc. grew to more than 650 stores worldwide in 1997 and was named the # 1 franchise opportunity by *Success* magazine that same year. After a dynamic new CEO, Robert J. Corliss, joined the company in 1999, the company experienced a year of record growth – opening 37 corporate stores in six countries and 87 franchise stores, the most franchises in company history. The other division, the operations team that managed company stores, also achieved significant success during this period. The company launched a new store design featuring an innovative, customer-oriented technology called the FitPrint System.[1] This innovation was to lead to a competitive advantage for The Athlete's Foot Inc. As a result of franchise oversight and marketing innovations, the company was awarded the "Trendsetter of the Year" award by the sporting goods community for 1999 and 2000.

The growth story of The Athlete's Foot became a model for franchising even as it successfully continued its almost three-decades-long tradition of domestic and international expansion. Many would-be entrepreneurs were drawn to the company, for reasons linked to the company's focus points: customer service, aggressive marketing, and control of the pipeline from production to point-of-sale. Comments from franchisees illustrate the company's magnetic effect on franchisee development. Jaclyn Hill from Auburn said that her "decision to join The Athlete's Foot was based primarily upon them having an established, customer-service focused program to sell athletic shoes." Powell's Kyle H. Johnson commented, "The Athlete's Foot was my choice when I decided to enter the retail industry for several reasons. Some are obvious such as access to vendors, reasonable franchise fees, and fair royalty rates. Beyond that, they offer a tremendous amount of support."[2]

12.4   An Athlete's Foot master franchisee in China

Rick Wang was one of many entrepreneurs interested in pursuing business opportunities in the footwear retailing sector; Rick, however, had not followed the less risky entrepreneurial path of franchising, but had struck out on his own, with problematic results. His research on the successes of The Athlete's Foot's management model led him to contact that company. At that time, Rick had little knowledge of how franchising worked, or what potential benefits he might realize. In fact, his ostensible reason for contacting the company was his belief that he might pick up some pointers from this more experienced retailer:

> I was not a believer in franchising, recalls Mr. Wang. I did not believe in franchising because I did not believe in paying so much money to buy somebody's brand and then putting more money in to build it. I can do by myself. But I decided to contact The Athlete's Foot because I really knew that I needed help.

Rick Wang decided to fly to Atlanta, to view the company's headquarters and evaluate the company and its team. This trip was fruitful. As a potential Chinese partner, Rick received a warm welcome from the CEO and the entire management team during his visit. He was especially impressed by the inventory control system in the merchandize department. Rick recalled,

> I wasn't very excited until I walked into the merchandize department and I saw their buying team, how they bought products. I saw how intensively they controlled the inventory system, using a very high-tech system. And then I started to learn the science behind the retailing. And I started to realize perhaps I need to pay the tuition to learn this. It's always the case: if you want to dance, you have to pay the band.

After Rick returned to China, he immediately started his franchise and retail plan. He first persuaded the board of RetailCo Inc. to agree to his idea of becoming the master franchisee of an Athlete's Foot structure in China. Second, he efficiently worked out a negotiations' plan with the U.S. franchisor on the subjects of sales territory and royalty fees. He suggested separating the huge Chinese market into three regions: the East China Area, North China Area, and South China Area. The region of East China, stretching to the cities of Chengdu and Chongqin, was the biggest and potentially the most important market in China; it was in this area that Rick planned to focus his efforts. The region of North China, including Beijing, although a potentially lucrative market, was to be a secondary consideration. Last, development of the South China Area was to be delayed until after the first two regions were penetrated: the proximity to Hong Kong, with its history of appropriating brand names and flooding the market with cheaper copies, made immediate consideration of this region a risky and ambiguous proposition.

In terms of royalty fees, Rick fortunately negotiated a fairly good deal with The Athlete's Foot Inc. The monthly royalty was to be 2.5 percent of net sales. Other initial-area development fees – including franchising fees, fees for additional stores, purchasing an MIS system, an employment-control system, etc. – totaled a few thousand dollars per store. In addition, Rick requested discounts related to any future fees for local marketing. All the funds for initiating business were to be self-financed.

When the deal was made, Rick, together with his six colleagues, went to Atlanta for the "New Owner Training" at Athlete's Foot's Inc. Within six weeks, they had completed their "On Site Training" and had practiced operating the business: they worked in a store, sold shoes, helped people with their fittings, and even worked in the warehouse, experiencing at first hand the realities of inventory control. They also learned how to work internal control systems and marketing procedures. Overall, their training covered issues related to marketing, merchandizing, operations management, and employee sales training. Rick commented: "It was just fascinating, like going back to school. It was very enjoyable."

Their efforts paid off. In September 1998, the first store of the nascent master franchisee's China operation was opened in the Parkson Department Store on the Huaihai Road in Shanghai – in the East China Area. The Parkson was the most popular department store with an ideal demographic: young customers between ages 20 and 35 – those considered most devoted to brand names and most style conscious – shopped on fashion-oriented Huaihai Road. Therefore, the first store was actually in the fashion center in a favorite venue for young consumers. The store was opened on the ground floor of the Parkson with the same store design and equipment as those in the U.S. Beautiful store design and abundant/diverse brand-named products made the store attractive to customers.

Rick achieved success in starting his retail franchising at a time when the franchise concept in the Chinese market was new and innovative, and the sports footwear market was underdeveloped. His business instincts, his knowledge of the Shanghai market, and his training at The Athlete's Foot Inc.'s headquarters combined to initiate a signal success in what was then a relatively new entrepreneurial concept.

12.5   Business context

12.5.1   Franchising in the Chinese market

The franchise concept first entered the Chinese market in the early 1990s with the emergence of reputable international franchising companies such as KFC and McDonald's. They first entered China at this time, building corporate stores to start with. After having achieved steady sales volumes and sufficient economies of scale, they cautiously, but aggressively, expanded. These pioneer global franchisors included dominant players in the fast-food industry and various master franchisors in other industries such as 7-Eleven convenience stores, twenty first century Real Estate, EF education, Avis auto rental, Kodak film developing, Fornet laundry service, etc. These firms contributed to China's franchising market development – and created an awareness among an increasingly entrepreneurial class that franchising held substantial positive outcomes for those able to enter into such relationships.

Overseas franchisors tended to adopt one of two approaches when operating in the Chinese market: the franchise of a product or trade name (product name franchising), or the franchise of a particular business model in exchange for fees or royalties (business format franchising). Corporations which had a strong capital background, like McDonald's and KFC, would choose an offshore franchise retail model (see Figure 12.2) to ensure effective control over product quality and company operations. Small- and medium-sized franchisors would often choose direct franchising by seeking a local franchisee. Franchisors, licensing to local partners, can take advantage of local knowledge, saving the costs resulting from distance – both in terms of logistics and culture.

Since the end of the 1990s, franchising has become a mature, steady growth opportunity in China. By the end of 1997, there were just over 90 franchisors in China and about 30 franchise stores. A year later,

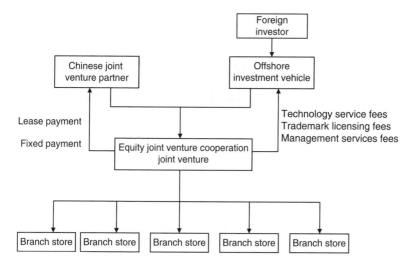

Figure 12.2 Offshore franchise retail model

Source: Mendel, Fraser "Legal Issues Related to Franchising in China", http://lawyers.law. cornell.edu/lawyer/f-fraser-mendel-832113.

however, the number had grown to over 120 franchisors with sales volume of over 50 million RMB (US\$ 6.05 million), among which 40 percent were franchise stores.[3] By 2000, the number of franchisors approached 600. The sales volume also increased dramatically, jumping by about 80 percent from 1999 to 2000.[4] This remarkable growth (at the time of writing this chapter, franchising is growing at a high double-digit rate) continued in the years that followed.

Franchised businesses in China vary along a wide spectrum of sectors. Companies in more than 30 industries have chosen franchising as a business model to sell their products and expand in the market. Retail and food/restaurant operations have always been the dominant franchising industries, accounting for 35 and 30 percent of total franchisors respectively.[5] Other sectors experiencing significant growth include education, business services, auto services, interior decoration, beauty and health, laundry, etc. The service sector has also grown in importance in recent years.

12.5.1.1 Market environment

In the late 1990s, as many in the global market were aware, China was becoming the land of opportunity. China's strong and steady growth,

Table 12.1 Consumption of recreation goods in entertainment and sports sector, 1997–2003

	1997	1998	1999	2000	2001	2002	2003
National	112.5	125.99	125.33	146.92	139.35	245.16	264.47
Shanghai	301.11	301.95	372.05	407.99	387.67	540.96	587.06

Source: China Statistics Yearbooks.

proven by ten years of continuing GDP increases, seemed unstoppable. Economic growth led to an increase in personal incomes, especially in larger cities. The emergence of a large middle class, often consisting of well-educated professionals, added to the consumer demand for globally recognized, quality products.

Domestically, the Chinese government made great efforts to regulate the market and standardize the business environment. To facilitate access to the World Trade Organization (WTO), China committed itself to removing more market-entry barriers, creating a more open market for international investors. In this way the laws and regulations governing franchise businesses were improved. On November 14, 1997, the Ministry of Internal Trade published and released the very first Chinese franchise law, *The Regulation on Commercial Franchise Business (for Trial Implementation)*. Afterward, the regulation was revised and improved several times: in 2005, *The Law on Commercial Franchise Business Administration* was eventually released as a basic rule for franchise operations in China.

Market competition in China was less rigorous than that in the U.S. In the athletics footwear retailing industry in China, for example, there were few capable players in the early to mid-1990s. Meanwhile, the demand for high-quality athletics footwear increased as consumers' incomes increased (see Table 12.1). Market research for 1998 indicated that people in Shanghai owned only one pair of athletics shoes. By 2005, they had, on average, three pairs. In terms of style, people's preferences changed from choosing footwear for functional purposes to opting for fashion. Athletics footwear retailers selling brand-named shoes had what seemed to be a promising future.

12.6   The glorious age

The success of his first store encouraged Rick to open more stores, more quickly than he had initially planned. In the months following his franchise premiere in Shanghai in 1998, Rick adopted an aggressive expansion strategy, opening a new store every 22 days. After spreading the business to the North China region, the company opened 40 corporate stores in seven other Chinese cities. The company realized a profit in its second year of operations, reaching a sales volume of US$14 million in 2000.

Every one of RetailCo's stores acted in accord with the standards of the global Athlete's Foot Inc. The stores, equipped with indoor music, sports videos, and fashionable designs, established a pleasant atmosphere for shopping. All stores provided the best possible service for their customers. The service staff in every store was trained before they began working – also in accordance with the model that Rick and his team had seen in Atlanta. In addition, every store was equipped with computers for billing and inventory control. In fact, the inventory-control system was an advantage that distinguished Rick's stores from other retailers. By adhering to strict, computerized tracking of product, store managers were able to react promptly to shortages or excesses of inventory. The company used the franchisor's proprietary pricing model by utilizing aggressive price reductions to manage inventory excesses. More important than the own-brand goods the store marketed were the famous internationally branded sports goods, such as Nike, Adidas, and Reebok, which were also available. A pioneering store atmosphere, an excellent inventory-management model, and the availability of famous brands quickly made The Athlete's Foot a premier competitor in the Chinese sports retailing industry.

Domestic promotion of The Athlete's Foot brand name was also done aggressively. Besides media advertising, the company put more emphasis on direct and in-store marketing. It organized three-on-three street basketball games and tournaments to grab the attention of young sports lovers. The company also sponsored high-school basketball teams to further inculcate brand-name recognition of both the franchise and its products among teenagers. In-store marketing activities included cooperation with the fast food giant, McDonald's; monthly newsletters advertising The Athlete's Foot were distributed in McDonald's restaurants. Nevertheless, the brand-building process was not as successful as it had been in the U.S. People responded to the branded products more than to the retail brand itself: consumers visited stores because they could find internationally known products, not necessarily because they were drawn to The Athlete's Foot as a brand. This customer motivation would lead to substantial problems for Rick in future years.

In 2000, Rick started, cautiously, to seek appropriate franchisees in an attempt to expand the business. Rick selected one sports' goods franchising exhibition in Beijing as the venue for promoting his franchise opportunities. Almost 500 applicants applied for franchises in one day, far exceeding Rick's expectations. Some applicants even came with large amounts of cash as testament to their financial abilities (and solvency). Rick was concerned, however, about the values of the applicants; he wanted to ensure that the selected candidates were service-oriented and fully understood the partnership requirements related to franchising. Carefully vetting all of the applicants, Rick short-listed 20 candidates. These finalists had strong financial capabilities as well as excellent educational backgrounds; they could understand the vital realities involved in franchising's partnerships. RetailCo invited these 20 candidates to come to the Shanghai Office and have face-to-face meetings with the board. Finally, one – out of the 500 – was signed with RetailCo to be the first subfranchisee of The Athlete's Foot Inc. Later, using the same careful scrutiny, 12 additional subfranchisee stores were developed in second- and third-tier cities such as Nanjing, Wuxi, and Ningbo.

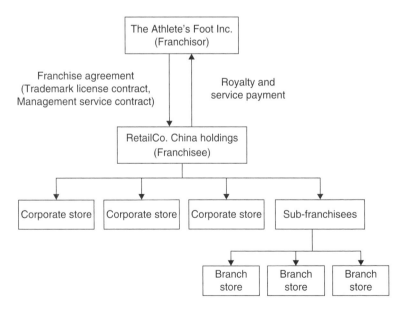

Figure 12.3   Franchise structures of the Athlete's Foot in China

12.7   Signs of problems

In 2001, in spite of – or possibly as a result of – its rapid growth, the company gradually felt pressures related to cash flow, marketing, and supply. The first "pressure" came from the need to commit large amounts of capital to obtaining retail venues. Since the location of retail stores is related to sales performance, gaining a quality location is crucial. Rick's good fortune in being able to open his first store at a high-traffic, upscale shopping area in Shanghai was often difficult to replicate at equally moderate rental rates. Obtaining a quality retail space in China usually requires at least a 24-month leasing commitment; in some department stores, a 36-month rental agreement is often the norm. To lock in quality locations in this competitive retail real-estate market, the company signed long-term contracts, looking to outdo competitors by securing desirable locations. This laudable approach to ensuring franchisee success, however, required an immense commitment of upfront capital. RetailCo took over prime spaces in department stores, but the cost of doing so was great. Unfortunately, when market conditions changed and sales decreased, the pressure caused by an insufficiency of ready reserves of cash inevitably increased.

A second pressure was related to a problem that many "breakthrough" franchisors experience in new markets: since 2001 the Athlete's Foot had started to lose its "first-mover" advantage. In 2000 China began to finalize preparations for its entry into the WTO. The global financial community was increasingly convinced by then that the immense potential of the Chinese market was soon to become a reality. As a result, the athletics footwear market – along with every other foreign franchise business – underwent major changes and foreign direct investment (FDI) increased. In department stores, the space allotted to sports goods enlarged dramatically from 300 square meters to 700 square meters, then 1000, 1500, and finally to an average of 3000 square meters. This meant that franchising space allotted to The Athlete's Foot was, as a percentage of total space, gradually diminished. More footwear retailing players joined the industry; for example, Quest Sports started to open stores in China in 2001. Competition also came from local players, who were able to insinuate themselves in this market through competitive pricing, enhanced customer service, and increased product quality. In other words, these local competitors learned from Rick's Athlete's Foot franchises what Rick had learned from the franchisor. A final problem occurred when individual brands opened more of their own stores.

As a result of its success in the market – partly related to the improved business climate in China as a whole – RetailCo/The Athlete's Foot was, paradoxically, losing its competitive advantage. In 1998, the average size of an Athlete's Foot store was almost 100 square meters, often occupying one-third of the total size of the sporting goods section of a large department store. The typical store was supplied by several world-famous brands, like Nike, Adidas, Reebok, etc. The rest of the sports goods space was devoted to selling locally branded products and sports equipment: footballs, basketballs, tennis rackets, etc. Although the goods sold in an Athlete's Foot store were exclusive and superior to others, the changes detailed above led to a tenfold increase in the amount of store space devoted to sports goods. The Athlete's Foot did not/could not grow as fast, now (post-2001) occupying merely one-fifteenth of the total space devoted to sports goods in a large department store. Size and visibility matter: the "idea" of The Athlete's Foot became increasingly insignificant in customers' minds.

Worse, for Rick, was the fact that his suppliers – the producers of the often popular styles and models his growing customer base demanded – began to increase their own penetration into what had previously been a fairly wide open market. The Athlete's Foot multibrand approach was forced to compete directly with brand-name suppliers who opened their own outlets in direct competition with him. Inevitably, Rick found it difficult to get the most desirable brand-name products for his stores; the company's headquarters – although committed to Rick's status as the master franchisor – was unable to put enough pressure on producers to stem the tide. Rick's stores were unable to stock the most recent styles and most in-demand products.

With declines in comparative store size and product varieties, and increases in competition from local and brand-specific market entrants, The Athlete's Foot found itself squeezed out of high-value department store venues. Department stores welcomed the single brand retailers because they were content with the smaller ratios of retail space; besides, grouping single-brand retailers together made a department store one, huge multi-brand store. The Athlete's Foot had to move to street-front locations which commanded higher rents and were less popular with the buying public. Thus, costs increased but revenue decreased.

12.8   What should Rick do?

Rick Wang realized the company was in risk of bankruptcy if he did not immediately address the radically changed demands of the marketplace.

Notes

1. According to The Athlete's Foot Inc. the FitPrint System is a proprietary state-of-the-art computerized technology that measures pressure points at different phases of a customer's gait.
2. www.theathletesfoot.com
3. ChinaOnline, August 2, 1999.
4. *Franchise: The International Management of Franchise.* Beijing: Xinhua Press, 2003: 181.
5. Ibid.

13
Final Reflections

Ilan Alon

13.1 Introduction

This book has attempted to capture some salient issues relevant to international franchising. Among the themes running through the book were internationalization, emerging markets, and franchising entrepreneurship which are worth continued to study. Franchising has been shown in industries as diverse as television programming (Thomas, 2006), healthcare services, technology, and childcare services. This current book has concentrated on the traditional industries employing franchising, notably retailing and hotels, across multiple countries and continents. Future studies should continue to add to the repertoire of industry and country studies that examine franchising in different institutional contexts and industry settings. Good theories of franchising that can explain the use, expansion, and internationalization of franchising should be able to hold true across countries and industries with only limited adjustments. Both resource-based and agency-based theories show promise. Together they may have greater explanatory powers (Castrogiovanni et al 2006). In the following section, I will comment on each of these franchising areas (internationalization, emerging markets and entrepreneurship) noting areas for possible future research.

13.2 Internationalization

Internationalization is a central theme in this book and in franchising research, more generally, and much of my own previous research on the topic can be summarized in Figures 13.1 and 13.2. Figure 13.2, in particular, shows organizational and environmental variables as

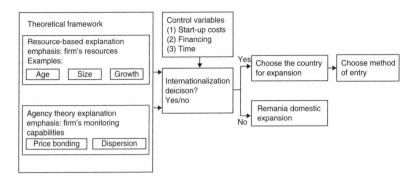

Figure 13.1   Conceptualization of international franchising
Source: Alon (1999).

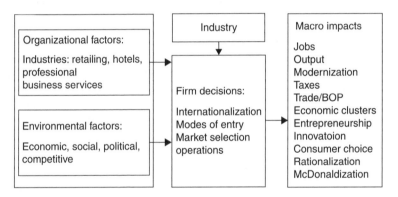

Figure 13.2   Service franchising: a conceptual framework
Source: Alon (2005).

contributors to a variety of firm-specific decisions relating to franchising. Both organizational and environmental factors are contributors to the internationalization of franchising. Firm-specific decisions, in turn, affect the relative impact of franchising on a particular society. In Chapters 3, 6, 9, 10, and 11 we examine some facets of the organizations extending their international presence. Other environmental variables that promote or impede franchising development are also reviewed in many of the chapters herein (Chapters 1, 4, 5, 6, 7, 8, 9, and 11). In sum, both organizational factors and environmental factors relate to franchise diffusion, internationalization, international market selection, international franchising operations, and franchise ownership.

Retailing has been widely investigated. Doherty (2007) examined the internationalization of retailing and found both organizational and environmental factors such as experience. Among the organizational factors, the availability of financial resources, the presence of a retail brand suitable for franchising, company restructuring, and the influence of key managers were important. Market factors included complexities, competitiveness, and the availability of franchise partners. Hutchinson et al (2006) investigated SME British retailing internationalization strategies and found that franchising allows retailers to overcome their size disadvantage.

Internationalization remains a big step for most franchising companies, testing their abilities to manage across heterogeneous locations. Franchising firms tend to go first after markets that are similar to theirs, such as hospitable neighboring countries (Hoffman and Preble, 2004). The firm's resources become stressed and new environments call for a new skill set to manage them. New agency costs and the need for effective monitoring become more critical and expensive and a variety of new organizational settings are created, such as master international franchising. Master international franchising as a vehicle for entering new markets, for example, is preferred when the economic potential and the level of corruption are low; and when the competitive intensity, demand variability, franchise knowledge, entrepreneurial culture, legal protection, and cultural and geographic distance are high (Alon, 2006b).

New internationalizing firms also need to select new markets (Alon, 2004b). International market selection for franchisors as a function of market size was examined by Alon (2006a). However, market size alone is not enough since personnel problems and cultural differences can overwhelm the success of the franchisor in new and emerging markets in particular (Frazer, 2003). Examining the life cycles of franchising organizations through their internationalization process and beyond could be useful for future research in order to connect studies that examine single points in time (Etemad, 2005).

There is also a need to examine the impacts on society of international franchising diffusion. Alon (2004a) examined both the negative and positive impacts of international diffusion of franchising systems. Grunhagen et al (2009) tested these propositions on a sample of Middle Eastern consumers and found that consumer agency moves the consumer from rejection to eventual acceptance of franchising concepts, with mixed feelings toward the service and its impact changing over time. More research is needed in new environmental contexts to measure the social costs and economic benefits of franchising from the standpoints of consumers, franchisees, and governments, as well as other stakeholders.

13.3 Emerging markets

Franchising studies of emerging markets have become popular. The books of Alon and Welsh (2001, 2003) were among the first on the topic, providing a comprehensive coverage of franchising in various regions around the world. Since then, there has been a plethora of studies on various emerging markets (Alon, 2006a), such as Russia (Anttonen et al 2005), East Asia (Choo, 2003; Choo, Mazzarol and Soutar, 2007), China (Alon and Bian, 2005; Frazer 2003), India (Allix-Desfautaux, 2006; Paswan and Sharma, 2004), Brazil (Perrigot et al, 2008), the Middle East (Raven and Welsh, 2004), Egypt (Grunhagen et al 2009), Israel (Pizanti and Lerner, 2003), Eastern Europe (Picot-Coupey and Cliquet, 2004), Poland (Lee, 2008), among others. Emerging markets constitute a heterogeneous group of countries with different developmental paths carved by unique historical context, ethnic makeup, and international relations. There is a continuing need for ongoing research regarding the particularized franchising environment that exists in this area. Case studies, empirical research, and conceptual studies can all contribute to our understanding of franchising as a global phenomenon.

Studying emerging markets with different characteristics allows us to isolate the relative contribution of the environment to franchising development, in relation to organizational and industry dynamics. Why is it, for example, that in the U.S., the UK, and France, franchising grew so well, while in other countries, such as China, Russia, and Israel, franchising is still in its infancy? Part of the answer lies in the environmental differences. In countries that protect intellectual property, follow the rule of law, and have an efficient economic system, franchising can proliferate. In countries where trust is low, or where the legal environment does not afford protection under the law, franchising may not realize its full potential.

Advice for franchisors operating in emerging markets abounds. Choo, Mazzarol and Soutar (2007) suggested that international franchisors should select franchisees who are financially strong enough to engage in aggressive expansion, sufficiently linked with relevant contacts, and able to capture key and scarce real estate for expansion. Miller (2008) suggested that when expanding to emerging markets, specifically

Poland, franchisors should use a modular approach to deal with the cultural and linguistic differences. By adapting selected elements of operations, branding, and marketing the firm can achieve superior results. The core of the franchising system must stay intact to preserve the franchisor's global identity, but peripheral elements that allow for better acceptance and diffusion of the concept can be adapted. Lee's (2008) views on restaurant franchising in Poland agree with Miller's view on the importance of customization and with Choo, Mazzorol and Soutar (2007) regarding dealing with international franchisees.

Emerging markets, in particular, do share a few characteristics that are worth mentioning as common denominators. Most of them are experiencing above world-average economic growth rates. Most are going through economic and political transition toward greater liberty in both. Most of them experience volatility that arises from a lack of institutions and accepted rules, uncertainty regarding the future environment, and political variability. Given these similarities, the experience of franchising in one area of the emerging world can have significant implications to others facing similar conditions. More research is needed to examine the patterns in franchising in emerging markets. Furthermore, emerging markets provide a useful social setting for experimental designs to test franchising theories.

13.4   Entrepreneurship

Franchising embodies entrepreneurship on several levels. First, franchisors who come up with the concept market it and grow it are entrepreneurs. Garg (2005) suggested that franchising is a sustainable form of cooperative entrepreneurship. Second, franchisees who are taking risks in order to buy a franchise concept and run a business are also a type of entrepreneur. Franchisees are also akin to employees by taking directions from the franchisor. This interesting mix of entrepreneur/ employee dichotomy was investigated in Chapter 2. Since the study was based on a U.S. dataset, it would be advisable to replicate it in different cultural settings. While various definitions of entrepreneurship exist, there are overlaps between some of them and the use of franchising both for the franchisor and the franchisee.

Much of the franchising research has until now focused on the point of view of the franchisor, with only a few exceptions. Roh and Yoon (2009) studied franchisee satisfaction among South Korean ice-cream franchises and found that, in South Korea, franchisees find out about franchising through friends and relatives. This is not surprising given the importance of relationships in East Asia. Do unique franchisee characteristics emerge in other countries? How do franchisees in other countries perceive franchising? How are franchisor-franchisee relations impacted by local cultures and cultural distance? These are all promising avenues for future research.

The evolution of franchising is ongoing across both continents and time. The evolution of franchising across space is evident as in the discussion on emerging markets. Different institutional contexts require franchisors to adapt their systems to local cultures, economic potential, and risk. Across time, industry dynamics and individual franchisor growth and change influence this evolution. Cochet and Garg (2008) examined the evolution of three German SMEs franchising contracts in restaurants, hotels, and retailing. They noted that it is hard for franchisors to anticipate all possible contingencies when working with individual entrepreneurs. Contracts change over time through learning, the desire for uniformity, and the presence of a franchisee council. Ownership redirection and multiple forms of franchising were found in varying degrees in the U.S., France, and Brazil (Dant et al 2008). Examining the impact of "internationalization" on multiple forms of franchising or the use of different types of franchising on internationalization can yield fruitful research.

The use of master and area franchising agreements of various sorts creates new permutations of entrepreneurship (Alon, 2006b). Various facets of master franchising systems were reviewed by Negre (2006). Etemad (2004) related international franchising to an entrepreneurial strategy viable for smaller firms in new markets. More generally, Garg and Rasheed (2006) suggested that multiunit franchising can be advanced by agency theoretic explanations especially in accounting for high cultural and geographic distance. Since franchising exhibits multiple forms and various types of franchising are, in effect, entrepreneurial permutations, franchising provides a good testing ground for entrepreneurship researchers.

Research on franchising success/failure and survival has great potential because the questions relating to franchising superiority are still unanswered. Juste et al (2009) suggested that an early entry strategy advantage has positively influenced survival across three markets: France, the UK, and Germany. Perrigot (2006) examined differences in franchising survival between retailing and other franchised services and found significant differences. A continued examination of franchising success/failure as an organizational form can contribute to the entrepreneurship literature.

We encourage researchers to continue the pursuit of developing knowledge specific to franchising internationalization, emerging markets, and entrepreneurship and hope that this book informs this future development.

References

Allix-Desfautaux, Catherine (2006). "Franchise Internationale et Marchés Émergents: Un éclairage sur l'Inde," *Décisions Marketing* (43/44), 109–21.

Alon, Ilan (1999). *The Internationalization of U.S. Franchising Systems.* New York: Garland Publishing.

Alon, Ilan (2004a). "Global Franchising and Development in Emerging and Transitioning Markets," *Journal of Macromarketing* 24 (2), 156–67.

Alon, Ilan (2004b). "International Market Selection for a Small Enterprise: A Case Study in International Entrepreneurship," *S.A.M. Advanced Management Journal* 69 (1), 25–33.

Alon, Ilan (2005). *Service Franchising: A Global Perspective.* New York: Springer.

Alon, Ilan (2006a). "Executive insight: evaluating the market size for service franchising in emerging markets," *International Journal of Emerging Markets* 1 (1), 9–20.

Alon, Ilan. (2006b). "Market Conditions Favoring Master International Franchising," *Multinational Business Review* 14 (2), 67–82.

Alon, Ilan, and Ke Bian (2005). "Real estate franchising: The case of Coldwell Banker expansion into China," *Business Horizons* 48 (3), 223–31.

Alon, Ilan, and Dianne Welsh, Eds. (2001). *International Franchising in Emerging Markets: China, India and Other Asian Countries.* Chicago IL: CCH Inc. Publishing.

Alon, Ilan, and Dianne Welsh, Eds. (2003). *International Franchising in Industrialized Markets: Western and Northern Europe.* Chicago IL: CCH Inc. Publishing.

Anttonen, Noora, Mika Tuunanen, and Ilan Alon. (2005). "The International Business Environments of Franchising in Russia," *Academy of Marketing Science Review*, 1. Retrieved August 20, 2009, from ABI/INFORM Global. (Document ID: 1040274701).

Castrogiovanni, Gary J., James G. Combs, and Robert T. Justis (2006). "Resource Scarcity and Agency Theory Predictions Concerning the Continued Use of Franchising in Multi-outlet Networks," *Journal of Small Business Management*, 44 (1), 27. Retrieved August 20, 2009, from ABI/INFORM Global. (Document ID: 969304021).

Chiou, Jyh-Shen, Chia-Hung Hsieh, and Ching-Hsien Yang (2004). "The Effect of Franchisors' Communication, Service Assistance, and Competitive Advantage on Franchisees' Intentions to Remain in the Franchise System," *Journal of Small Business Management* 42 (1), 19–36.

Choo, Stephen (2003). "Valuable Lessons for International Franchisors When Expanding into East Asia," in *International Franchising in Industrialized Markets: North America, Pacific Rim, and Other Countries*, Dianne Welsh and Ilan Alon, eds., 249–268.

Choo, Stephen, Tim Mazzarol, and Geoff Soutar (2007). "The selection of international retail franchisees in East Asia," *Asia Pacific Journal of Marketing and Logistics* 19 (4), 380–97.

Cochet, O., and V. Garg (2008). "How Do Franchise Contracts Evolve? A Study of Three German SMEs," *Journal of Small Business Management* 46 (1), 134–51.

Dant, R., R. Perrigot, and G. Cliquet (2008). "A Cross-Cultural Comparison of the Plural Forms in Franchise Networks: United States, France, and Brazil," *Journal of Small Business Management* 46 (2), 286–311.

Doherty, Anne Marie (2007). "The internationalization of retailing: Factors influencing the choice of franchising as a market entry strategy," *International Journal of Service Industry Management* 18 (2), 184–205

Etemad, Hamid (2004). "International Entrepreneurship as a Dynamic Adaptive System: Towards a Grounded Theory," *Journal of International Entrepreneurship: Special Issue on International Entrepreneurship in a Dynamic Complex Open Adaptive System* 2 (1–2), 5.

Etemad, H. (2005). SMEs' "Internationalization Strategies Based on a Typical Subsidiary's Evolutionary Life Cycle in Three Distinct Stages," *Management International Review*: Special Issue (3/2005) 45 (3), 145–86.

Frazer, Lorelle (2003). "Exporting Retail Franchises to China," *Journal of Asia Pacific Marketing* 2 (1), 1–11.

Garg, Vinay Kumar (2005). "An Integrative Approach to Franchisor Strategy in Large Chains," *Journal of Applied Management and Entrepreneurship* 10 (2), 58–74.

Garg, Vinay K., and Abdul A. Rasheed (2006). "An Explanation of International Franchisors' Preference for Multi-unit Franchising," *International Journal of Entrepreneurship* 10, 1–20.

Grünhagen, Marko, Carl L. Witte, and Susie Pryor (2009), "Impacts of U.S.-based Franchising in the Developing World: A Middle-Eastern Consumer Perspective," *Journal of Consumer Behaviour*.

Hoffman, R. C., and J. Preble (2004). Global Franchising: Current Status and Future Challenges. *Journal of Services Marketing* 18(2), 101–113.

Hutchinson, Karise, Barry Quinn, and Nicholas Alexander (2006). "SME retailer internationalisation: case study evidence from British retailers," *International Marketing Review* 23 (1), 25–53.

Juste, Victoria Bordonaba, Laura Lucia-Palacios, and Yolanda Polo-Redondo (2009). "Franchise firm entry time influence on long-term survival." *International Journal of Retail & Distribution Management* 37 (2), 106–25.

Lee (2008). http://www.entrepreneur.com/tradejournals/article/188641880_2.html, http://www.highbeam.com/doc/1G1-188641880.html

Paswan, Audhesh K., and Dheeraj Sharma (2004). "Brand-country of origin (COO) knowledge and COO image: investigation in an emerging franchise market." *The Journal of Product and Brand Management* 13 (2/3), 144–55.

Perrigot, Rozenn, G. Cliquet, and R. Dant (2008). http://papers.ssrn.com/sol3/papers.cfm?abstract_id=1113935

Perrigot, Rozenn (2006). "Services vs retail chains: are there any differences: Evidence from the French franchising industry," *International Journal of Retail & Distribution Management* 34 (12), 918–30.

Picot-Coupey, Karine, and Gérard Cliquet (2004). "Internationalisation des Distributeurs dans les Pays en Transition d'Europe de l'Est: quelles Perspectives pour le Choix de la Franchise comme Mode d'Entrée?" *Revue Française du Marketing* 198 (3/5), 19–35.

Pizanti, Inbar, and Miri Lerner (2003). "Examining control and autonomy in the franchisor-franchisee relationship," *International Small Business Journal* 21 (2),

131. Retrieved August 20, 2009, from ABI/INFORM Global. (Document ID: 351530421).

Raven, Peter, and Dianne H.B. Welsh (2004). "An exploratory study of influences on retail service quality: A focus on Kuwait and Lebanon," *The Journal of Services Marketing* 18 (2/3), 198–214.

Roh and Yoon (2009). http://www.ingentaconnect.com/content/mcb/041/2009/00000021/00000001/art00006

Runyan, R., and C. Droge (2008). "A categorization of small retailer research streams: What does it portend for future research?" *Journal of Retailing* 84 (1), 77–94.

Thomas, Amos Owen (2006). "Cultural economics of TV programme cloning: or why India has produced multi-'millionaires.'" *International Journal of Emerging Markets* 1 (1), 35–47. Retrieved August 20, 2009, from ABI/INFORM Global. (Document ID: 1139556141).

Index